Erna Walraven was born in the Netherlands and moved to Spain as a young adult, before moving to Australia in her late twenties. She worked as a translator and interpreter of Dutch, German, French, Spanish and English, as well as a kennel-maid, zookeeper, petrol pump attendant, waitress, aged care worker, farmhand, conveyancing clerk, debt collector and a dog washer. She eventually settled for zoology, as Senior Curator at Taronga Zoo in Sydney for two decades, where she was responsible for the care of some 400 wild animal species. Erna's career has inspired her to write many non-fiction books about animals. Her latest, *Wild Fathers: What Wild Animal Dads Teach Us About Fatherhood*, was published by New Holland in 2021. She has travelled to most of Earth's continents, and she's currently planning a trip to Antarctica to achieve her life goal of seeing all the penguin species of the world. Erna's long-harboured dream of living in Spain again came true when she and her husband, Alex, returned in retirement and bought a falling-down villa to make their home.

Sunset in Spain

Erna Walraven

affirm
press

affirm press

First published by Affirm Press in 2022
This edition published in 2023
Boon Wurrung Country
28 Thistlethwaite Street
South Melbourne VIC 3205
affirmpress.com.au

10 9 8 7 6 5 4 3 2 1

A catalogue record for this
book is available from the
National Library of Australia

ISBN: 9781922992130 (paperback)

Cover design by Christa Moffitt/Christabella Designs © Affirm Press
Cover image via Shutterstock
Typeset in Sabon LT Std by J&M Typesetting
Proudly printed and bound in Australia by McPherson's Printing Group

MIX
Paper | Supporting
responsible forestry
FSC® C001695

for Carla and Bob

The names of some villages and some
people have been changed.

Contents

Chapter 1

The Stuff of Dreams

We've done it! We've surprised ourselves actually – we're really doing this big thing. We've left behind bushfires and droughts and are on our way to the lush valleys of the Rio Duero in Spain. I've dreamed about Spain so very often since leaving her behind four decades ago, a dream akin to a longing to finally be reunited with a lost lover. Always, when I wake up, I promise myself I will live there again – one day. Today is that 'one day'.

I wake up in Madrid, slightly groggy after a deep jetlag-induced sleep, the first day of our new lives on Iberian soil. I turn over to find Alex still fast asleep. My love for Spain never diminished after living here in my teens and early twenties, and neither has my love for this man, sleeping beside me. For many years I did not think I could have both, but I'm starting to wonder: maybe I can?

Lying as still as I can so that Alex can sleep some more, I close my eyes again and relive my very first glimpses of Spain on a sunny spring day in the 1970s. An eighteen-year-old on her first holiday without parents. It was also my first time on a plane and my first trip to Europe's south, as opposed to the usual family outings to the Alps or the Black Forest. I recall my excitement as the plane banked steeply, heading for the runway: the panorama below coming into focus, the sky the bluest of blue and the water below shimmering and sparkling. The view from that plane window was a world away from the cold and grey Dutch village where I grew up. On leaving Amsterdam earlier that morning the world looked small, cloud covered and dark. On landing I saw a curtain of cream-coloured mountains running parallel with the blue of the sea, clumps of green pine trees starkly outlined against white rocks and pink almond blossom lining the valley in orderly rows. This exotic country promised palm-fringed beaches, endless sun, music and fun, everything I'd fantasised about. My love affair with Spain began the moment that charter flight landed at the small airport of Alicante on the Costa Blanca. I stayed for seven years until an Aussie backpacker swept me off my feet and I followed him to the other end of the world. Love will do that.

Alex, the Aussie backpacker, and my 'other' love, stirs and wakes up, which brings me back to the here and now. Soon we'll be on our way to start our new life in Castilla y Leon.

~

Only a few short months ago we celebrated our retirement with a trip to Europe and paid a brief visit to my nephew Josh and his Spanish wife, Maya. Josh recently moved from the coast to the province of Soria, north of Madrid, a scarcely populated district of Spain. Soria is not on the coast, which is probably the reason it's still so authentically Spanish, with little or no outside influence from tourists seeking sun and sea.

As we sip coffee on a terrace in the centre of town, the tableau has all the flavour of my fondest memories of Spain. Old buildings surround a cobblestoned square; trees in autumn colours cast a shade over benches where people sit and chat. Then the church bells ring, triggering a visceral emotion.

This moment, this scene and the sound of the bells takes my breath away. It is as if my simmering passion for Spain has suddenly become a giant bonfire consuming all my oxygen. My love for this country comes rushing out, refusing to go back in the box where it's been kept, dark and silent.

'I want to live here,' I say a little breathlessly to a surprised-looking Josh and Maya. I think I've just surprised myself!

I look at Alex next. He returns my gaze with raised eyebrows and a bemused smile. I'm on a roll.

'I want to shop in the markets, see the red poppies in the fields. I want to sit in a bar somewhere and join the locals discussing the latest events.'

All of a sudden I know exactly what I want to do with my life. When I lived in Spain all those years ago I felt I was where I was meant to be. Being in this square now with the church bells ringing recaptures that feeling of being exactly where I'm supposed to be. What does this mean? Why are these feelings so strong? Is it because we've recently retired? I've struggled with the idea of retirement, but we wanted more time for travel, to experience more of the world. We do travel, but eventually we always come home again to find ourselves on the northern beaches of Sydney living a pleasant enough life. But I feel unsatisfied, unfulfilled. Something is missing.

These are feelings no doubt related to giving up a job I loved, leaving behind the animals and the workmates I cared about. When I first became a zookeeper more than thirty years ago, I knew I'd found my tribe in Australia. My job became my identity. Now in retirement I feel a bit lost. I have to create a completely new life. At the same time, I'm seized with a kind of indefinable nostalgia for Spain, the last place, before the zoo, where I felt I knew who I was. Maybe it's time to go back there? But would Alex be happy? Can I have both the country I love and the man I love?

~

As soon as we're alone Alex wants to know what's going on in my head and in my heart.

'I don't think we are living the life we could or should be living,' I say tentatively. I'm still trying to find the words to articulate that rush of emotion I felt in the square.

I don't miss working, the deadlines or the report writing. At the same time, I feel guilty. We have so much more than most people on the planet. Privileged and spoiled for choice. We're so lucky already. We have a nice life, but I keep thinking there could be more.

We retired early so we'd be fit enough to do the kind of adventurous travel we like to do. Travelling has been fun, but as a traveller you're observing the world, moving through it without being part of anything significant. Life on the northern beaches of Sydney is perfect in many respects but it has few challenges, if any. I want to live more deliberately, more connected, or challenged, whatever that means. We have an entire future to invent.

'I've been thinking about that too,' Alex confides. 'How to make the most of that one precious life and not waste any of it. Not quietly sitting by and letting the years roll into another.'

Fortunately, Alex also loves the country where we first met all those years ago. We quickly agree that Spain would be the place to find that different, more stimulating life we both want. I may get to explore those ill-defined feelings of identity and being in the right place. As an immigrant, the subliminal search to find 'your special place in the world' is ever-present. Not only longing for pretty places and great food, but for that sense of belonging. A couple of months after this epiphany, we packed up, left our house in the care of a stranger and hopped on a plane.

~

A day and a half of travel gets us to Madrid to pick up the leased car. We're on our way to the house we found online. It will be our home for the next few months as we sort ourselves out and decide where we want to settle more permanently. Our wish list was for a modest house, with two bedrooms, no further than fifty kilometres from the capital of Soria province (unimaginatively also called Soria). In Australia, we scanned the internet for places while Josh and Maya had some leads on places through word of mouth. If you want to know anything about any topic, ask in the bar. Everybody will get involved. Everybody will have an opinion, often conflicting, but you do find a happy medium eventually.

We got lucky and found a very appealing house in a small provincial town of about 5000 inhabitants called Almazán. It's a couple of hours north-east of Madrid and only half an hour to where Josh lives. Not too close – we don't want to smother him – but close enough to share an occasional meal. Maya drove over to inspect the place on our behalf. She was let in by Maite, an Almazán resident and a friend of the absent owner. '*Precioso*' (gorgeous), Maya reported on the phone the next day. Turns out the owner is a Dutch woman called Renske. She rents out her cottage when she is in the Netherlands for half of the year. Enough time for us to have a roof over our heads while we look around to find the perfect spot to put down roots. However much I had anticipated this moment, there's some trepidation. I am nervous about what may come next.

~

After an hour, we pull up on the outskirts of a small town. Renske recommended a quick stop in a village called Torija along the way.

It boasts the first castle on the way from Madrid to Almazán. We're now in Castilla y Leon, the old kingdoms that joined to form part of modern Spain. It is here that the most authentic, beautiful Spanish is spoken – Castilian. This is of course debated by every Spaniard who is not from Castilla! Castilla y Leon is the biggest region in Spain, while also having the lowest population density. According to the travel guide, there are more castles here than anywhere else in Spain. Even the name of this district, Castilla, comes from the word 'castle'.

We park the spanking new car on a bit of dirt on the outskirts of the village and stroll to the nearest cafe. Everyone stares at us with intense interest. It is around ten on a Tuesday morning and the place is already packed with locals. We take the free table in the corner by the door. We soon realise the table is free because the door opens every now and then to let patrons in or out while bringing in a blast of cold air straight off the nearby snow-capped mountains. We order some coffee and a slice of Tortilla Española, the celebrated Spanish potato omelette. Alex relishes his first bite of tortilla as he envisions the culinary delights he's yet to discover.

'Maybe we could explore the entire peninsula to find the best Tortilla Española, and then move there,' he suggests.

'Or maybe the best Ensaladilla Rusa,' I add. It's one of my favourites, a wicked potato salad served in nearly all bars.

After the coffee, a short walk further into town takes us to the jumble of turrets and towers that is the castle. The cobbled streets lead to the Plaza Mayor, the main square in the village, where another couple of bars also look inviting. All cafes are called 'bars' in Spain. All sell alcohol, but also coffee, breakfast, tapas and main meals. The Plaza Mayor is lined with stately London plane trees, branches intertwined and joining the neighbouring tree, like garlands festooning the plaza. Benches in the square are an important aspect of a town's social network. This is where the old people meet to sit and chat about the time when they had things to do other than sit and chat, where mothers with prams gather as children play. Even now in the meagre winter sun a few brave geriatrics congregate. In summer, these majestic trees shade the benches from the hot Castilian sun. I love how good urban design in these old towns contributes to maintaining social networks. Old folks here are not short of other folks to talk to. They come to the Plaza Mayor and sit on a bench, and someone will inevitably join them for a chinwag.

~

Another hour along the freeway gets us into Almazán, a medium-sized town on the banks of the Rio Duero. As we get close the car's GPS sends us up a steep road next to massive ancient town walls. The dirt track up to the cemetery is a shortcut to one of the town gates. Calle Junto al Campanillo (the Street Next to the Church Bell – I love the pragmatic street naming in Spain) is inside this town gate called Puerta del Mercado (Market Gate), a short street with houses on one side and an empty field on the other. The house we're heading for is a modest place painted pink and blue, with a great double barn door.

The bell brings Renske to the door, who welcomes us with a hug. Well, she has no choice. I forget the Dutch three kisses and the Spanish two kisses and I clasp her in an Australian embrace with a squeeze. Never mind. I don't think she is concerned about the lack of cultural appropriateness in my greeting. Renske, about my age, is a recently retired academic. A tall, slim woman in stylish jeans and a colourful jacket I secretly covet. Perhaps she'll forget to take it with her? (She doesn't, unfortunately.)

We're enchanted as she shows us around. The house is even cuter than we gathered from the photos online. We truly did luck out stumbling onto this delightful place. A mixture of traditional Spanish design with Dutch styling creates a warm, cosy and extremely comfortable home.

'The pigs used to run in from the street, along the corridor through the middle of the house and up the steps, through the garden and to the pigsty,' Renske explains.

I imagine the stink they must have endured just after the pigs came home for winter. Urine and faeces of scared beasts would have wafted in from the corridor to the kitchen and beyond.

From the converted sty there's a door to another terrace, right on top of the medieval ramparts. The old defensive stone wall around the town overlooks the cemetery first, then the Rio Duero and fields beyond. The fields we can see from the terrace are surprisingly small, handkerchief-sized, in different coloured soils, looking like a mosaic in the landscape. This terrace is a delightful addition to the house. Perfect for a glass of wine at sunset or a bit of birdwatching during the day.

'Let me show you around the old part of town before I go,' Renske offers.

The house is in the *casco antiguo* (the old town). We walk through narrow cobbled streets lined with old houses and very few new buildings. After a few minutes we get to the Plaza Mayor, where one side of the square is taken up by a palace. Our landlady, quite the historian, has an astonishing amount of local knowledge.

'Almazán's most prosperous era was in the sixteenth century, by then under the control of the Mendoza family who built this palace.' She points to the *palacio* on the left of the square.

'It's also where Queen Juana la Loca (Joanna the Mad) lived for some time, the daughter of Queen Isabella of Castile and King Ferdinand of Aragon. Together those two were known as Los Reyes Católicos, the Catholic Kings.'

Alex asks, 'How did they get the lofty title of Catholic King and Queen?'

'It was bestowed on them by Pope Alexander in 1494. Their reward for being quite helpful to the Church during the Spanish Inquisition!'

Renske enjoys her role as our tourist guide, adding, 'The unification of Spain as we know it is traced to the marriage of these two second cousins. Their marriage brought together the most powerful kingdoms in the peninsula at the time.'

At the bar, we order a couple of beers, a wine for me and some *torreznos* to nibble on, a type of pork crackling, a snack for which this province is known. It's crunchy, chewy and meltingly soft at the same time. Vegetarians would have a bit of trouble in this nation. Fat dribbles down my chin. I can feel my veins clogging with every bite, but it's worth it.

Enjoying our drinks as much as the tapas, we chat about history and why poor Juana was known as 'la Loca'. Perhaps the repeated marriage of royal cousins throughout the previous generations did not help her genes. I remember there's always been some debate about how mad Juana really was. Maybe she did suffer from mental illness, as she lost her mother, her siblings and her husband in short succession and was probably not a happy little royal. Some histories tell the story differently. The alternative version says she inherited her mother's titles, but her father, Ferdinand, sent her to a convent so that he could keep calling the shots a little longer. So, the question still remains, was Juana really mad or was she the victim of ruthless men meddling in her life? Renske further tells us that Isabella and Ferdinand were also the ones who commissioned Columbus to go and 'discover' America.

These buildings drip with history, adding to the excitement of being here. Our first day in Spain, sitting in a bar, looking at a palace and talking about Juana la Loca, I feel a lightness and excitement I've not felt for a while. I'm filled with joy … unless it's the wine before lunch. Whatever it is, I am relishing this, being here, as well as the fat-dripping *torreznos*.

After our drinks Renske is off to catch a bus to Madrid. She's kindly made up all the beds before she left. Our body clocks are still trying to tell us it's four in the morning rather than two in the afternoon. Alex suggests a little nap and I'm all for it. Time for a jetlag-induced siesta in our new home.

'Thank you,' I whisper into my pillow.

Chapter 2

Butcher's Secret

We wake up to a freezing morning. Winter still has its hold on this region. Our first walk on Sorian soil takes us to Parque de la Arboleda, which has a circular walking track along the Rio Duero. I can't wait to have a look around. There's so much anticipation about what we will do, what life will be like. I picture us sitting on beautiful village squares sipping wine in the late afternoon. I've missed the atmosphere of ancient cobblestoned streets and dialects that change with the architecture, not to mention the home-grown cuisine. I want to see the big black bull silhouetted on the hills, advertising Soberano brandy (the only billboard allowed to remain in most places as it's loved by all).

The path along the river shoreline is lined with gigantic poplar and willow trees. The trees' bare winter appearance looks stark against the bright blue sky. The leaves that fell in autumn are still on the ground, uncovered again after the last snowmelt only days ago. As we set off for this wintery exercise, we rug up big time. In the early morning we're the only ones out and about. Other Almazán residents who use the path to keep fit and get some fresh, crisp air must wisely do so later in the day. Most sensible people in this part of the world wait for the thermometer to rise a fraction above zero before they go for a walk. Not us though. We set off as the grass is still frosted white. The icy grass crunches satisfyingly underfoot. It's not long before I'm freezing, the wind whipping around my ankles, my beanie, scarf, gloves and puffer jacket barely enough to keep me warm and make this a pleasant walking experience. A normally slim Alex looks like a plump bank robber in his big puffer jacket with a black beanie almost pulled over his eyes. Still, we're here and it's a splendid walk, cold or not, we tell ourselves. After a brisk semi-jog, the reward is a warm bar for some excellent coffee. We find a table right in front of the big window overlooking the plaza. The elderly barman proudly tells us a bit about the history of our temporary hometown as he serves our drinks. The local grapevine has already informed him we're the foreigners that rent a *casa* right on top of the fortified wall that surrounds the town.

'That wall where your house is,' he says, 'was built in 1088. The name of the town Almazán is Arabic and means "the fortified one". The ruler at the time, Abderramán III, was the one who built that wall.'

Other customers come in and he leaves us to drink our coffee looking at the palace. It takes pride of place in the middle of town, although the square is deserted now in the early morning.

~

On Sunday afternoon we find the streets eerily quiet. That is until we get to the Plaza Mayor, where the populace has gathered in droves to drink, eat and be merry. Another bar to the side of the *palacio* is open today and in the wintery sun the terrace is chockers with revellers dressed in their Sunday finery. It looks like people here still dress up in Sunday best. Everyone appears schmick – little girls in dresses with bows in their hair, little boys in suits like their dads. The palace is obviously still a focal point for the local population.

The *palacio* is in private hands now and desperately needs some repairs, but we're told that the current owners don't have the money to restore such a large building. An all-too-familiar story in Spain, where priceless, ageless buildings crumble as families can't afford the upkeep. Often these buildings are inherited and not sold, kept for sentimental reasons. Many have been in the family for generations and selling is not easy as there's no great demand for old houses in these parts. Everybody has one or more antique buildings in the extended family, mostly a burden they can ill afford.

~

We're keen to meet our neighbours. The rubbish bin seems like a good place to start. Rubbish collection is a communal affair here. Garbage in Spain is collected from a central point at the end of each street. Often the bins are hidden underground, while a smart and modest steel structure above ground is where one makes deposits. When I lived in Spain in the 1970s, everybody put plastic bags in tin rubbish bins with an ill-fitting lid by the side of the road for collection once a week. During the night, the ubiquitous stray cats and dogs would attack the bins, rip the plastic bags open and in the morning the rubbish would be strewn all over the street. Now, there is no individual house collection. It's picked up daily, so the fish heads don't stink out the whole street. The recycling bins too are at fixed points every few hundred metres and residents are used to the system. It's doubtlessly much cheaper and more hygienic, and encourages residents to think about waste. As I get to the end of our short street to throw out some rubbish, I spot a neighbour. The first one I meet is Mariana, who lives some four doors away in the yellow house on the corner. Mariana comes out to smoke on the raised porch, which gives her an excellent view along not one but two streets. She also has full view of the bins and who throws out what. I bet she knows what's going on.

I introduce myself so she can tell the rest of the street about the Australianos who have moved in at Number 15. Mariana has two teeth left. Both proudly sticking out of her lower jaw. She uses the gap between them efficiently to lodge the fag when she's talking. I am mesmerised by this skilful use of what's left, a good example of making the best of what you've got. We chat for a bit, but I have to dash back to the house eventually as I'm freezing. Note to self: Put a coat on before taking out the rubbish.

Later the same day we meet our next-door neighbour Constanza as she comes back from the shops with bulging bags of fresh vegetables. She has all the teeth she needs, as far as I can see. Constanza is a neat-looking woman in her late fifties and seems genuinely lovely and welcoming. Chatting away about this and that, she tells us they owned a shop selling *electrodomésticos* (small electrical appliances). Their two children do not want to sell electrical appliances for the rest of their lives and have their own careers. They tried to sell the shop but, in the end, they simply closed it and retired.

'We're *contentos* in retirement though,' she assures me.

She is content in retirement, so why do I find the adjustment to a life of leisure so difficult? I guess she has her roots firmly planted in this village, this region where her ancestors have probably lived for many generations. Maybe it's about putting down roots?

At sunset, as we're sipping a wine on the top deck, Constanza's husband, Lorenzo, sticks his head over the hedge that divides our terraces. A booming voice rings out, '*Bien venido!*' (welcome). Lorenzo looks like a genial fellow with a big open smile. Like his wife, he's spruce, hair neatly combed, clothes smart and ironed.

'We are like your family in Soria. If there's anything we can do, or anything you need, please let us know.'

I think he's genuine and would help us out of any scrapes. He also tells us they have a spare key should we ever lock ourselves out. That's good to know too. Lorenzo, too, looks like he's a contented fellow. We toast each other through the bushes that separate our terraces, high on the fortified walls of the village.

~

We settle comfortably into our new life. Ever since I first lived here, Spain has had a magnetic pull on my soul. I relish being back here. We potter, go on long walks, drink coffee in bars in the morning and wine in the evening. I read and write. In my notebook I let my thoughts about identity and belonging pour out, hoping to understand more about myself if I let the words flow freely. There is no television to waste time on awful Spanish game shows, of which there are many. No radio either, but there is good, fast internet.

When I lived in Alicante, I loved the markets. Chaotic, smelly and full of banter as everyone haggled and talked loudly. They were literally an assault on the senses. Forty years ago, these places were not for the fainthearted. We've set ourselves the challenge of finding Almazán's grower's market, which we're told is held on a Tuesday on the other side of town. Much has changed in the market scene too, it seems. Rather than chaos, there are attractive displays of fresh vegetables and fruit grown on Iberian soil, pickles, olives, even frozen *bacalao* (cod), nuts and dried fruits. In Spanish, only walnuts are called 'nuts' (*nueces*). All other nuts have their own names. For example, peanuts are *cacahuetes* and hazelnuts are *avellana* and so on. I love rolling my tongue around these almost-forgotten words again. To my ear they sound like poetry. The sheer joy of opening the filing cabinets in the brain and drawing out words that have been dormant for several decades seems like a miracle.

On market day, a couple of streets are blocked to general traffic so the stallholders can come in with trucks and wagons to unload their wares onto big tables. There are forests of herbs, cheeses made from sheep's, goats' and cows' milk, and every type of sausage imaginable. The vendors are cheerful, flirting with the frosty matrons buying the weekly supplies. They joke and compete for shoppers. The Almazán housewives are loud, bossy *señoras*, pushing in whenever I hesitate. Alex has backed off.

'Your Spanish is better than mine.'

Somehow, I make it to the front of a couple of stalls and hold my nerve long enough to order something. I proudly walk away with glossy dates still attached to their branches. At another stall I get a kilo of strawberries in a wooden basket. At yet another stall we manage to hold our own against the dominant locals to buy a most beautiful bunch of white asparagus. For a first trip to the markets, we're satisfied with our achievements.

I am not a vegetarian but not a big meat eater either. As a result, I don't frequent butcher shops often. Even though I'm a feisty woman I must admit that I'm sometimes intimidated by butchers. I'm sure I'm not alone. They have such a know-all approach to meat products that I am overcome with doubt, of which they seem to take full advantage. Generally, this is what happens: I go into a butcher shop all pumped up, ready to ask for something specific to use in a recipe – lamb chops, for example. Before I know it, all intentions to stick to my plan have come crashing down and I have agreed to take pork mince instead of lamb chops. They are all 'love' and 'darling, what can I get you today?' with their big-bellied attitude I find difficult to combat. In the end I always seem to go home with what they want to sell, rather than what I want.

There are a few butchers here in town and I venture into the one close to the markets. It seems to be a local favourite so it's likely to be a good one. There's a long wait. I am in the queue for a while when I hear a woman's voice behind me saying to her companion, 'Ah, that's my new neighbour.'

It's Mariana from the yellow house on the corner of the street. She has all her teeth in today, so it takes me a moment to register who it is. Soon there's lively discussion in the line of waiting punters. They are curious about us strangers. Why are you here? How long are you staying and why have you chosen this town above all others? These seem to be the standard questions we are asked by most people we meet. Everyone enjoys hearing we've chosen to come here from the other side of the world. It seems to validate the love they have for their hometown.

The butcher shop even has a rattan seating arrangement in the corner to cater for the long waiting times. I like the butcher here. He takes his time with each customer, sharing his recipes no matter how many shoppers are lined up behind. He has a fine performance, brandishing sharpened knives, while charming the elderly matrons.

'Dad is the one who knows it all,' says the butcher's son with an admiring nod to his old man, who is standing in a corner of the shop. He's not a pushy butcher and seems prepared to give me what I ask for. I am quite pleased with myself when I walk out with sausages, ribs and chops for a barbeque. Later I twig. It's all pork! The sausages, the ribs and the chops, the whole lot. I did go in for some beef, chicken and other types of meat but each time the butcher suggested something else that would suit better for a barbeque. There is an oversupply of pork here, no doubt. The smell of pigs is faintly in the air when we stroll back to the house.

~

Being in our rented *casa* means we can cook food at home some days. What we eat at home is usually healthier than the bar and restaurant food when eating out. The restaurants seem to rely heavily on pork and its tasty fattiness, but the Mediterranean diet, lauded for its basis in olive oil, fish, lots of fruit and vegetables, is the typical fare on the kitchen tables of Galicia, La Mancha and Castilla y Leon. Home cooking is usually vegetable and pulse-based, with a little chorizo or ham being used for flavour more than anything else. The kitchen in Almazán inspires country cooking and I enjoy making traditional Spanish dishes with white beans, tomatoes, lentils and chickpeas.

Despite the visit to the butcher, lunch today is a salad with huge fresh white asparagus just bought at the market. They come from Navarra, the neighbouring province to the north. White asparagus shaved and then cooked in boiling water with some salt and a sniff of sugar for ten to fifteen minutes, served with a mayonnaise dressing and a poached egg, has no comparison to the bottled white asparagus in the supermarkets. A fresh crusty loaf comes from the *panadería* on the Plaza Mayor. A glass of white wine to accompany the salad and bread, and life is exceptionally good indeed.

~

After a few more days we're getting over our jetlag, managing to stay awake after nine or ten o'clock in the evening. We meet Josh and Maya in the Soria capital in a bar on the Plaza Mayor, where the inevitable *torreznos* appear with the beer and wine. More tapas are ordered: garlic mushrooms, juicy green olives, slices of ham and kidney in sherry sauce. Then we progress to a minuscule dive of a place, once an old bullfighters bar, which only holds some twenty drinkers standing close enough together to become more than merely acquaintances. It was probably handed down by the owner's father, grandfather and so on, judging by the similarities in the photos on the wall, each depicting a proud barman. It's still immensely popular with the locals – on a weekday evening the place is crowded.

As we're savouring our tapas, Josh explains that the word *tapa* comes from the Spanish verb *tapar*, to cover.

'In the olden days in the south near Andalucía, glasses of sherry were covered with a slice of bread with something on it like a slice of ham or chorizo. This was to stop flies from falling in the sweet sherry.'

Tapas have a more sinister history too.

Josh continues, 'During the time of the Spanish Inquisition, tapas were used to unmask false *conversos*, Jews who claimed to have converted to Christianity. If the *conversos* were reluctant to eat whatever ham or non-kosher tapas was offered to them, this was taken as a solid admission that they had not abandoned their Jewish faith. Tapas, delightful as they are, were a tool of the Spanish Inquisition!'

After two bars and several tapas in each, we are finally going for dinner at nine o'clock, although we hardly need it. This is early for Spaniards, but it's in recognition of our still-fragile jetlagged state! There's nobody else in the restaurant when we arrive and the waitstaff look surprised to see diners appear this early. They are still setting up the tables. After the *torreznos* and the *jamón* (Spanish ham), I'm ready for a change. As pork features heavily on the menu here too, I struggle to find a pig-free meal and I ask the waitress for a recommendation. She suggests the local trout.

'Straight out of the Rio Duero,' she assures me as she points vaguely in the direction of the river below.

Some ten minutes later it arrives at the table beautifully presented and wrapped in crispy bacon. Bacon? Maybe the butchers in Soria have as great a sway over the restaurant chefs as they seem to have over me.

Chapter 3

Foreigners in Town

We head home to Almazán on pitch-black roads. It's midnight and foggy. The leased car has French number plates, which was cheaper for some reason. At the entrance to town, two Guardia Civil signal us to pull over. They must have noticed the foreign number plates. They're always in pairs. This branch of the law has never been known for employing the brainy recruits, and then they top it off by giving them a gun. The Guardia is the oldest law-enforcement mob in Spain, originally established in the nineteenth century to ensure safe passage on rural roads, where bandits had begun holding up carriages. Spain also has its Policía Nacional and Policía Municipal, who work together in some way, and all have slightly different roles. I've never worked out how exactly their differing jurisdictions work and I don't think many Spaniards have either.

I'm a little nervous. Both officers clutch a semi-automatic weapon and I vividly remember the abuse of power by the Civil Guard from my time in Spain in the 1970s. They were a force to be reckoned with during the Franco regime, when they were universally feared, and it seems they still try to maintain that aura today. We're on a deserted road out of town; there's no one else around. If we disappear no one will know. We open the window on the driver's side reluctantly, letting in the icy wind, so the officer can see inside. One looks deep into the car and confirms he's dealing with strangers. Foreigners are a rare sight around here. He probably suspects that we're up to no good.

'*Pasaporte*,' he barks, a puff of cold breath punctuating the command.

We do a desperate dive into handbags and pockets to produce what's asked for. Meanwhile, his partner keeps watch over his *compañero* and points his weapon at our front tyres in case we're planning a quick getaway. We had some wine with dinner, not too many we hope …

Once he has a look at the *pasaportes*, he grunts, '*Licencia*.'

'Licence, Alex,' I say quietly. Our guard swings his torch over to see who's talking. Blinded, I explain that my husband does not speak as much Spanish as I do, so I interpret for him.

~

This interaction with the Guardia Civil takes me back to one of my first nights in Spain as an eighteen-year-old. We were four young northern-European girls renting a holiday house on a hill by the sea. We were confident and strong; that is, until we heard what we thought was an intruder. One of my friends woke up screaming that she'd heard someone slowly walking around trying to open the screen doors to each of the bedrooms. Instantly we were all awake, huddling together on the terrace. Seeing two Guardia Civil stationed next to their motorbikes on the road below, we called for help. Spain in the 1970s was still a dictatorship with El Generalísimo Franco at the helm, and the Guardia Civil 'protecting' the villages and the roads. It seemed the *guardias*, with their green uniforms and ridiculous triangular black hats, initially seemed to take their guard duties quite seriously that night.

The two officers ran up the steep sandstone steps, one of them clutching a transistor radio. It wasn't the kind of weapon I would have brought to confront potential intruders, but we gave them the benefit of the doubt. We had no common lingo between us as I did not speak Spanish back then. Perhaps they didn't understand why we'd called them. Maybe we weren't making ourselves clear. It didn't seem to matter much. We were fully expecting them to examine the flimsy locks on the doors, one of which looked like it had been forced a bit. But they didn't seem overly interested in looking for evidence of a break-in. Instead, they switched on their radio and *Ole!* the *guardias* skilfully began to demonstrate flamenco paces, arms held high, stamping their feet and clapping their hands to the rhythm. They insisted that now was the perfect time to learn the national dance. At two in the morning, we weren't so keen. We wanted a bit more attention to our problem: examining the evidence, taking fingerprints, calling for reinforcements, searching the surrounding bushland, anything but dancing the flamenco. After some time, I realised the *guardias* were not going to be useful in any way. We'd have to get rid of them. But how?

'No *comprendo*,' the taller officer with the lazy eye repeated several times as I used what I thought were universal hand signals. Pointing at myself then two hands together, as in prayer, under my cheek with head inclined. I was pretty sure this meant 'sleep' in Spain too, then I pointed at the officers, next indicating the direction of their motorbikes. The *guardias* feigned incomprehension. Finally, the short stocky one with the jug-handle ears, possibly accustomed to rejection by the opposite sex, gave up. The *guardias* were persuaded we really wanted to go back to bed ... without them.

From that night onwards until the end of our holiday, each evening, a pair of officers of the Guardia Civil were stationed on the road below the house, possibly waiting for us to call them again.

In hindsight, I strongly suspect that the *guardias* themselves were the 'intruders' that night, creating the opportunity for flamenco dancing with the obvious hope of more action. I've always been a bit wary of this mob since that first encounter.

~

On the road outside Almazán, the officer studies us carefully for a good while. After what seems like an eternity, Alex finds his papers and hands over both his Australian and his international driver's licences. Again, the officer takes his time to examine both documents with a strong flashlight. He compares the details in the passport against the driver's licence, shines the light in our eyes once more, then over the back seat, asking us to open the boot, which he checks for contraband. He saunters back to the front of the car for round two. Snowflakes are falling. He must be freezing his arse off but evidently his duty to this potential threat to national security overrides the falling temperatures.

'Car papers.' Alex finds them quickly and hands them over. 'Why are you here?'

If he continues to look at us this way, I feel like I could confess to any bank robbery or unsolved crime that may have happened in recent years.

'We're renting a house in town,' I say.

'*Por qué aquí?*' ('Why here?') he repeats.

That's hard to answer. I don't think saying 'I don't really know' or 'I'm trying to find myself' would cut it, so I murmur something about liking the birds and the beauty of nature in this province.

Finally, disappointed perhaps that he can dig up nothing untoward, he waves us off. I hope we entertained him for a bit on this long, cold night. Slightly relieved, we go on through the deserted streets, over the Duero bridge, past the strikingly illuminated

St Michael's Church and the palace, and along the fortified town wall. Alex keeps repeating, '*Por qué aqui?* Why here?' It rolls of his tongue by the time we head up the dark track towards the cemetery and enter town at the Puerta del Mercado, reaching our safe little house on the fortified wall. *Por qué aqui*, indeed!

~

The following morning, we are ready to explore the countryside around us and keen to find some local maps. The town square has a tiny Tourist Information Office in the walls of the old palace, mostly for Spanish tourists rather than foreigners like us. The woman behind the desk is beside herself with excitement at finding out that we are from Australia. She's a tidy-looking woman with a pitch-black fringed bob. Never has she heard of any Australians visiting the town. She immediately assumes we are related to Renske, our landlady, the only other foreigner they know. She's surprised to hear we found the house online and not because we know our landlady.

She keeps asking: 'But why here? Why this town?'

For a person paid to promote the town, she doesn't show a lot of confidence in its merits. I ask for some brochures in English so Alex can understand them easier. She only has one that's not in Spanish she tells us. It covers the whole province of Soria.

'Fantastic! That's a start,' I say.

This leaflet provides us with more entertainment than we assumed at first glance. Spain has never been big on having things translated professionally. Often, if someone's teenage son or daughter studies English at high school, they get to translate whatever official information is produced. I assume that nowadays Google Translate also works overtime on Spanish pamphlets. These are then printed before any English speaker gets to check them. Spanish writing is often florid and does not handle automatic translations well. The result is often hilarious. To quote the very start of Alex's tourist brochure:

> Two hills and a lengthy collection of poems cradle rhymes and memory in Soria. City of ink, paper and beauties, the capital is nothing but a hill on which promenades can be prolonged as words do, while images of an intimate world crowd together its typical Castilian streets.

There is also:

> Romanesque, tiny, tender province city with small streets and lace curtains, the city of the river Duero offers walkers a wonderful destination for the emotions that interweave slow.

We have to see this city that caters for the emotions to interweave, slow or otherwise. As lovers of rail travel, we decide to take the train from Almazán to Soria capital. The Madrid to Soria line comes past our small town to pick up and set down passengers. It's a short hike to the station, where we buy a ticket from the stationmaster, a profoundly serious man, buckling under the pressure of managing two trains a day. He still seems to have a bit of time to lovingly tend some flowerbeds on the main platform, where snowdrops are just poking up out of the soil. He's less interested in travellers wanting to actually catch trains. We finally manage to get him to leave the weeding to sell us some tickets.

The train winds its way through delightful pine forests with an understorey springing into effervescent green. The pine trees are milked for their resin, which has a host of different uses, including glue, varnish and sealant. Cuts are made in the bark, from which a trickle of resin drips into a cup. There's quite a pine resin industry here, judging by the number of trees we see with cups attached.

The train is not very full and few travellers get on or off. Presumably, it's heavily subsidised by either the federal or the regional government. This train helps to keep the least populated part of Spain connected to the capital, Madrid, in a couple of comfortable hours' journey.

Despite the confused words of the tourism brochure, the capital of Soria province, also called Soria, is a lovely city worth visiting. The plan today is to wander around to see some of the old buildings in town. We appear to be the only non-Spaniards here. People stare as they pass us on the street and some even turn to have a better look. We cross the road to walk in the sunshine as it's still bitterly cold.

Some palaces and castles have been converted to government offices and public places. One of these has an exhibition of photos depicting the landscapes of Castilla y Leon accompanied by the poems of Antonio Machado, a venerated poet who taught in Soria for several years. The *Sorianos* adore Antonio Machado, and his poems are writ large on buildings throughout the city. He has a host of things named after him: a luxury hotel, streets, plazas, bars, buildings and I believe a type of pork sausage (although I may have made that up!).

The college where he taught is still used as a school. We seek permission to enter and are told we can have a look around the ground-floor corridors, which circle a large patio. A grey-haired woman sporting a bright pink streak of hair above her left eyebrow watches us with interest as we go around. When we're about to leave she asks us if we would like to see the schoolroom where Machado taught.

'Well, yes, indeed. We'd love that,' we reply.

Pink Streak takes us up the stairs to the next level and takes out a bunch of keys hidden under her jumper.

26

'This is the room Antonio Machado taught in for many years,' she whispers almost reverently. 'It's exactly how it was. We've not changed a single thing.'

The room has large windows filled with opaque glass.

'Perhaps he was a boring teacher and the opaque glass stopped the students looking out the window,' Alex whispers under his breath.

Rows of narrow antique desk-and-seat combos are assembled for some fifteen students. Machado's desk is tall, towering over those of his pupils. It may have helped to establish who was boss in the room. Pink Streak strokes Machado's desk lovingly. His buttocks would have once slid across the polished wood of the seat, after all. It's obvious she adores this room, the place where greatness once taught literature to the local teenage boys, instilling a love of poetry that even now, several generations later, is still celebrated in this town.

Our guide rattles off the poet's full name: Antonio Cipriano José María y Francisco de Santa Ana Machado y Ruiz. Sensibly, he's known by two of these names only: Antonio Machado. This we assume is the finale of the performance and we thank Pink Streak profusely for her kindness as she takes us down the stairs again. We're about to head off when she asks if we'd also like to see the museum, normally closed to the public. Would we?

'*Sí, por favor!*' says Alex. I nod enthusiastically too.

We're so lucky. This chance encounter with Pink Streak leads us to a scientific treasure trove not many would be fortunate enough to see. The small museum is housed in a single room jammed with glass cabinets. There's only enough space to squeeze sideways between the displays, which are filled with stuffed birds, fish, mammals, an extensive insect collection and many of the instruments early 1900s scientists would have lusted over. Pink Streak looks at us expectantly.

'What do you think?'

'*Magnifico*,' Alex exclaims with that beatific smile of his. She beams in the light of those blue eyes.

Pink Streak has done us a splendid favour. I'm sure not many foreigners get the royal tour that we have. We depart and thank her for her time. She's pleased with her good deed for the day and we're grateful for a unique experience; everyone's a winner.

~

Although we haven't seen any other foreigners, there are Spanish tourists in town. In Spain, it is customary to bring home a delicacy for the rest of the family, something emblematic of the location visited. Waiting at the airport in Alicante in the 1970s and 1980s, you could recognise the passengers coming off the plane from Mallorca because they would all be carrying big round cardboard boxes labelled Ensaimadas de Mallorca, a soft, sweet pastry typical of the Balearic Islands. Spanish folks, so very fond of food, celebrate the regional gastronomic differences at every opportunity. A sweet from one region is often not available anywhere else.

There are several specialty shops in town, with foodie treats specific to this region, catering to this custom. One of these in the main street looks so good from the window display we have a peek inside. The woman at the till is quick off the mark, ready to offer some sheep's cheese.

'Would you like to try?' she coos to Alex as she holds out a plate.

'Don't mind if I do,' Alex replies in English.

He tastes it and swoons. Whatever she's given him has hit the spot. He's drawn further and further into the bowels of the shop, making his way innocently towards the owner's husband, who stands ready to offer him more cheeses to try. Alex falls for it hook, line and sinker, walking out with two half rounds of sheep's and goats' cheese, some chorizos and a jar of truffle honey. The shop owner drizzled some truffle honey on a sharp sheep's cheese, which was all Alex needed to be sold on that idea. Not quite the price of liquid gold but not cheap either.

We return to Almazán with cheeses under our arms, sausages in our pockets, and stop off at the local patisserie, which makes a unique sweet we've heard about. The shop has been around since 1820 and is now run by Celina, a descendant of the original owner. These handmade treats are called Yemas de Santa Teresa, a concoction of egg yolk and sugar. They're extremely sweet.

Once we offload the wagon wheels of cheese, the chorizos and honey, we contemplate the tourist brochure once more and consider if our 'emotions interweaved slowly' as we walked around town. The jury may be out on that one.

~

In town later that evening, we see our first ever female Guardia Civil. Goodness me, how things have changed. For a woman who has always believed and fought for equal rights, I shouldn't be surprised to see her, but I am. I've obviously never even considered that female Guardia could exist. It gives me such a thrill to notice that not only is she here, in uniform, but she's at least a head taller than either of the three male officers standing next to her. The *tricornio*, the strange three-cornered hat, is now reserved for parades and ceremonies only. The day-to-day uniform with less unusual headgear has a fresh look and in it the woman officer looks striking, capable and strong. This Amazonian Guardia Civil is another example of the positive changes in modern Spain. With changes like these afoot, it's less likely they'll want to teach us to dance the flamenco.

Chapter 4

Meeting the Visa Police

Alex, as an Australian citizen, can stay in the Schengen Area (that whole bunch of European countries that have a common border) for only 90 days in any 180 days. Unfortunately, we realise this only a couple of days before we plan to leave Sydney. It's a weekend and we can't call anyone for advice. We're planning to be in Spain indefinitely, and that's a lot longer than 90 days. For some reason it had not occurred to us that there would be a limit on Alex's stay as an automatic visa is always granted upon entry. We only now realise these are only valid for three months. Bugger.

We panic, thinking the whole living in Spain idea is about to come crashing down. Once we recover from our dismay, we take a deep breath and decide to take the risk and see what happens when we get there.

The Police for Foreigners Department is just off the main square. Once inside, the offices are well guarded by a duo of a police officer and a Guardia Civil.

'What are you here for?'

'A visa extension,' I reply, smiling politely.

We're asked to explain in more detail what we want, why we are here. After some consultation between the different branches of the law, we get directed through the doors to the left. A fellow with a very deep, gravelly voice, contrasting his fragile frame, also asks what we want.

'A visa extension,' we explain once more.

He stops us from going any further, sending us to a waiting room to the right. After a few minutes we can proceed to the inner sanctum. The office has six desks set up in a U-shape. The bureaucrats at each station seem to ignore their visitors and chat to each other animatedly while looking at one another's screens. We get a stern-looking officer, a woman of fifty or so who likely has not smiled in the last decade.

'He is legal for now and he should come back towards the end of his 90 days and then we'll decide if we'll let him stay longer,' she says as she nods towards Alex.

'She can give you some forms,' she grumbles as she waves her hand vaguely in the direction of the next desk.

To be fair, these public servants are not likely to come across many non-nationals like us, grey nomads. There is a word they use for people in our situation: *guiris* (pronounced 'giri'), a colloquial slur used in Spain and applied to older foreign tourists, particularly from the rich countries to the north.

We had a coffee in a different bar this morning. The proprietor called out '*buen viaje*' (travel safely) when we left, as if he could not conceive that we could be doing anything but travelling through this place after a quick pit stop. Nobody assumes we'd stay here for any length of time as there are so many more suitable destinations in Spain that have famous tourist sites or beaches.

Sourpuss on the next desk does not seem any friendlier or even faintly more interested than the original Iron Lady. She gives us some forms to take away and fill out. If we bring proof that we have travel insurance, tickets home, enough funds to support ourselves (original and duplicate, and translated into Spanish by a qualified translator) *and* exceptional circumstances to support our request for a visa extension, they may consider our application.

'What may exceptional circumstances entail?' I ask.

'We'll decide that when you bring the papers back to us.'

As we leave, Sourpuss gives us a suspicious, lingering look.

~

While I'm scribbling away in my notebook, Alex spends a day getting paperwork together for his visa extension. There's a fair bit of swearing coming from the loft as Alex tries to print out our bank statements, travel insurance and all the other documents the authorities have requested. He tries for ages to get the old printer working, swears some more and eventually gives up. The *librería* (the bookshop, not the library) is run by a wiry, efficient-looking middle-aged woman called Ester. The bookshop sells a few books but mainly piles of other paraphernalia like schoolbags, toys, art materials and knick-knacks. The *librería* also does photocopies and printing for its clients. Ester charges a pittance for the printing but takes the time to ask what we're doing here, how long we're staying and why on earth we chose Almazán?

Armed with all the paperwork we think we need, we make the second assault on the immigration bureaucrats. We are directed to a man with a receding hairline, dressed in a bright pink woollen jumper. The office still looks bare and unloved. There's a dying pot plant in a corner. We explain what we're after to Pink Jumper this time. As we do, Sourpuss right next to us starts to interject. At hearing this the Iron Lady comes over from her desk at the other end of the office.

It's not going well at this point.

Smiling my best smile, I say, 'What can we do about this situation? We are retired, have money to spend and would like to spend it in this province. Surely there is a way you can make this happen.'

Alex tells me later that it was at this point that their facial expressions changed. Suddenly, there's a distinct transformation in the Iron Lady, who seems to carry a lot of street cred with the rest of the office crowd. Understanding we have money to spend, she is now patting me on the shoulder and I think I can almost see a smile.

The Iron Lady tries to say that we should put in the application for an extension just before the 90 days are up. They will doubtlessly take an awfully long time to deal with it and possibly that will be enough time for us to get a longer term visa via the Netherlands using my Dutch passport. She tries to say it in such a way that I must read between the lines. I'm obviously a bit thick or my Spanish is still rusty because she has to make it clearer and clearer.

Now this is the Spain I remember! A land where the rules will bend if they like you. Wanting to spend our money in the province must have struck a chord, for the atmosphere has become a bit more positive now. We pack up and disappear with goodbyes to all.

'See you in 90 days. Thank you for your advice.'

'Quick Alex, before they change their mind,' I whisper as we scurry out the door.

Chapter 5

Living Like a Local

One test of whether I'm truly living like a local or just pretending includes the dreaded proposition of finding a new hairdresser. Going to a stylist on the other side of the world strikes fear into the heart of many a woman, but I tell myself it's just a practical exercise in observation and deduction: find a woman with a reasonable haircut, be brave and ask her where she gets it done. Having waited as long as possible, the time has come. I see a middle-aged woman in the supermarket who looks quite stylish with a trendy haircut, so I approach her.

'I like your hair.'

'Thank you,' she says, looking at me suspiciously at first, wondering if she should be flattered or worried about this weird foreigner complimenting random people on their hair.

'I'd love to know who cuts your hair. Is it someone local?'

I'm sure she can tell I need this. She has a quick glance at my locks and concludes my need is genuine. She gives me a name, Piedad, which literally translated means piety, still a commonly used name and wished-for character trait in this Catholic nation. It seems to me a name more suited to a nun than a hairdresser.

The next morning on our bike ride, freezing at 1 degree Celcius,

I investigate the shopfront of Piedad's salon in the newer part of town. Fearlessly, I go in and show Piedad a photo of the haircut I am after.

She tells me quite firmly, 'You can't have that! Your hair is not suitable for that cut!'

Far from being demure and benign as a nun, Piedad seems a bit of a dragon. I don't tell her this is the haircut my Sydney stylist has done for me for a couple of years now. She's off my list of potential hairdressers. I ride my bike towards the next *peluquería* (hairdresser) in the street. This is obviously the salon street, as there are several in a row. The next one looks good from the outside, photos of models with fashionable haircuts in the shop window.

As soon as I open the door, I know I've made a mistake, but I'm committed now to going all the way in. At least seven older women in various stages of having their hair tinted in inappropriate shades of orange or red note my arrival with shameless interest. One leans forward so far she almost falls off her chair.

'What do you want?' she calls out.

Turns out she is not the proprietor or even someone who works there, unless they employ octogenarians. All eyes are on me, mouths almost salivating with the excitement of a stranger in their midst. The owner comes out to see what the fuss is all about. She's in her fifties and seems to be wearing her teenage daughter's clothes, including tights in multi-colours that fail to hide the lumpy cellulite on her thighs. Her top is stretched over her ample bosom, boobs struggling to get out, hair badly bleached, while her eyeliner meanders randomly across her lids. There's no way I'm going to let her loose on my head. I mumble that I would like her business card so I can call later to make an appointment. A big fat lie, but I'll say anything to get out the door as fast as possible at this point. The scrutiny of these elderly *señoras* is too much to bear.

How can I even contemplate that we could fit in here? I stand out like dogs' balls with my steely grey head and tall Dutch genes, towering above the villagers.

During one of the many processions, looking over the heads of the other spectators in front of me, I notice that there is hardly a woman with hair in its natural colour. Occasionally, there's one grey female head in the crowd, but the rest make up every shade available at the beauty salon or the hair product aisle in the supermarket. Only girls up to fifteen or sixteen have their lovely natural dark brown or black hair. When I lived in Alicante in the 1970s blonde hair was the aspiration of many Spanish women. Matrons who could afford it would bleach their dark or greying tresses. The ads on TV showed almost exclusively blonde women to advertise wares in a country with an overwhelming majority of brunettes, as if the fridge or vacuum coveted by a *rubia* (a blonde) was way more desirable than that of a brunette. Before school, mothers used to comb their children's hair with a comb dipped in peroxide water, slowly creating the 'naturally' blonde children they wished for. It seems that folks here continue to favour any hair colour other than their natural one.

I still need a haircut. There are other hairdressers in town to choose from so I try again. By the time I work up the courage to go into another hairdresser, I am in the old part of town again. Boldly I push open the heavy door to reveal only one client inside, unlike the entire women's league of the other shop. Patricia, the owner, looks quite stylish with a Cleopatra style black bob and black tunic with chunky boots. When I show her the photo of the desired haircut, she seems to have no problem with that, inspiring enough confidence to make a booking. She tells me to come back at midday.

When I arrive, Patricia is doing a blow-drying job on a blonde lady who is more likely grey without Patricia's help. I sit down on a two-person couch next to another elderly woman, but I'm ushered to the basin without delay by Patricia's offsider. The seat massages my back as I sit down, while the assistant washes and does things to my head. I'm not sure how many times it is necessary to put goo in my hair, move it around and then rinse it out again, but my scalp gets a lovely massage in the process. While I am shampooed and rinsed, Patricia finishes the blow-wave and cuts the hair of a raven-haired man in record time. I'm delivered to Patricia herself, timed to coincide with her availability, and transferred to a chair in front of the mirror where she does her magic. I try to show her the image of the desired haircut, but she only gives it a cursory peek before she's off and shearing. A woman of few words it seems, and extremely quick to get to work. She wastes no time with small talk and attacks my head silently with a type of long razorblade. I view her technique with a degree of trepidation, but I'm trapped now.

When I lived in Spain in the 1970s, I had a classic hippie look, straight long hair parted in the middle. As a result, I lack any Spanish hairdressing vocabulary. I don't know the words for *trim*, *thin*, *texture*, *spikey*, *gel*, *mousse* and so on. Patricia, as a woman of few words herself, doesn't seem to expect me to say much either. In Australia you generally have to put up with vacuous conversation along the lines of 'got any plans for tonight/this weekend/your next holiday?' But not Patricia. Concentrating on the job, she remains silent. She was equally silent with the blonde woman and the raven-haired man. I'm all done in fifteen minutes flat. This is the fastest haircut (shearing?) I've ever had but the result is fine. Not spectacular but adequate. It makes me think my hairdresser at home fluffs around a bit for an hour to justify the $100-plus price tag. The bill here is a big surprise. A fifth of what I'd pay in Sydney and in a quarter of the time.

~

After this super fast hairdressing experience, there's plenty of time left for lunch. The weather's warmed up since this morning and it's pleasant enough for a barbeque. We've bought sausages and lamb chops (I managed to buy something other than pig!), which we'll have with a salad. It's still barely 12 degrees, but in the sunny walled garden it's simply perfect. From the upper terrace we marvel at the top of the timeworn stone gate into town, which is just visible. Beyond the gate, the backdrop is dotted with fields and piggeries. In the other direction, over the roofs of the houses, the old church towers high and mighty over the age-old town.

If we're truly living like locals it would be wrong not to have at least a glass of red wine during an outdoor lunch. Maybe, just maybe, a siesta after that. When in Rome, after all! Siesta time is still observed in Spain. Businesses and shops close in the afternoon, from one till four o'clock, or from two till five. Not everybody goes home anymore but one would not think of calling a tradesman or anyone between these times at least. The main meal of the day is usually eaten between two and four o'clock and in the evening folks have a lighter meal at nine or ten o'clock or even later.

After a siesta, the rest of the day sort of mellows into the evening. But, before the evening meal, a drink at a bar and some tapas are in order. We're trying to find out where everyone goes for evening drinks and a tapa or two in our adopted town. This is important business requiring a systematic approach. The bars closest to us get our attention first. What time to go? Work finishes at eight or nine o'clock at the earliest, so no point going before that time. We still leave home too early at eight. The two bars closest to home in the Plaza Mayor have a sprinkling of people. The next nearest is Bar Archi on the Plaza de Santa Maria, next to the church. It's busier here. Despite the cold, some tables outside are occupied by families so the kids can play in the square while the adults smoke. So different from Australia where, following some unwritten rule, children are in bed by seven-thirty or so. Inside there are small groups playing cards, others looking over their shoulders. Occasionally one or another gets up to get their nicotine fix outside. All new arrivals go around and kiss at least a few of the other patrons, who are presumably friends or family. Anyone in a town like this must do a lot of kissing on any given day, as all friends and family are greeted and farewelled with two kisses.

A drink in Bar Archi leads us to think about what other bars may have going on. Down the road, next to the other stone gate into town, is Bar El Arco. We've had some morning coffees here and it's a super busy place. Not at this time of day though. Now it's pretty much empty. It must either get going late at night or it's a morning bar. I'm sure there are unspoken agreements between the residents about which bar to go to at what time. If we want to live like the locals, we'll have to uncover the secrets.

~

We feel more and more like we're living here rather than being tourists on an extended holiday, even if the locals still ask us why we are here. We don't go sightseeing every day but spend some time going for walks or just at home, reading, writing, cooking and answering emails. The days are warming up a bit. All around us the fields are now ploughed or already seeded or planted. The soils are dark red. The Rio Duero shimmers silvery in the late afternoon light. The river scenery is dotted with distant villages surrounded by terraced hills.

At sunset, out of the wind, the views from the upper terrace are enchanting. This is the perfect place for a quiet drink. We're trying the truffle honey bought in Soria town with a mature manchego cheese and thin slices of bread. A divine combination, despite the odour of hog from the piggeries nearby. A fitting rural smell, we tell ourselves. As the sun sinks in the sky, the pencil pine-lined road to the cemetery is bathed in a pink hue. A lone widow dressed in black is doing her final visit to her husband for the day, may he rest in peace. Or at least that is what I fancy she's doing.

Earlier today we walked around the graveyard we can see from the terrace. Cemeteries are a sight to behold in this area. One family grave is more elaborate than the rest, immodestly decorated with an oversupply of angels, cherubs and flower garlands. Many graves have a photo of the dearly departed in their heyday. Walking around the cemetery I think about the lives lived here. It's strangely absorbing to go from grave to grave wondering who knew each other. Were they friend or foe during the civil war in the 1930s? Were they classmates in school or did they have a fling later in life? It's sad to see the number of tiny graves. Neonatal survival was poor even as late as the middle of the last century.

Funerals are generally held the day after a person dies. This custom is cultural today rather than a necessity. In the past, lack of refrigeration would have made such speed a good idea, particularly during the heat of summer. Burials are still the go here. People don't go much for cremation and the cemetery is a lively part of town, as visiting one's departed loved ones is still very much in practice. There is a special day (another fiesta of course) called the Day of the Dead. Over the first two days of November families go to the cemetery and clean the grave, have a picnic and perhaps pour some rum on the remembrance stone for Grandad, who loved a tipple. Each family has its own traditions to honour their deceased relatives.

There are also different regional traditions around the Day of the Dead. In Castilla there is a myth that the dead leave their graves on the night of the second of November, mostly to scare those who have partied out late. Some towns have processions in the streets around the cemetery while praying the rosary by candlelight. In

Galicia, the traditional belief is that the dead attend the mass offered on their behalf. Yet another way to combine myth and traditional beliefs to everybody's satisfaction.

I pinch myself as I sit here on the terrace on top of the ancient stone wall surrounding the medieval village. What a lucky duck I am to be here sharing this dream with Alex. Picking up a penniless backpacker in a bar in Spain forty years ago has turned out to be the best thing I ever did.

I think about how 'living like a local' is panning out so far. Today, more than any other day, the views and the smells give me the sense of being in the heart of my beloved Spain once more. I have conquered the local haircut, the morning coffee bars and the evening tapas bars, but would I extend living like a local to *dying* like one? Would I ever be local enough to be buried in Spanish soil? I'm not sure, but I do fancy the idea of my relatives and friends having a party on my grave on the Day of the Dead!

Chapter 6

Quién es El Ultimo?

I love waking up to a dawn chorus of birdsong. The wooden shutters on all the windows make the bedroom as dark as a tomb, so the birds reassure me every morning that I'm not dead. I poke Alex in the ribs to make sure he's not dead either. He's not!

Once up and about and on our walk I notice anthills forming in the cracks in the concrete footpath. It's the first time I've seen any ants since we arrived. Obviously, the weather is warming up. Is there some ant advisory board that tells all ants to get up and at it, as summer is on the way? We hear new bird calls too. The forests of Europe are often quiet compared with the Australian bush, but in this lonely province of Spain birdsong is ever-present. I've been wondering which bird makes a specific call I often hear. It sounds like the beep of a car reversing. I soon realise it's the hoopoe. I'd seen them before but didn't know their call. The hoopoe flies more like a butterfly than a bird, an interesting fluttering flight, and today we see one just as he calls out so we're able to put two and two together.

A longer hike along the Rio Duero today takes us around the other side of the park to the newer part of Almazán. It's a fairly unattractive suburban environment comprised mostly of brick high rise, yet most people now seem to prefer this over the older houses inside the old town walls. A strong rural smell comes from the direction of the pig farms as the wind blows into town today. There's hardly anybody about this early; it's a holiday again. We'd thought it might be one of the many religious holidays, but we learn that it's Community Day for the autonomous region of Castilla y Leon.

The Spanish love to commemorate uprisings against authorities, even unsuccessful ones, as was the case against King Charles in 1521. The populace revolting against authority is a repeating pattern across Spain. Even though the Battle of Villalar was a failure, it is still worth celebrating the bravery of ordinary Spaniards rising to protect their rights, some five hundred years later.

Many shops are closed today except for the petrol stations, which are always open on Sundays and fiestas. The smell of bread wafts through the air as we get closer, replacing the smell of pigs. Not only do they have bread, but the service stations bake it freshly on the premises. No self-respecting Spaniard would go without freshly baked bread when they may be holding a barbeque or a special lunch because it's a public holiday. When everywhere else is closed, the petrol stations always have bread, ham, cheese and alcohol.

There's a bar right next to the petrol station unambiguously called La Gasolinera (The Gas Station). Smokers stand in the door, so we know it's open, even though the dark glass and low light inside doesn't make it look like anybody's home. Pushing the heavy door, we're surprised to find the place packed. We take a seat at the counter. The massive U-shaped bar already has some twenty patrons sitting and standing around it. They're all eating tapas and drinking coffee or even wine at nine o'clock in the morning. A common morning drink in Spain is a *carajillo*, a coffee fortified with rum, whiskey or other spirits. Two *camareros* (waiters) are run off their feet delivering fortified drinks and tapas to the patrons around the bar. They call out to the customers seated at tables to 'come and get it' – no table service here. Rows of tortillas line the bar, the traditional ones with potatoes and others with spinach, ham or prawns. Also on offer are meatballs in tomato sauce, boiled egg with anchovies and chunks of canned tuna and, of course, the inevitable *torreznos*. So this is where everyone in town goes for breakfast, it seems.

Thoughts of serious weight gain enter my consciousness every time these crispy pigskin *torreznos* come into view. How is it possible that everyone manages their weight here? I see very few obese individuals. Chubby, yes, and stocky, most of them, but very rarely anyone who is truly obese. I read a few days ago that the Spanish are due to overtake the Japanese in a few years' time as being the longest lived people on Earth. This is supposedly due to the beneficial Mediterranean diet. They must be eating that healthy food at home because what's on offer in the bars, while scrumptious, doesn't look like it would extend one's life for very long. Not to mention, Spaniards still appear to smoke like chimneys. Every bar has a few smokers standing outside in the cold. The ubiquitous smell of much-loved brands like Fortuna and the heavy-duty Ducados is thick in the air. Often, we push through a curtain of smoke before getting to the door of a bar.

~

We traipse about the countryside looking at houses to rent in scenic villages around the capital of Soria. The owner of our rental place will be back in Spain in a few months and we're searching for somewhere to rent longer term. We're pretty sure now that this is the area we'd like to be. The Costa Blanca, where I used to live, is not the place to return to, transformed as it has been by foreign investment and greed. We want to be somewhere untouched by crass tourism and precooked frozen paella being flogged to holidaymakers. Castile and Leon seems to be that place. It's much more like the Spain of my best loved memories. It has endless green mountains, exquisitely clustered farmhouses and winding roads. Small hamlets are unspoiled by rampant progress, the lovely old buildings preserved in perpetuity, many under World Heritage protection, and the locals live their lives unaffected by the fever of the tourist dollar.

Every now and then little niggly thoughts come into my head. Is this the right thing? How will I cope being a stranger somewhere yet again? A migrant once more. Will we miss friends and family? Is this even fair on Alex? He has much deeper roots in Australia than I have. My Spanish is better than his. We talk about this as we're travelling on rural roads in a landscape with distant castles, passing villages defying gravity as they hang off rocky cliffs. Any qualms are dispatched as we are both taken with the thrill and excitement of being here. But some niggles remain ...

~

This province is full of all the things Alex and I both love: nature, history, birds and good food with excellent wines. We meander along the back roads of vineyards and almond orchards, discover pretty villages with a Romanesque church or a good bar for lunch. Both are worthwhile finds. Today we're off having a look at some houses west of the capital, near the town of Ucero. We meet Josh and Maya in a bar near their village at noon. First, we must have a drink, of course. By the time we get to Ucero, it is nearly lunch time, so we eat. This is so Spanish. In the end the stops for drinks and food are so plentiful that we run out of time for any of the planned house hunting. Needless to say, a good time is had by all.

The place we eat at is a renowned and exquisite restaurant called El Balcón del Cañón on the banks of the river Chico. In the sun it's warm enough for a table outside by the water. A gaggle of geese noisily make it clear that they are anticipating some table scraps. They tread water right in front of us until some bread gets tossed. The menu is full of pig in whatever way you may like it prepared. Inevitably, we start with some *torreznos*, mushrooms, for which this zone is also famous, grilled pork, pâté with goats' cheese and a salad, followed by some *postres caseros*, home-cooked desserts.

The plan is to do a hike after lunch in the nearby nature park, called Cañón del Río Lobos (Wolf River Canyon). A couple of glasses of wine while sitting in the sun makes me joyful but doesn't inspire vigorous bushwalking right after. Fortunately, the rest of the day unfolds languidly. The walking is not arduous, only one kilometre gets us to the Ermita Virgen de la Cueva (Virgin of the Cave Hermitage). There is indeed a cave, devoid of virgins though, it seems. A few kilometres further along a well-trodden path following the river, we spot the vultures we've come to see. The park is home to a dense forest of junipers and clusters of pine, as well as pairs of griffon vultures. It's also an important reserve for golden eagles, Egyptian eagles and falcons. Although there are no wolves here anymore, there are deer, boars, squirrels, otters, badgers and wildcats, none of which we see, but we're pleased to know they are here.

Once the effect of the wine has worn off, I thoroughly enjoy strolling through this park. Along the way there are some ancient beehives perched on a rock wall. These are supposed to have been built by Templar monks hundreds of years ago, fashioned from hollow trees with bark lids. Looking for virgins in caves, seeing vultures soar and old beehives in one afternoon, what more could I ask for? Well, a castle, I guess. Towards Ucero there's a Knights Templar castle, no less. The same Templars that built the beehives. A combative mob, these monastic warriors were known as the Poor Fellow-Soldiers of Christ, and they left behind imposing castles and fortresses throughout the twelfth and thirteenth centuries. Not so poor after all, perhaps. Many of these castles remain standing today, including this one. Worth a visit for the castle itself but also the vista from the top of the hill, overlooking the impressive topography towards Ucero.

Along the way we have a look at a few houses for rent, but nothing spectacular leaps out. They either have no garden, are dark inside or disappoint in some other way. Perhaps we need to consider buying something if we really want to settle in this region which boasts both majestic vultures and quality restaurants.

~

We shop mostly at the weekly Almazán markets and they are on again today. My memories of the old Spain involve a lot of markets. You still had to haggle and all prices were given in duros, five peseta entities of the old money. Something might be 20 duros, meaning a hundred pesetas. I've not seen any haggling in the markets here. The wares have prices on cardboard signs and shoppers order a kilo of this or 300 grams of that without the enjoyable argument about the price. The old market in Alicante was somewhere I liked to take friends and family from northern Europe. You could smell the markets three blocks away. Hardly any refrigeration, just some melting ice to keep the fish and meat cool while it reeked to high heaven. My northern friends and family would almost retch with disgust at the olfactory onslaught, much to my delight, allowing me to show off how much I had 'turned native'. There's none of that now. The market today is as hygienic as anyone could wish for. Displays of fish, meat, cheese, sausages, fruit and vegetables are tasteful and hygienic and the sellers look more sophisticated too. Spain is proud of its *gastronomía* and deservedly so. The food in the region is of the hearty variety rather than, for example, the more modest elegance of French food, but it's made from quality fresh ingredients and is usually delicious.

We've been to the markets a few times and have only now recognised an extremely important cultural custom. When you arrive at a stall from which you want to purchase, you ask loudly: '*Quién es el último?*' (Who is the last one?) This is so that you know when it's your turn. We'd seen arguments at the markets about 'who is next' but have only just detected the 'who is last' rule. I never witnessed this when I lived in the south, so I'm glad to have finally cottoned on. Proud to display my newfound knowledge, I ask each time I arrive at a new stall who the last one is. We now understand this market etiquette, but it seems that those who invented it do not play by the rules. At each stall there is at least one argument while I am waiting for my turn.

The most spirited ones are those nuggetty, diminutive matriarchs who obviously have no time to waste. At their age, perhaps they don't. Alex stays right out of it. He's not doing battle with the locals about whether it's his turn to order tomatoes. All conversation goes extremely fast as the women seem to have a go at the older men in the queue. They may be experienced at intimidating men like their own husbands. One tough old gentleman is not having it, and he continues with his order to the stallholder, even engaging in some banter about whether the garlic was early this year and where it's coming from. He seems to be enjoying the distress he's causing to a couple of argumentative women. I am impressed with his garlic savvy. He holds his ground and knows something about most produce he orders. He asks where the cheaper sultanas come from as opposed to the more expensive ones and he has an opinion about the two types of walnuts available, small and large. He advises another customer to get the smaller ones as they will be tastier.

The Spanish are so deeply passionate about food. They talk

about where to buy the best quality produce, how to cook it, and they love telling you about the finest meals they've had. There are so many foodies here, and I love the willingness of people to fuss over gathering the right wood to cook paella and then to spend a good part of the day getting the fire exactly the right temperature for the all-important meal.

Meanwhile at the markets, Ms I-Was-Here-Before-You calms down once a second stallholder appears from nowhere to take her order. Excitement, intrigue and almost violence among the vegetables today. The stallholders, cleverly, stay out of the whole 'whose turn is it' business. They must have worked out ages ago that they can't win shoppers by getting involved. They call out 'Who is next?' and leave the arguing up to the customers. Finally, it's our turn to order. We buy fruit and vegetables for the week, some lovely prunes, dates and some biscuits, the type eaten for breakfast with a milky coffee or a hot chocolate.

Walking back to the house, Alex relives the moment we understood Spanish market etiquette, repeating '*Quién es el último?*' as he races me back up the hill.

Chapter 7

Bringing Jesus Down

This weekend is the beginning of the significant Easter Holy Week, Semana Santa, and everyone in town is talking about 'bringing Jesus down'. Holy Week in Almazán has an elaborate program of activities, which includes Jesus visiting various places. From Palm Sunday to Easter, thousands of brotherhoods around the nation march through towns and villages in emotion-laden processions. Accompanied by a band, brotherhoods carry statues of Jesus and the Holy Virgin. I check the town council website and find there are many dates and times to see these Easter events. Today, Good Friday, is considered the most important procession as it involves the Bajada de Jesus, the bringing down of Jesus. A statue of Jesus on a donkey is brought from the Santa Maria Church via a procession to the San Pedro Church. There are two brotherhoods, like fellowships, involved in this ritual, one from each church. Both are Catholic of course.

The San Pedro Brotherhood is dressed in voluminous green capes. The Santa Maria Brotherhood, dressed in black hooded capes, are the ones bringing Jesus down. The entire town has gathered on the Plaza Mayor for this annual spectacle. There's drumming in the distance, getting louder and louder. Finally, the procession comes around the corner, accompanied by music, the people swaying side to side while carrying Jesus and his donkey on their shoulders. Only eight men do the carrying; some are elderly, worryingly so for the task at hand. The statue carriers have the black capes but not the hoods like the rest of their brotherhood, presumably to avoid tripping over and toppling Jesus. Jesus looks about life sized, but his mount is a petite grey donkey. Any bigger and the whole thing would be too hard to carry. Christ looks relaxed on his ride, sitting sideways, his feet nearly touching the ground. He wears a flowing white robe and a red cape, while expensive flower arrangements cover the statue's platform.

The brotherhoods meet on the Plaza Mayor, where everyone has congregated. Most believers hold an olive branch or a palm leaf to commemorate Jesus coming into Jerusalem on a donkey. I assume he was welcomed then too by supporters waving olive branches and palm leaves. The palm leaves are crafted into magnificent folded and plaited masterpieces, some so tall that they are used as walking sticks. Christ is followed by other statues, of Maria and other smaller Jesuses, splendid statues draped in priceless garments that must weigh a ton.

Not so long ago, these affairs were men's business only. These days the brotherhoods include women and girls too, still a minority but significant all the same. Children grow up in the brotherhood of their parents and grandparents and participate from the time they can walk. What child doesn't like a dress-up party and a parade? This participation from a young age strengthens these traditions. The brotherhoods are social networks and the children carry on the age-old customs. The brotherhood from the Santa Maria Church has some tiny kids marching. One looks about three, dressed in a severe, black hooded cape like the rest of his fraternity. His mother walks alongside, not in the procession but on the spectators' side, keeping up with the parade. Beaming, she only has eyes for her child and regularly stumbles on and off the footpath as she tries to keep up with him, snapping pictures on her phone. She's at serious risk of a sprained ankle for the sake of documenting this proud moment. Motherly pride on display, as much as Jesus on his donkey.

Once both brotherhoods are in the square, a priest goes around the gathered crowd spraying holy water to bless the faithful and their branches. Despite being at the rear of the masses during the holy water blessing, I don't miss a thing. Almazánians are short stocky individuals and it is easy to look over the tops of all heads and get a good view of what's going on. Most would be blessed indeed to make it to 160 centimetres in their stockinged feet. Alex is running around with a camera, like a mad thing. I lose him in the crowd every now and then. He's a head taller than most so he's easy to find; he's also the only man wearing a colourful beanie. Beanies are not considered to be manly unless it's really freezing, which we softies think it is.

Some of the faithful, holding the now blessed branches, make their way to the Church of San Pedro, presumably to get a good seat. Others wait for the brotherhoods to lead the way, accompanied by the band. The brotherhood members carrying Jesus appear mesmerised, swaying to the rhythm of the now more solemn music as they carry their precious cargo through the narrow streets and up the hill. The formal party is joined by Almazán notables such as the mayor, the uniformed head of the police and the top Guardia Civil in town.

The crowd follows the procession up the hill to the San Pedro Church, where mass will be held and Jesus will stay for a few days. Once the faithful enter the church clutching their blessed branches, the band leaves to go home to change into something more comfortable or to stop at a bar for a drink. We follow some walkers up the hill to our street. As we get closer, we recognise our neighbours Constanza and Lorenzo walking home with a friend. Lorenzo is dressed in the dark blue suit of the band uniform and carries a clarinet. He's been in the brotherhood band for fifty years he tells us.

'Practice is once a week and I enjoy it very much.' He's also in a brotherhood band in Soria. 'Also, a lot of practice there too,' he says.

He almost winks at me at that point. I get the feeling he's intimating he gets up to a bit of mischief when 'practising' with the band in Soria.

Not long after we get home the doorbell rings. As I open the top half of the solid barn door there's Constanza, our neighbour, holding out a plate of torrijas, a typical Easter treat she's made and would like to share with us.

'Would you please come in?' I ask.

'No *gracias*, I have things to do. I just wanted to share these sweets with you. *Aproveche!*' She calls out and she's gone.

There's no good English translation for *aproveche*. Literally it means to take advantage, but culturally it means 'enjoy your food'. Sweet-toothed Alex has not tasted torrijas before and sings Constanza's praises. With every new bite he raises a toast to the wall that separates us from our neighbours and calls '*Aproveche!*' Little by little, he's adding words to his vocabulary.

Many religious holidays in Spain have specific food prepared as part of the festivities. Although the tradition of fasting during Easter is now largely overlooked, the making and eating of Torrijas luckily is not. Torrijas are sugary golden slices of fried bread, crisp on the outside and soft inside. They're a relatively simple dish, like French toast. Old bread is soaked in milk sweetened with honey or sugar, and beaten egg, and then fried in olive oil. Sprinkled with copious amounts of cinnamon and sugar, they are simply scrumptious. Many family-recipe variations exist and, as with so many dishes in Spain, there will be no consensus on the absolute best ones. Everybody's mama makes the most delicious ones! They can be bought in shops and bars but the homemade ones like Constanza's are the finest. They signify more than a sweet treat to me. I'm chuffed, not only because I love food but because her neighbourly gesture makes us feel included in these community activities. I feel a little less like a stranger. This is the first time anyone has come to *our* house and her gift feels like a token of acceptance into the neighbourhood.

~

On Good Friday evening, the rain stops and the drums get louder and louder. Alex whistles 'Fernando' by Abba, which immediately becomes an earworm in my head. 'Can you hear the drums, Fernando?' In a city of five thousand residents, the band has chosen our corner for all their last-minute rehearsals. We've heard drums all this Holy Week as the different brotherhoods practise outside the town gate. Close to the cemetery would be a good choice, you'd think, but the drumming happens to be right by our house! While they may not wake the dead, they certainly keep *us* awake in the meantime. Finally, we give in. We're tired, it's cold, still drizzling a bit and dark, but the drums are calling us. The streets are deserted again until we get near the Plaza Mayor. At eleven o'clock in the evening, we find the square packed wall to wall with adults and kids, even small ones in prams. It's even busier than the daytime procession of 'Bringing Down Jesus'. The drummers have done us a favour; this fiesta is totally unique and we're lucky to be here to experience it. Had we given in to our desires we'd be tucked up in bed and missing this spectacle. Hard as it is to get used to the night-owl timetable it's worth it to participate in important events like these.

The processions are very sombre this time, the music dramatic and haunting, the mood exceptionally dark. More brotherhoods are involved in this event, evident in the many different outfits marching in groups together. The oddest are the unnerving black Ku Klux Klan-type pointy hoods. Others wear balaclava-style masks, like an executioner. They can obviously see where they are going as no one falls over while drumming away. Many things are carried in the procession this time too, a statue of Mary, crosses, flags, a miniature Jesus on a cross, all moving at a slow and dramatic pace, swaying from side to side to the beat of the drums. A group dressed as nuns hold electric candles, evidently having given in to modernity. Nobody likes burning candle wax on their hands, I suppose. I don't think they are true nuns as some have bleached blonde hair.

Again, the parade is joined by high-ranking officials like the mayor, the police and the Guardia Civil. This gloomy and funereal procession is very different from the one earlier today. People now are subdued and sombre because of what history tells us happened to Jesus next. I really only know this from the Monty Python movie, *Life of Brian*, but the spectators here are much better informed than either Alex or I are.

~

After Jesus stops in the San Pedro Church for a couple of days there's movement again. Close to noon the drums start up once more. Fiesta time! We ignore them for a while, but they get us in the end. Wrapped up warmly, Alex and I head for the Plaza Mayor, where all processions seem to end up. Today a statue of a resurrected Jesus is carried to the square, where he will meet a statue of his mother, Mary, 'rejoicing'. This is what the council website has told me we are about to witness. Mary arrives in a 'black cloak of sorrow', which is removed after she sees Jesus 'alive'. The 'nuns' then change her black outfit for a white cloak with gold-thread embroidery and she 'rejoices'. Extraordinarily awkward as it is for a statue to 'rejoice', the bearers do their best to help the statue show joy by dancing her about a bit. Girls and women dressed as nuns shower Mary with flower petals and offer her bouquets before she approaches Jesus again. This looks very much like an adult puppet theatre with adult-sized puppets. The rejoicing is further demonstrated by the bearers bobbing up and down slightly, as much as they can carrying a statue weighing several hundred kilos. At the precise moment Jesus and Mary meet in the middle of the square the church bells ring twelve noon and keep ringing to spread the news of the resurrection. The square falls silent except for the bells pealing. It's an evocative moment and I feel slightly guilty having stifled a chuckle when Mary 'rejoiced' earlier on.

Then the music starts up once more and the procession leaves the square for the Iglesia de San Pedro, where all the statues are united again. Jesus now has a staycation until his next outing in six months' time. The music is much more uplifting now. None of the sombre mood of Good Friday, the tunes are classical but joyful, cheering with Mary. As before, once they get to the church, the band leaves immediately, returning to their warm houses or a bar to relax with family and friends.

We too go home, pour a wine and thaw out frozen limbs. Reflecting on all we've seen over the last few days it seems that, although the church does not have the sway over people it once had, faith holds firm.

'I'm a bit envious of their ability to believe,' Alex contemplates. 'All these individuals come out on freezing-cold days and nights to perform these rituals. They all believe in the same things. I can feel the positive impact of what religion and its formalities potentially do for a society.'

Even though I giggled about the statue of Mary 'rejoicing', I too respect what these rituals potentially do. The significance of reliving these all-important moments in history together is profound. They are moved by what happened two thousand years ago and they are experiencing these emotions as a group bonded by their belief. Will we ever find the place where we feel as one, as this society does through their shared beliefs? Religion aside, I'm moved by the spirit of community. Although I'd like to joke about it, I was touched to see how affected the people were. They're united in a way that I don't think I've experienced.

Chapter 8

Patron Saints and Old Churches

One of the delights of Soria is the extensive network of walking trails throughout the province. *Senderismo* (walking, hiking, tramping) is immensely popular in Spain. The international fame of the pilgrim walk, the Camino de Santiago de Compostela, undoubtedly contributes. Walks are advertised on big billboards on the edge of many towns and many trails link up with other trails to keep you going on ancient paths from hamlet to hamlet.

Alex and I treat ourselves to the next instalment of the English version of the tourism pamphlet, which to our delight has some words of wisdom about walking in Soria:

At the risk of provoking opinions, we will start formulating a saying that we strongly believe in; walking is the purest essence of any travel you can experience.

The leaflet goes on to say:

It is not easy to defend this while they discover water on the moon and they talk about communities living there. We are in the age of rockets and huge planets rather than trainers' soles, but it is also true that rambling is becoming a strong form of tourism.

We, too, think walking is the purest form of travel and enjoy a ramble in the woods. We register for a 15-kilometre hike in the forest nearby, which we see advertised on a poster in a bar. To register one has to go to a bakery, Patiseria Gomez, pay three euros each and write your name on a bit of paper. Our names were against numbers 54 and 55. We notice the walk is organised by the Brotherhood of San Pascual, the patron saint of shepherds. How the Brotherhood gets to organise walks in the forest is also not entirely clear to us but we speculate that shepherds and goatherds do wander around the mountains, so that could be the link.

Committing to the Spanish timetable, we've been going to bed later and getting up later each day so we can join others at dinner after 10pm and avoid nodding off in the middle of pudding. Shock, horror! We're to meet our fellow hikers at 8.30am. We only discover this as we head for bed well after midnight. We set alarms on both our phones hoping this will be foolproof. It is, and we arrive at the appointed meeting place at the Plaza Mayor at 8.20am. We've not seen a soul on our five-minute journey to the plaza. Almazán does not wake that early on a Sunday.

In the Plaza we anticipate seeing perhaps fifty or so other walkers, but the vast square is deserted, save for two short, middle-aged men chatting under the columns. Have I mentioned how diminutive the local Sorians are? Anyone over a metre and a half would stand out in a crowd. The two men saunter over. Neither are dressed as warmly as we are. They may be short but it seems they're tough buggers. They must have been, to push the Moors out of their territory in the twelfth century. We've researched the Brotherhood a little to try to understand who we'd be walking with, but we learn the trek has, unfortunately, been cancelled due to the severe weather forecast. That's understandable – it's bloody freezing, the icy wind going right through my trousers.

However, every walk ends in a bar, even when it's cancelled. We order *dos cortados*. In Sydney, the barista would call these a macchiato, a good strong espresso with a tiny dash of milk. *Cortado* means 'cut'. The coffee is literally 'cut' with a bit of milk.

~

Instead of a walk, we decide to go for a drive and then a walk. We leave Almazán via the old bridge over the Duero. On the other side of the bridge, in front of Mateo's Bar, a tiny, very old man stands a little hunched over. He's sticking up his thumb and clutching a shopping bag in the other hand. He looks to be an octogenarian, in the latter half of that decade. We stop and ask where he would like to go.

'Matamala,' he says, 'just up the road.'

Matamala is about 10 kilometres along quiet rural roads. Although 'walking is the purest essence of any travel' for many, this old bloke is certainly not up for 10 kilometres lugging his shopping. I hop out to help him in. He stands stock still, immaculate in his suit, collared shirt and tie. He needs a hand to get in the car and neither of us is sure how to make a start on that. I sort of lift him under the armpits a bit to get him on the back seat. I should have given him my front seat, but it's too late now, he's half in, half out of the back seat. For his sake I hope I manage to get him in the seat in a dignified manner. I'm sure I don't look very dignified with my bum sticking out of the car as I manipulate this tiny man. I do up his seatbelt, make sure he's got his shopping tucked beside him and we're off. Once we're going, I turn around in my front seat to chat with him.

'Have you been shopping in Almazán?'

'Yes. There's not much in Matamala these days,' he replies.

As he talks, I can smell alcohol. He's obviously enjoyed some time at Mateo's Bar, the added advantage of being in town.

'Have you always lived in Matamala?'

'No, I was born there but moved to Madrid to find work. I left when I was eighteen years old and now I'm back. I was a draftsman and worked all over Spain to draw the plans for many projects.' He sighs as he continues. 'I came back to the old house in Matamala so my oldest daughter and her children can live in my house in Madrid. They couldn't find work in the town they were living and Madrid has more possibilities.'

I ask how he finds being back.

'I'm glad to be living in my childhood home again,' he replies. He tells us about his neighbours, most of whom he's known all their lives. He still has a few old friends he went to school with and they meet on Matamala's Plaza Mayor for a chat most days.

As we enter Matamala, Juan Andres, as our hitchhiker is called, directs us to his house. It's in a short, neat row of whitewashed buildings on the edge of the small town.

We farewell Juan fondly – he's been a lovely and sweet interlude in our day.

'*Muchas gracias y adios!*' he calls out, smiling an almost toothless smile.

~

After we drop off our pocket-sized hitchhiker, we drive to the town of Berlanga de Duero to do some 'pure essence' walking. The tourism flyer has some encouraging words to say about our hike:

In the accumulation of plains and stubbles, dovecots are against the light with their usual vertical position. They watch the traveller passing by from the fields and the villages and they show their popular architecture of the region of Berlanga.

The dovecots are now left to decay. It is much more common these days to buy meat at the butcher rather than catch pigeons for dinner.

The impressive Catholic church is about to begin the twelve o'clock mass. If we went in right now, we'd make a nuisance of ourselves, so we wait until mass is over to have a look inside. We return as the parishioners are streaming out. Some other visitors are also lining up to get in. As we get closer, we see that the priest has brought out a table at the entrance, where he is setting up to charge an entrance fee. Alex is appalled as the Church has already made quite a bit of money from its faithful over the centuries.

'You'd think that with the current child-abuse issues some good public relations would be useful. Getting people in rather than charging them might be a better idea,' Alex snarls in English, so the priest is probably none the wiser.

~

Berlanga de Duero is a remarkable town with colonnaded houses in the old centre. There's a magnificent, ruined castle too, of course. The castle dates from the fifteenth century, when it was built over a tenth-century Muslim fortress. It originally belonged to the Tovar family and played an important role in defending the lands along the Duero riverbanks during the Muslim conquest. There are nearly three hundred castles in Castilla y Leon alone, in all sorts of places from the middle of towns to isolated hills in the countryside. Medieval and imposing, they are a common sight. On the way back towards Almazán we stop off to see the mist-shrouded castle at Gormaz. The guidebooks describe it as one of the largest in western Europe, overwhelming the terrain from its vantage point high on the hill. It dominates the skyline in a rather bossy way. This one was built during the early years of the Reconquista over the ruins of an old Roman fort. The Gormaz castle was on the border of the Ándalus (Moorish) and Christian kingdoms. In 975, it came under Christian control and has remained so. There was obviously a good reason for so many medieval castles in Castilla y Leon: this was a war zone for centuries. Castles and fortifications were built here as far back as the eighth century, to defend against the Moorish invasion.

This is one of the things that thrills me about the Iberian Peninsula; anyone who's anyone has been here at some time in recorded history. Celts, Phoenicians, Romans, Visigoths, Vandals, the Alans (Iranian nomads) and of course the Berbers and Muslims who came from the south and stayed for four hundred years. Their departure is still celebrated in excessive style in many towns and villages, with loud music and processions in costume. One evening on the day of these fiestas in Valencia, I had dinner in a Moroccan restaurant with family and friends. The noisy celebrations during the fiestas of the Moros y Cristianos commemorate the ousting of the restaurant owners' Moroccan ancestors. It felt weird to us; if it did to the restaurant owners or waiters, they didn't show it.

~

The twelfth-century church in Los Llamosos, a nearby village, is also open this weekend. Adorned with ferocious-looking gargoyles, the church is known as the Church of the Virgin Mary Ascending to Heaven. Josh told us that, if we find it closed, we should go find Pedro, who lives behind the church and keeps the key. Naturally, the church doors are firmly locked when we get there. We're not sure which house belongs to Pedro but there's a group of people sitting on a front doorstep chatting. It's a long weekend, which brings crowds to the ancestral villages. Villagers who've moved away for study or work come as soon as there are a few free days in a row, as most are still deeply attached to their community and the old family home.

This group all know where 'Pedro of the church key' lives, and a spritely man in his eighties personally takes us to Pedro's house, three doors down. Pedro comes to the door and is pleased indeed to show us the church. Short, like his compadres, in his seventies, with a gigantic grey handlebar moustache, Pedro is not only delighted to show us the church, but also obviously immensely proud. A massive iron key, the length of a good-sized baguette, opens the solid wooden doors.

'This is one of the oldest churches around, built in a Romanesque style in the twelfth century with Muslim influences.' Pedro is in his element, focusing our attention on every little detail the church has to offer.

The cornices are decorated with plant motifs, animal heads, contortionists and other human figures, which he points out individually. There are murals of biblical scenes, including *The Last Supper* and the *Arrest of Jesus in the Olive Grove*. Pedro knows everyone in the mural by name as if he's pointing to a family photo.

'These murals are dated to the fourteenth century and have recently been restored with a big grant from Madrid,' Pedro reveals proudly.

Alex sees me glancing at my watch, which I hope will show it's almost wine o'clock. He winks conspiratorially.

'This baptismal font is thought to be of Roman origin, some two thousand years old,' Pedro continues.

I get the feeling Pedro could potentially continue all day. How long will it take to examine each and every artefact in the church? Pedro is enjoying himself immensely.

He tells us, 'You're the third Australian couple to have come specifically to see the church. There was one couple last year and another couple the year before that too.'

Last week, Josh recounted a story Pedro told him last year. Sometime shortly after we'd been in this village, but not the church, Pedro told him that a couple had come all the way from Australia purely to see the church. He'd shown them around himself of course. He described Alex and me precisely, but we'd never even met him or been inside the church at that time. We're amused to think we have doppelgangers who've visited the same place.

Politely we murmur that we're not surprised that many Australians would come to see this magnificent church. Pedro is happy with that response and urges us to pass the word around about this church to as many fellow Australians as we can. This makes me think, if there were other Australian couples, just like us, in this remote part of Spain, would they be like us? Would they be visiting the church in Los Llamosos? Would they be crazy enough to move to the other side of the world? Would they risk their 'perfect' lives at home for whatever it is we are looking for?

It takes some time for us to get around to seeing every bit of this little church, but we're grateful to our passionate guide. We're not sure that everything he told us was necessarily fact. Just like the oversupply of Australian couples, the artefacts' history may also have benefitted from a lively imagination. Two hours later we're outside again and Pedro and his huge key cross the street to go home for a coffee. I'm sure that if he weren't caffeine deprived he could have gone on far longer.

Opposite the church is a lovingly maintained cemetery. Statues of Mary under glass domes are widespread, as are the ubiquitous plastic flowers. The recent Easter holidays were evidently a good time for the graves to get a spring clean, as living relatives were around to tidy up the final resting places of the dead ones. Every grave looks spick and span – not a weed in sight, flowers blown about by wind put back in vases, glass-domed Mary polished and clear of cobwebs.

The sign on the ornate metal gate to the cemetery intrigues me. The *memento morí* reads:

Mortal mira y considera
con atención cual estoy
Lo que tú eres, yo era
Tú serás lo que yo soy

Mortal look and consider
with attention how I am
What you are, I was
You will be what I am

A poignant reminder of our mortality. Life is short and we should live it to the fullest.

Fluffy snowflakes drift around as we drive home. The weather forecast was right – it's even colder now than earlier this morning. We did not get to enjoy the company of the Brotherhood of San Pascual, but we did experience the 'purest essence of any travel' as we walked around exploring. When we got too cold on the way home, we stop for a bite to eat in a bar on the square of yet another quaint village. Alex is keen to avoid more pig and orders lamb chops. A mountain of delicate chops, piles of chips and roasted peppers arrive at our table. As San Pascual of the Brotherhood is also the patron saint of hearths and cooks, the theme of the day came together nicely in the end.

Chapter 9

La España Vacía

The cold spell passes quickly and the feeling of spring in the air is back. Along the Rio Duero I hear the first cuckoo today. At the house, with the bird guide at hand, I identify it as the common cuckoo. From this moment onwards the insistent call of the cuckoo rings out over the landscape. We've been walking the route for a few months now. Spring has sprung and changes are evident every day. There are still trees in their winter mode, with no leaves at all, whereas others, like willows, elms and poplars, are sprouting merrily. The new leaves are a delicate green, soft and fragile looking. Let's hope a late snowstorm doesn't kill them off. Some trees in the walled house garden are starting to blossom already, protected by the walls. Some are almost in full bloom. In the morning light, their sweet smell fills the crisp air. There are also tulips, daffodils, rosemary, lavender and an array of other flowers. The courtyard buzzes with the sound of bees. So many different species. Some I recognise as the normal European honeybee, but there are also blue bees and some other kind that I simply call 'big bugger bees'. They're vast black things, like a small hovercraft on a kamikaze flight.

We take our morning stroll at more or less the same time each day along the Rio Duero. The regulars are becoming a familiar sight and the *holas* are getting friendlier. Some passersby almost smile.

I stop to take a closer look at the sign at the entrance of town, which highlights a long-distance trail in this locality. The sign is essentially a map, with the largest section of text dedicated to the gastronomy of this locality rather than walking. Highly recommended are the *torreznos*, of course. There's also a great deal of pride in the local fungi – mushrooms and truffles. A shepherd's dish called Migas, made with old breadcrumbs, which tastes better than it sounds, also gets a wrap. The area also prides itself on a variety of flavoured butters.

Spanish cuisine is still rich in regional differences: gazpacho (cold tomato soup) from Andalucía, lamb from la Extremadura, ham from Castilla, paella from Valencia, the Catalan *natillas* (caramel custard) and so on. The desire for traditional dishes is undiminished, and simplicity and quality rule. Fresh food direct from the market is still preferred but many women now work outside the home, making this kind of shopping difficult. Reliance on the supermarket is a necessity, but even there the quality and freshness of the food is outstanding.

~

Alex and I are settling in and falling into new habits: morning coffee is often at a bar looking out over the square towards the palace. The woman behind the bar now brings us the two *cortados* unbidden. We leave 2.40 euros without asking 'how much', as that is the price for two coffees in every bar in town.

One morning as we have a drink in a different bar near the market, a man in his fifties holds court on the topic of the 'empty countryside'. In Soria province, the least populated region in all of Spain, this topic is extremely sensitive. He draws in all who will listen as he talks about the lack of government action to stop the countryside from emptying out further. He is nearly in tears as he states: 'This is not the Spain I want to leave for my children and grandchildren. What's the government doing about it?'

Elections are coming up in a couple of weeks. In this region, depopulation is a hot topic for political debate.

'What we need is more *autopistas*. The government that gives us money to build more *autopistas* will get my vote,' states a stallholder on his break.

'That's not going to change a thing,' retorts the teary bloke. 'People don't want to drive too far to go to work. We need businesses to come here.'

A third punter puts in his two bob's worth: 'The winters are too bad here. Nobody wants to travel home in the dark, with snow on the road. Even if it's on an *autopista*.'

Roads crisscross this province linking towns and villages to nearby capitals, but many Sorians do want more *autopistas*. Protest banners in the streets promote fast highways that will allow travellers to reach cities like Logroño or Valladolid more quickly.

'The young ones don't want to work hard,' adds another. 'That's the problem. It's nothing to do with the roads. They don't want the hard life of a farmer. We give them an education and then they leave us for city jobs.'

This view gets silent approval and nodding. Then a few start talking over each other and it's hard to follow where we're up to.

The original teary man sums it up: 'We need the government to invest in Soria.' He leans forward for emphasis as he adds, 'They need to put up the money, make it attractive for businesses to come here.'

An older man, guzzling down a beer at ten in the morning, agrees. 'Then our children don't have to move away. They can be here when we are old and need them.'

'But which party to vote for? Which one is actually going to do something about it?' asks the teary man despondently.

Madrid, at two hours away, is too far for a daily commute. Even Soria capital, at a leisurely 20 minutes' drive, is considered too far for a daily commute by many. If someone finds work in the capital, they can usually also afford to buy an apartment there with all the mod cons.

Unlike the coastal areas of Spain, these parts do not attract much tourism. Here there are no tacky souvenir shops with Mexican sombreros sold as 'Spanish' to naive tourists. Holidaymakers are not likely to save this region from the emptying trend. Here folks have worked the land in small plots for generations. Young people with better education than their parents and grandparents are not attracted to this tough rural life. Bit by bit the plots of land are sold off or left fallow.

Alex shakes his head, saying, 'This is just so sad. These beautiful places dying a slow death before their eyes. I wonder what can be done about it.' Flippantly he adds: 'Buy a village and do it up?'

~

Spanish country towns are slowly dying as residents move to the big cities in droves. *La España vacía*, the 'empty Spain' is a national tragedy. Whole villages are abandoned. The shops close one by one, the last school shuts down, church bells stop ringing and eventually the whole town dies. There's even a route to drive that goes around a bunch of uninhabited villages called the *Ruta de los pueblos abandonados*. We visit one of these places on a mountain top called Peñalcázar, deserted since the 1960s. The road climbs up and up, getting narrower and steeper. We reach a point where manoeuvring the car up any further is not safe. The dirt road has not been used for some forty to fifty years, deteriorated to the point that cars can't get up anymore. There's now a steep climb on foot for the last half hour or so. A once lively township is now crumbling. Houses, which I imagine were once lovingly built for a new bride, rooms added as children were born, now stand empty. Roofs sag and windows are broken. The church, prominent on the hill, has half its roof collapsed. The altar is still there, with a fallen roof beam resting where once the priest would have placed the communion wine. Some villages have only a handful of people or even a single inhabitant remaining, like a last sentinel keeping vigil over a lost world. Often it's an old woman who can't bear to leave the ancestral home or perhaps has nowhere else to go. Once surrounded by a dynamic society, they now face the neighbouring houses with dread as roofs cave in, wooden window blinds and solid entrance doors crumble as woodworm takes hold.

In this rural landscape many homes are locked up most of the time while the family visits only in summer for a few weeks or the odd long weekend. Unwilling or unable to sell these homes, families hang on to them in the best way they can. Often incomes are not enough to keep up with the maintenance and selling is not realistic either. Houses in empty villages don't sell well. Some are for sale for as little as 5000 euros but much more is needed to bring the decaying, gorgeous facades back to being liveable homes. Sometimes, these seemingly abandoned houses surprise and reveal a person lurking in a doorway, stubbornly hanging on against the tide of departures. Councils do what they can to keep these places viable. Even if the population only swells on weekends or in summer, they often retain the essential hub of town: the bar. Locals then take it on themselves to open the bar and serve other locals. After all, it is the focal point for residents and a magnificent way of keeping the community connected to the village and each other.

There is one way families manage to keep the old ancestral home in good repair. They sometimes fix it up and rent it out short term, which pays for the upkeep and sometimes provides a modest income. In this part of the country the focus is on promoting national tourism, so this only works if the house is in a place where holidaymakers want to spend a weekend.

Even in Almazán, with a population of over 5000, the old part of town is slowly becoming less buoyant. Several shopfronts stand empty and look as if they will never open again. The *carnicería* (butcher), the last *ferretería* (hardware store) and two bakeries in the old part of town have closed recently. Several bars appear to have closed their doors permanently as we never see them open (although they may not open until after midnight when we have gone to bed). Admittedly, some houses have been done up, but many of the characteristic older ones stand empty, flanked by newer and decidedly uglier versions. On our daily walks through the old part of town we mostly encounter the elderly, shuffling about with canes, now having to travel much further to buy the daily *barra de pan* (loaf of bread). At least our presence in town provides them with something to look at on the way. A friendly '*Hola, buenos días*' often leaves a stunned geriatric stranded in a narrow alleyway questioning what has happened to the world.

~

After visiting the abandoned village, we take the long way back to Almazán. Narrow, winding *caminitos* (small roads) getting us home slowly rather than an hour on the highway. We see brilliant towns and villages along the way. Some are near empty, others still have some life left in them. In the town of Salmerón we look for a drinking fountain to fill our water bottles. An elderly woman comes out of the church as we get to the main square. She's short, grey haired and dressed in the kind of housecoat women more often wore in Spain when I lived here decades ago – a mixture between a dress and a pinny in a cheerful pattern.

'Excuse me, is this water good to drink?' I ask.

She replies, 'I drank it all my life. It's exceptionally good water, straight off the mountain.'

I thank her and turn away to fill up our bottles. She calls after me to say, 'Come back and have a look at the church.'

We don't want to pass up the opportunity for a guided tour, so we hurry to follow her. Our guide, Valentina, appears to be in her seventies. She begins the tour by telling us about the church she's obviously mighty proud of.

'It was built in the fourteenth and fifteenth centuries with both a Baroque and a Gothic chapel.'

She sounds like she's done this before and has a spiel. Bleach hits our nostrils as soon as we step over the threshold. Inside there's a hive of activity with some twenty aging women racing about with brooms, mops and wet cloths, wiping statues of Mary and Jesus. The chatter sounds like an excited flock of budgies. They dust down pews and clean the gargantuan cavern with a fervour reserved for the deeply religious.

'Our beloved Father Jose died early this morning,' Valentina says. Her voice quavers a little as she delivers the bad news. She's upset, but more than that she seems preoccupied. 'We're getting the church ready for the funeral tomorrow.'

I remember that it's customary in Spain to bury the dead as soon as possible, usually the very next day.

'Was Father Jose from Salmerón?' I ask her softly.

She nods. 'He was born here and served his village faithfully his whole life. Mourners will come from the surrounding villages to farewell him tomorrow. Many priests and mourners from the region will want to pay their respects,' she says. 'The church will be full,' she adds a little worriedly.

I look around. The church is big and can comfortably seat a

couple of hundred mourners.

'There may be more people than seats,' Valentina bemoans. Her son has been roped in to bring foldaway chairs from the town hall on the opposite side of the square. I look around at the elderly women polishing the church until it shines. It must sparkle to show the villagers' respect for the much-loved dead man. Some of the women cleaning today have come back to the ancestral home to grieve with their neighbours. Regardless of the circumstances that brought them together, once more they're obviously enjoying each other's company. I overhear them egging each other on.

'Ah, you're getting old Pepita, can't you go faster than that!'

'I remember you jumping over those pews Maria. What's up with you now?' Pepita replies.

Despite their teasing and joking, their dedication and loyalty to the priest is palpable, and their deep respect for him touches me. Each time we chat with locals we feel their pain at the loss of their society. Valentina too laments the ever-diminishing number of inhabitants in Salmerón. She points to a little chapel on the side of the big church.

'This is now where most services are held,' she tells us.

The chapel has three short pews, hardly enough to sit the number of dedicated women cleaning the church now. While I am looking for belonging, these people have always known where they fit in but their communities are dying a slow death as the world changes around them.

'On the bright side,' Valentina says about the little chapel, 'we can heat this space in winter, which is lovely.'

Someone comes over to let Valentina know she's needed to order her son around. Before she leaves, she hands us over to guide number two, Maruja, a sprightly octogenarian with bright orange hair, who relishes her guide duties. She too wears one of the Spanish housecoats, hers sporting bright slices of watermelon, the colour contrasting nicely with her orange hair. Maruja came 'home' a few days ago when she heard her treasured priest was about to meet his maker.

'I was born in Salmerón but I've lived in Barcelona for more than sixty years. I miss being here all the time now,' she tells us. 'I'm old,' she says, 'I want to be here with my own folk, in the home I grew up in.'

Maruja takes us to the sacristy, where all the official vestments are kept. There's a slightly musty smell here. She opens one of the huge doors of the wardrobe with reverence, exposing the treasures within. Embroidery of gold, silver, purple and vermillion greets our eyes. These boys sure know how to dress-up! There are three massive cupboards in total, each revealing riches within. Maruja strokes the priceless hand-stitched robes and her voice breaks a little as she talks about Father Jose being the last priest in town.

'Who will wear these garments now?' Alex gently asks her.

'Nowadays, since Father Jose became too sick to preach, there is no permanent priest in Salmerón. We share priests with other parishes nearby. When these visiting priests come to town, they use the vestments in these wardrobes.'

As Maruja looks up at us, her eyes are a little teary. It is hard not to be impacted by her dignified sadness. Her devotion to the church and her clan is tangible. These beautiful costumes are kept in pristine condition by these devout women. As we chat to locals like Maruja and Valentina we're struck again how their sense of community is what brings joy to their lives. Perhaps the answer to all my questions is community. Every time we talk to locals it is clear that their sense of belonging and kinship is what matters most.

The last permanent priest will be buried tomorrow, another sign of an emptying Spain. All that is left in many villages like this one are a few women of advanced years who keep these places from being completely vacant in the face of a rapidly changing Spain. A culture will die with them. Once they are gone what will happen to this once vibrant settlement?

Chapter 10

Falling in Love

One day, on another sightseeing trip, looking where we might like to rent a house, Alex stops to take photos of the distant mountain views. Snow-capped peaks, blue skies and a light breeze. I remember this moment vividly. It's funny how the brain retains all the seemingly insignificant details leading up to key life events, like a fuse being lit in the brain. We drive through a small hamlet first. A farmer hears our car stop and walks around the corner to investigate what we're up to, a village vigilante in case we are intending to rob one of the houses. I explain we're only taking some pictures of the view. Satisfied we're genuine sightseers, he points to the house we're standing next to and says, 'That house is for sale you know.' Perhaps he's also the local real estate agent.

I turn and notice the For Sale sign. And then I notice how Alex's eyes light up.

And that is the start of it all. A simple twist of fate. I know Alex well enough to see he's visualising the stunning views through the window frames of this house, if they were not bricked up. I know him well enough to see that he's already imagining sitting on a yet to be built deck, overlooking the sunset, with a red wine in his hand.

Later, when we get back to the car, he turns to me and says

suddenly, 'I think we should buy that house.'

What? Did I hear him right? Maybe he's joking.

I smile, indulging him. 'Oh really? What do you like about it?'

'Did you see the views over the rolling hills? Those pink and lilac hues, the red poppies in the fields, the snow-capped mountains behind.' He's waxing lyrical and it surprises me. Alex isn't a philistine, we've seen plenty of breathtaking views in our time and his sudden passion for this one sets off an alarm bell in my head.

He takes a breath, solely to continue: 'That mountain range in the distance would have some fabulous hiking options!' His eyes glaze and I know what's coming next. 'We could build a lovely deck outside to take in those views.'

The panorama from the house is stunning, I agree. There's a valley of small-scale cropping, grazing and forestry in the foreground, which combines with the rugged backdrop to create a setting alive with colour and variation. Large patches of natural bushland surround the hamlet and have survived in good shape over the years, the faraway peaks offer dramatic depth and the roadside abounds with flowering rosemary, the scent wafting through the air. But most of all I fear Alex likes the idea of the project needed to restore the house. The challenge of saving a charming stone cottage from eventual collapse seems to appeal to his idealistic notions. Have these been triggered by the 'empty Spain' conversation we heard in the bar a couple of days ago? He joked then that maybe we should buy a village to help save it.

I'm playing this cool and decide not to react too much. Up until this point I thought we were going to look around, see where we wanted to be and then rent somewhere nearby. It looks like Alex was not joking when he wanted to buy an abandoned village and do it up. This is an almost-abandoned village and certainly needs to be rescued before it crumbles altogether. Saving it one house at a time.

Mountains and poppy fields and wafting rosemary aside, the

house is pretty much derelict. It's the last house on the road out of town, a three-storey stone farmhouse built in the traditional Spanish way, with its own well and an almond orchard in full blossom, which, Alex is keen to point out, adds to its appeal. What it does not have is a working roof. Its major windows have been bricked up. Alex writes down the seller's telephone number from the sign tacked to the stone wall. I realise he's taking this to another level. Contacting the owner to have a look inside takes us well beyond the familiar territory of daydreaming, to the shaky ground of home renovators in a foreign country. This means I can't easily change my mind about living in Spain 'permanently'. Once we buy a house, a ruin, we're much more committed, financially and emotionally. Is that what I want? It scares me.

I'd never imagined that moving to Spain could involve home ownership and renovation. Renting a cute little cottage in an authentically Spanish village was as far as we had planned. This is utter folly and we both know it. As he drives, Alex looks at me sideways to gauge my reaction. His face seems to be saying: For a very affordable sum, we can save this captivating, historical site from ruin and get a home in Spain in the process. My face is saying: That 'affordable sum' is the cost to buy only; we have no idea how much it will be to add on a new roof, stabilise the crumbling wall, add a kitchen and bathroom and all the other essential amenities, especially a good heating system. This is an extremely cold part of northern Spain, on the mesa, sitting at around a thousand metres above sea level. Even now, in early spring, there's an impressive amount of snow on the tops of those mountains. But I keep my cards close to my chest for now. Alex's excitement tends to be contagious, but I'm determined not to run with this idea for a while. The house has been for sale for some time, it seems from the faded and barely legible For Sale sign. It's not likely anyone's going to snap it up now. Not any sane person anyway.

~

We chat about the ruined house over the next few days. Mostly we agree that it's a stupid idea. Our lives are rather good right now. Why would we want all the stress of going into battle with Spanish tradesmen to get a derelict building to a liveable standard? We decide to give up on the whole idea, only for Alex to raise it again the next day.

'Maybe we should take a look inside? If it's particularly bad, then all well and good. I'll have got it out of my system.'

Funny, sweet Alex, the love of my life, never stops surprising me, but he's outdone himself this time: he's fallen in love with a view. Perhaps with a house *and* a view. Wasn't coming to Spain supposed to be about *me*? Wasn't it supposed to be *me* reliving the past and rekindling *my* love affair with the Iberian Peninsula? Of course, I didn't expect him to simply be a spectator in my late-life crisis. But I hadn't quite imagined my mostly sensible husband would fall head over heels for a dilapidated house in an almost-abandoned village.

I suspect I'll never hear the end of it if he doesn't get to scratch this itch. I look at his faraway blue eyes staring at the owner's number pinned to the fridge. I've never been able to resist those eyes.

'Okay,' I tell him. 'Let's call them. We can have a quick look inside at least. What harm is there in that?'

~

It was those blue eyes that first reeled me in forty years ago. After living in Spain for seven years my Spanish was good enough to act as an unofficial translator for the village. One morning in early May, I ran into Dorothy, an English friend, who asked me for a favour.

'Could you help out a friend of mine and go to the Banco Alicantino de Comercio with him? He's had money transferred but it hasn't arrived.'

I'd performed tasks like this often for tourists on my patch. There weren't many people fluent in Spanish as well as English, German and Dutch, and my translation skills came in handy with plumbers, doctors, dentists, as well as the authorities.

'Sure,' I told Dorothy. 'Ask him to meet me in the bar tomorrow at eleven.'

The back of the bar was dark as I walked in the next morning, but out of that gloominess appeared the bluest eyes I'd ever seen. The bluest of blue. A fraction later, I registered long blond curls and a mischievous grin to go with those eyes.

'Hi, I'm Alex. Are you the person who's volunteered to take me to the bank?'

'Yes ... Hi ... I'm Erna.' I felt myself blush as I tried to keep my cool in the presence of so much piercing blue.

I'd never heard an Australian accent before. On this part of the Iberian coast, I heard British accents of all varieties, a sprinkling of American twang, but not this novel pronunciation. The accent and hippie-surfer look reeled me in straight away. Was this the point where I fell in love or did it take a little longer? I recognised this person. I felt like I'd known him a thousand years. We took our *café con leche* outside and Alex filled me in on the details of his banking woes: he was running out of money for a planned bicycle trip around Europe.

'I wanted to start here and cycle north, but it looks like I'm stuck. I've been travelling in the US for a year and sent the last of my savings to a Spanish bank. That was a couple of months ago now, but they keep saying it hasn't arrived.'

I hoped I wasn't gushing as I said, 'Sure, I'll try to help with that. Let's go and see what we can do at the bank.'

I tried not to fall over my own feet as we got up. I get clumsy when I'm nervous and those blue eyes made me nervous alright.

On the way to the bank Alex went through the sequence of events so I could interpret for the teller on his behalf. As we pushed through the heavy glass doors, I saw an acquaintance, Sergio, behind the counter. He's a good bloke; he'll be helpful, I hoped. I explained the issue to Sergio and he lamented with us, making all the right noises and facial expressions. Ultimately, though, he said he was afraid he couldn't help.

'All money coming into Spain from anywhere in the world goes to one place – the *Banco de España* (the Reserve Bank). They then release any money to the allocated bank after they are satisfied.'

'Satisfied with what?' I asked.

Sergio shrugged, 'With what, we don't know.'

'How long before they are satisfied, usually, on average?'

'That too is unknown.' Sergio seemed truly sorry to share this less than useful information. 'All the Australiano can do is come back a couple of times a week to see if his money has arrived.'

The wait was long enough for Alex to completely run out of cash. He took on odd jobs in the village and made the best of his time waiting for the Reserve Bank to be 'satisfied'. He sold his fancy bike so he could buy food for a few weeks and helped out behind the bar for some extra pesetas. His charisma made him popular in town and the locals nicknamed him 'Jesus' for his kind blue eyes, blond hair and tendency to go barefoot. He organised 'State of Origin' tennis matches, imported versus locals, and taught Spaniards to surf when the Mediterranean showed some rare wave activity. He moved into a multinational sharehouse, also famed for being that summer's 'party house'. We hung out in the same crowd and got to know each other well. Very well.

Perhaps I didn't try quite as hard as I should have to get news about his money at the bank. The rumour among the expats was that the Spanish Reserve Bank holds on to all foreign exchange coming into the country for at least a few weeks, sometimes even months, making a bit of interest on other people's cash before handing it over. We never found out if this was true or not, but either way Alex was forced to hang around for months waiting for funds to finish his tour of Europe. He was stuck because he could only collect the money from the branch where it's been sent. Although he had a return ticket home, his bank account in Sydney was empty and there was no more to transfer to Spain. He simply had to wait around until the bank handed his money over. On the umpteenth visit to the bank, Sergio greeted us with the widest smile.

'Your money is here Alex.'

My heart sank. He could leave now. Luckily, Alex, like me, was too far gone to say goodbye for good. We were both deeply in love and our fates were sealed. I now thank the antiquated Spanish banking system for meeting the love of my life. Alex and I were thrown together by Spanish bureaucracy. But, as one love begins, another inevitably ends. Meeting Alex eventually spelled the end of my time in Spain.

~

Little did we know that several decades later we would both be here, together and living back in Spain. What I did not expect either is that my loved one would fall in love with a ruin. As Alex loves this house in Ventosa, it's changing the ideas about the sort of life we are going to live. Renovating a ruin was not the plan, or so I thought.

But we're committed to looking at this house. Alex and I agree that we should compare it with a few others in nearby towns just to get a handle on the 'abandoned ruins' market, if there is such a thing. An internet search gives us a list of comparable wrecks in the area surrounding the capital, Soria. But why look here, we ask ourselves. Well, why not? It's a beautiful spot, nature is abundant and humans are not, plus it's only a couple of hours from Madrid airport. It's also on a train line and has a highway connection to major cities like Zaragoza, Burgos, Logroño, Bilbao and Valladolid. In short, it's a little-known part of Spain that has not been corrupted by uncontrolled development, and the abundant nature all around appeals to us.

On a map of the Soria province, Alex plots the other ruined houses we've found for sale. He's determined to save a ruin or maybe a whole village. For all these locations he also googles the number of registered inhabitants. This scientific approach is more like the sensible Alex I know and love, even if the purpose behind it is still crazy. Most of the houses appear to be in places that are already completely abandoned or are close to getting there. The population statistics for some places list five or three or no inhabitants at all. Driving through these almost deserted settlements we sometimes see one or two of the residents left behind. In one hamlet, a couple of old women dressed in black sit on a bench outside the church, conceivably the same bench they sit on every day to have a chat and catch up on any overnight news. They carefully watch our car approach, no doubt discussing who we are and where we might be going. In the rear-vision mirror I can see them, like a pair of crows, eyeing us until we disappear in a cloud of dust on the road out of town. Many older women still wear mourning black (*luto*) after the passing of their husbands or a close relative, sometimes for years, or even the rest of their lives.

~

I call and leave a message with the owner of the house Alex has fallen so hard for. While he anxiously waits for an answer, like some hopeful besotted lover, I'm keen to check out a house for sale in a nearby town called Muriel de la Fuente. If he's getting more and more serious about doing this crazy thing with each passing day, I'm at least determined to do our homework before we rush into it.

Muriel de la Fuente is a quiet hillside town with a cemetery on the top of the hill. Less travel time to the pearly gates, I joke to Alex; at our age that could be an advantage. The house seems an attractive proposition, online at least. Three photos show an alluring stone building with three floors, another traditional farmhouse typical of this area. The ad further states it has four bedrooms and a bathroom and could be ours for the very reasonable sum of 34,000 euros. The house right next to it is also for sale for an additional 50,000 euros and it is suggested the two could be renovated together. After going round in circles for a bit in the car, we grasp that we've passed the property several times already but haven't recognised it from the internet photos. That's probably because what we're standing in front of now is a derelict cottage with an entirely missing wall and a caved-in roof. So that was the reason there was no fourth angle in the advertisement shots. The ad did say it's 'ready for renovation'. A complete rebuild, more like. It's hard not to feel cheated as we pull away. It's still early enough in the search to stay philosophical about it though. We're doing our factfinding and learning from experience as we go along.

'Now we know to always ask if the property has a roof and all the required walls!' I tell Alex. But I can see from his expression, he's already somewhere else, sipping wine on the deck of a cottage overlooking poppy fields and mountains.

Chapter 11

Daytripping and House Hunting

New habits develop, but we continue to have a good walk before breakfast most mornings, finishing with a coffee somewhere. We try another bar this morning, as Alex has spotted a fancy-looking place in the main street with lots of gold trimmings, reminiscent of the 1980s. Bar Gill turns out to be quite a find. So far, it's the best coffee in town. The barman dances behind the bar in a graceful and yet extremely efficient way. Obviously, he's a man for whom personal grooming is a high priority. He's not afraid of solid work either. He manages singlehandedly to serve some twenty coffees in a few minutes, about the time it takes to get a takeaway in Sydney when there's no queue. Along the long bar, rows of saucers with a spoon and sugar cubes are lined up ready to receive a full cup. No one waits long to be served. He also slices cakes and delivers all sorts of goodies from the attached bakery. He does this all on his own while maintaining witty conversations with the regulars. He proudly says goodbye to us in English when we leave. If, by some cruel twist of fate, we must limit ourselves to one bar only for our morning coffee, I may have to choose this one.

~

Fortified with excellent coffee, we set off on yet another journey of discovery. It's Sunday and there are noticeably more cars about. It looks like we're dawdling about the countryside, but we do have an actual destination in mind. Looking for a place to live gives an intense focus. We're aiming for a town that made an impression on our first visit to this region last year. Maybe it's a place we'd like to settle? We forgot the name of it or even where it was located, as it was one of those places one stumbles across. Alex systematically searches Google Earth until he thinks he's recognised the tall gate into town, the triangular 'square' with a fountain, the church and the general lay of the land.

We're off to see if it's the town we remember. We meander through the country, passing villages and vineyards. On the way we miss a turn-off and end up in a hamlet called Rello, an unexpected bonus. Rello has stone houses, mostly dilapidated, some missing their roof but there's a picturesque church that is still standing. Some homes continue to be lived in by the remaining, mostly elderly, residents. There's no longer any shop, bakery or butcher in town. Where do these oldies go for their shopping?

Mass is held even in the tiniest of parishes that still have a priest or can convince one to travel. With surprisingly good luck, a church service has just ended as we approach. About ten parishioners are gathered in the overgrown churchyard holding fresh branches of rosemary. Two older gents, a celestial spirit fuelling their energy, are sweeping the entrance of the church with their rosemary branches, brushing away the leaves the wind has blown in under the massive old doors during the congregation's absence.

'Could we please have a look inside?' we ask politely.

'Yes! The *cura* (priest) is still inside,' replies a man in a suit that undoubtedly has served him for decades of funerals and church services. We enter and I'm surprised to see such a young *cura*. He's carefully wrapping up something that looks like a chalice in a fancy embroidered cloth. He's ready to leave but greets us warmly with a solemn priestly voice.

I smile and say boldly, 'You're the youngest *cura* I've seen in a long time!'

Young priests are a rare sight nowadays. Most young people have stopped attending church and even fewer are attracted to a career in the ministry. If he's offended by my boldness, he doesn't show it.

He laughs and says, 'Yes, I'm a rarity! I wish there were more of us. There's a big shortage in the rural areas, so I'm kept busy. I have six parishes to serve. If only I could be everywhere at once.'

He looks around this fine-looking church once more as he prepares to lead us out the door. There's room for about one hundred faithful, but the pews are now empty most of the time. An ancient church and centuries of tradition are steeped in this soil, a full stop on hundreds of years of village history may come soon, as the last resident gives up the ghost and the *cura* has one less parish to serve.

As we are searching for a community to join, these poor people have lost theirs little by little, some leaving and some dying. Now I have some distance from our old lives I think a lot about what it is that I want from this phase of my life. I'm looking for belonging but also identity and purpose. They are clearly related. I will poke them all with a stick as we go around these gorgeous places and see what comes from it all.

~

Google Earth and Alex's determination eventually lead us to a town called Atienza. We approach Atienza from the opposite direction to last time. Before the town comes into view, the enormous, bulky Castillo de Atienza can be spotted from kilometres around. The castle stands like a sentinel on a rock escarpment, the height adding to its dominance. Lower down, more tall walls add to the defences. Atienza is another medieval town with a long history of protective fortifications. The information board at the bottom of the hill tells the story of the castle. Exactly when it was built is not known. The castle was constructed on the site of earlier Roman and Visigoth fortifications, so it's at least twelve hundred years old. Like many hillside towns, the battlements are immense, walls as thick as a metre or more and as tall as a four-storey apartment block. The constant threat of invasion would have been extremely stressful, as castles, lands and villages changed hands frequently. Anyone thinking the times we live in now are dangerous should look at how communities hundreds, even a thousand years ago, felt about the risk of invasion. For at least two thousand years the Iberian population has been conquered by one force after another. This may well be the most peaceful time these soils have known for an exceptionally long while.

~

I feel particularly peaceful myself after two glasses of wine with lunch. The restaurant on the square oozes charm. It's in a delightful courtyard right next to the church on a colonnaded square with pebbled paving. The highlight of their menu is estofado de rabo de toro con boletos, braised oxtail with wild mushrooms, which we both order. A few weekend daytrippers are about today. One table intrigues me. Three couples so representative of what I remember of the *pijos* (the posh or preppy class). The men with their foppish hair gelled back, dressed in polo shirts, chinos and step-in shoes. The sweater is always draped over the shoulders with the cuffs of the sleeves rolled together slightly. Who ever thought of that and why did it catch on big time with this cohort? This is the weekend outfit that serves as a uniform for the conservative upper class or those who'd like to be in that league. The women, all late forties to early fifties with long bleached blonde hair and manicured nails, are dressed in obviously expensive clothes. I am nearly blinded by the sun refracted off their diamonds. They wore the same style when I lived here decades ago. The conservative uniform evidently does not change quickly in Spain. The class system I saw in operation in the 1970s and 1980s still seems to be around. The *pijos* continue to be arrogant when they talk to the serving staff in bars and restaurants. (*Pijo* also translates as prick, which is not a coincidence, I think.) The *pijos* retain an aura of privilege. It was common then and, in some places still is, to call the upper classes Don for man and Doña for a woman, rather than *señor* and *señora*. The titles Don and Doña are considered titles of respect. Maya tells me her boss still insists on being called Don Manuel although he's quite a bit younger than she is.

~

Sightseeing does not get Alex's mind off his idea of buying a ruin. We drive past the house in Ventosa a few times, which seems to reinforce his desire. He's obsessed with it and can't stop thinking about it. Walking through some other hamlets Alex points out features of the old or restored houses.

'See those eaves? We should do that to the house at Ventosa.' Or, 'Wow, I like the way they brought light in through that wall.'

He tries to explain to me why the Ventosa house is specifically the one that has captured his imagination.

'Why not live in a livelier place with a few shops and a bar?' I suggest.

'It's the location,' he says in a dreamy voice, 'the view, the way the light shines on the panorama, the way the church sits behind it. It's the last house in the village on the way to the public fountain.'

Oh, my goodness, he's getting almost poetic now. I would never have thought that the church would be something he cared for. He's really got it bad …

'I'd rather have a bar at my back,' I say. 'Would be more useful to us in the long run. We'd use it every day. How often would you use the church, you non-believer?'

Wisely, Alex ignores my jibe. I guess the church is an even bigger pile of stone in need of severe reconstruction. Come to think of it, I'm lucky he has not fallen in love with one of those.

Several days ago, I found the Ventosa house listed for sale on a website and left another message. I also rang the mobile number signposted on the house itself again. It rang out, so I left another message. No one has replied. It could be because I rang from an Australian mobile phone. After all who'd want to return what might be a prank call from a foreign number? We might ask Josh to call from his Spanish phone next week when he's back from his business trip. Alex sees all old houses we've seen today as inspiration for *his* house in Ventosa. As we're driving home, he confides that he'd like to kill his infatuation for the whole notion of buying a house and doing it up.

'It is obviously a bad idea,' he says.

Unfortunately, like being in love, he can't help it. Right now, he's driven by his heart, not his head. Alex came to Spain to support me in my search for whatever it is I need to find. Surely I need to let him explore his fancy for this house. He says he hopes that once he has a look inside the house, and it's in a bad state, he can give up on the dream. When we get home, a bright yellow leaflet has been pushed under the door. It's an advertisement from a company that can give your old house a new roof.

'That surely is a sign,' says my scientific, not-ever-superstitious husband.

He will use anything now to justify his obsession with this ruined house. We agree to keep doing our homework, visiting more houses around the same distance from the capital Soria. We'll compare prices and see what we can learn from the experience. After all, it's quite good fun going to see unknown parts of the countryside with a purpose in mind, meeting some people to let us have a look inside interesting properties and having a drink or lunch in the village or the next one along. We still have a few months left in our current rental so there's no hurry. In the end, we either buy something or we kill the idea once and for all, but we'll have a good time deciding.

~

The next day we catch up for a coffee with Josh. Alex urges him to ring the owner of the house he fell in love with. He's still very keen to have a look inside. It's more than a week since I called and left a message. We ask Josh to call. There's no answer and Josh leaves a message. The owner rings back a few minutes later. The woman's name is Maria de la Paz Gomez Gomez. Her first name means Mary of the Peace and the two following names are her father's surname combined with her mother's surname, as is the custom. The choice of partners was extremely limited in some places and the marriages of cousins was common, possibly resulting here in the same surname twice. Josh explains that he's ringing on behalf of his family about the house for sale in Ventosa. Mary of the Peace discourages him as much as she can.

'It's in terribly bad shape,' she says. 'It needs a lot of work. It may not be worth the 18,000 euros we're asking,' she adds.

It's also very difficult to have a look inside, as she lives in Murcia, some 600 kilometres away.

'I have a sister visiting Soria this week, but she has no car. I don't know how she'd get there. There may be another family member in the area next week, on a Sunday. Maybe ...'

Alex is straining his brain to understand the rapid Spanish Josh is speaking with Mary of the Peace. His face is all concentration, nearly bursting with excitement. I'm still flabbergasted by this, although I'm not sure why. I know he's adventurous and this would certainly be a renovation adventure. But I'm not sure how I feel about it. I can't help but be simultaneously thrilled and terrified by his obsession, as if we're travelling to an unknown destination at high speed and I'm not anywhere near the brakes. I want Alex to have his dream, but I feel I'm out of my depth.

Once more the owner tries to convince Josh it's a lost cause.

'Do you know there's a hole in the roof?' Mary of the Peace adds just before she hangs up.

Not at all the attitude of someone who wants to sell a house. The conversation ends with Mary of the Peace saying she will ring again next week sometime once she knows if someone can meet us in the village. We don't expect to hear back from her. Nevertheless, Alex has his hopes up and deliberates what we can do. Offer to pick up the sister in Soria? Pick up the keys from the sister in Soria? Ask her to mail the keys? Maybe we wait for a bit to see what happens next, if anything. As we hope to hear from Maria de la Paz, life goes on.

Chapter 12

Uncle Domingo's House

Walking home from the markets, we stop for a coffee at the Plaza Mayor, at another one of our best loved bars. It's named after the poet Tirso de Molino, born in this town, whose statue stands on the plaza. This bar is a favourite because they give you a nice biscuit with the coffee and I've not had breakfast yet. As we leave the cafe, Alex notices he's missed a phone call from Josh. We ring him back sitting on a cold stone bench looking at the palace and the statue in front of it.

'Mari-Paz Gomez Gomez can have someone with the keys in Ventosa if you can get there by 11.15,' Josh reports. (Mari-Paz is short for Maria de la Paz). 'She's still telling me it's not in very good repair, but she's organised her sisters to meet you at the house.'

'Yes! Yes, we'll be there!' Alex says excitedly.

We look at each other and Alex smiles a funny kind of smile. We have our separate emotions about where this is going. Alex is obviously delighted, while I feel my face contorting into something more like a grimace pretending to be a grin. This is moving from 'house appreciation' to 'house viewing'. Holy crap. It's getting real now.

'I'm surprised she's called back,' I say breathlessly as I put on speed to keep up with Alex, who's running up the hill with our shopping.

'Can't wait to get in and take a look! How good is this!'

It still feels like he's suddenly developed a crush on someone or something, and I'm excluded from what's happening.

'Can we make it there in time?' I ask doubtfully.

'Sure, we can,' is his answer.

I'm not so sure. It's already 10.25am. The car is at the house, a few minutes' walk away. We need to take the market produce home and get going straightaway. I do a slow trot as Alex runs up the hill to the house high on the town wall. We get in the car by 10.40. I punch Ventosa in the GPS and we're off. During the drive, Alex thinks out loud, linking the market experience and the house.

'*Quién es el último*, who was the last person to live in the Ventosa house? Who was the last person to go into it and have a look around?'

'And for that matter, why didn't they buy it?' I say. I'm being a spoilsport and don't like myself very much right now. I try to make up for it by being a little more positive.

'Now that Mari-Paz has called to say we can come and have a look, it's our turn, just like at the markets. It's up to us what we do next.'

~

We get there first, of course, and wait in the car for a while. Then we get bored and wait outside, wandering around the house without going into the garden. Alex loves the simple address: Tras Iglesia 1 (Behind the Church, Number 1). A few minutes later a car arrives. A woman emerges, stumbles onto the verge, gets caught in the brambles and eventually gets to where we stand at the back of her car. She's not young but she's sophisticated, well dressed and beautifully coifed, with a nice alert face and a friendly smile. I greet her with the customary kiss on each cheek, even at first meeting, and tell her our names. Hers is Lola.

She says, 'Ah, but you're not Spanish!'

'No,' I say, 'we're Australian.'

She asks how long it takes in a plane from Australia to Spain.

'A bloody long time!' I reply.

Lola explains that her sister is getting the keys as they are kept in another house in the village. After a couple of minutes, the sister comes walking down the road. She's a tall woman for this part of the world, dressed in a practical way: jeans, sneakers and a puffer jacket against the cold. She has a head of short silver hair and a bright, inquisitive look about her. Her name is Lucy.

'Well, actually Lucia,' she tells us.

Some fiddling with the keys lets us into the house and the door makes a satisfying groan after having been closed for a long time. The house belonged to their Uncle Domingo, Lucia and Lola explain. It was inherited by their elder sister, Mari-Paz.

'Domingo was a bachelor all his life. He went to Argentina after the Spanish Civil War and made some money,' Lucia tells us. 'Enough to buy a modest stone house when he came back. It's the last house in the village on the way down to the fountain.'

The sisters tell us that's where they had to get water every day when they lived in the village as children. Just after Uncle Domingo's house they filled up at the fountain and then carried the full jugs of water back up the hill. Often, they would stop and ask him for flowers for their mother.

'Uncle Domingo had the most attractive garden full of flowers,' Lucia tells us. 'We loved it and thought it was the prettiest home we knew.'

Inside, we are pleasantly surprised by the space. Alex is walking around as if in a trance. It's bigger than we assumed from the outside. The large entrance hall leads to a staircase with one set of steps going up to the loft and another one down to the barn below.

The kitchen has an old fireplace where once all meals would have been prepared. The roof has collapsed in this part of the house and there's a leak.

'What's that?' I ask Lola as I point above our heads through the hole in the roof.

'Pigeons,' she says. 'People kept a girl pigeon in a cage in the roof. She would call and a boy pigeon would come. The pigeon boys could get in but not out. Uncle Domingo ate them for dinner.'

The rest of the roof seems in reasonable shape. There's a compact dining room next to the kitchen. Small rooms would have been easier to keep warm in winter. The sisters run around opening the wooden shutters to let in some light, as there's no electricity. The open windows bring in the breeze and with that the smell of almond blossom. Most of the shutters have deteriorated during the years the house has stood empty.

On this entrance floor, apart from a rudimentary kitchen, without water or electricity, there are what may have been two bedrooms and a large room, not used as a sitting room but perhaps more for drying and storing food in the winter. There are sticks suspended from the ceiling with rope and things still hanging off them that look like dried capsicums and strings of garlic. We venture upstairs carefully, as the stairs look like they may collapse. They don't, but the loft is scarcely tall enough to stand up in the middle. It's also full of junk, mostly huge wine barrels and empty beer bottles. It looks like Uncle Domingo made his own booze and liked a tipple. There are too many treasures to take in properly but I spot riding boots with spurs, old tools, hats, trunks, ceramic jugs and platters.

Downstairs on the ground floor are the animal stalls. Domingo kept pigs, of course, as everyone does in Soria. Cows and sheep were kept here too. They all came into the barn through two big doors that open to the fountain road below. The animals would have kept the house above quite cozy and warm in winter. At the far end of the building, an opening goes through to a hayloft. More animals were kept underneath with the hay on the next level above. This is the space that is most evocative of the romance of these old houses. The barn still has the wooden feed troughs, pitchforks, thrashers for the wheat and many other farming tools.

'All this old farming gear would be wonderful to decorate the house after restoration,' Alex whispers. He squeezes my hand; I squeeze back.

So much for 'I just want to see it and hopefully it's so bad I can get over it.' This doesn't sound like he's getting over his infatuation at all. He's still smitten.

Lucia asks, 'But why do you want to buy a house here?'

I explain that we had no intention of buying a house in Spain until very recently. We were looking for a house to rent. They are delighted to hear Alex fell in love with their uncle's house when we drove through the village on a daytrip. They are still so proud of their birthplace and love the fact that someone from the other side of the world has fallen in love with it too.

'Imagine,' Lola exclaims, 'you come from the other side of the planet and fall in love with the house of our Uncle Domingo. Of all the houses in Spain, this one in this village caught your imagination!'

To emphasise that it is a really unique place, Lola points to the north from Domingo's house.

'See that hill there? That's a Roman settlement. We used to find pottery there all the time. One time, when I was a child of nine years old,' Lola reminisces, 'my friend's father found a big jar with gold coins.'

The intrigue of Romans at the end of the garden is getting to Alex in a big way. His eyes shine and he has a permanent grin on his face. He's not 'getting over it', not even a bit, and Lola and Lucia are not helping either!

They point once more to the hill. 'The Roman garrison was thought to be over there. All in all, there were three places we called the Triángulo Romano (the Roman Triangle). There has never been a proper archeological dig, but there should be!'

If we buy Domingo's house, we'll look out over a Roman garrison with a long-distance view to the snow-capped Sierra de Inodejo mountains. This knowledge, of course, only serves to get Alex more excited about the prospect of buying this old ruin.

~

After seeing Uncle Domingo's house, the sisters take us to their old home, which has been kept in the family after their parents died years ago. Lucia and Lola's parents' house is in the middle of the village. They tell stories about their ancestral home, their family and the history of the house. Alex understands some of it and I interpret the rest.

Lucia points to a ceiling hook in the corridor. 'This passage was where animals were slaughtered. We used the hook to hang the carcass to bleed out.' She pauses to make sure I can interpret for Alex before she continues. 'The whole house was the kitchen and two bedrooms. The corridor we're standing in goes to the barn at the back of the house. The animals came in and out of the barn through this corridor.'

The corridor runs between the kitchen and the bedrooms. The family members would have squeezed past a bleeding cow or pig carcass to go to bed. The sisters grew up in Ventosa during the 1950s and 1960s, sharing a single bedroom. There was no bathroom and they cooked over a fire in the kitchen. Later as the children grew up, their father bought part of the house next door, opened a hole in the wall and, presto, two more bedrooms were created. In the kitchen Lola points to a wooden stand holding four earthenware carafes.

'These were the ones we had to go and fill up at the fountain. We'd carry them all the way up here. We even had to wash in the river, breaking the ice in the winter first, and washing sheets and clothes there too.'

There were four siblings in total; they have a brother and the other sister is Mari-Paz. Exceptionally for the times, all four siblings are university educated. They were dirt poor but were fortunate to have an aunt who was a nun and a teacher. She made sure they all went to school and applied for scholarships on their behalf to continue their studies, a remarkable achievement for these kids, escaping the poverty of rural life and going to university. Their story exemplifies the reasons for the 'empty Spain' phenomenon.

All of them went on to different parts of the country to receive their education, which resulted in them all living across the length and breadth of Spain. Mari-Paz lives in Murcia. Lola's from Madrid, Lucia from Barcelona and their brother lives in Santander in the north. When Lucia tells us how many siblings there were, she recounts how she's named for her dead sister.

'Two months before my mother gave birth to me, my older sister called Lucia died. I was named for her.'

She adds: 'The cemetery is on the hill just behind us. The first baby Lucia is there, as well as both our parents and our grandparents.'

The ancestral home, shared between the siblings, has been updated and now has a bathroom. The barns have been converted to a large open-plan living and dining room. The old village still pulls at their heartstrings and they all return periodically to spend some time here. Lucia tells us about the old Ventosa primary school.

The building still stands and a recent reunion brought many back to the hamlet. Between the old pupils they are trying to refurbish the building with old school desks and blackboards.

These two women are close to me in age, and yet I can't help thinking how different their early lives have been from mine and how similar our lives are now. In the 1950s and 60s, the dictator Franco kept a very tight rein on Spain. The advance into the post-war era did not start until after he died and the country returned to democracy. From his death in the mid-1970s until now, Spain has had to jump forward into the twenty-first century with enormous leaps and bounds.

The Ventosa sisters were living an incredibly harsh life at a time when I was doing the hippie thing in northern Europe. I protested the indulgent and wasteful society I lived in when 'all we needed was love'. I did have a bathroom though, and central heating and running water. I didn't have to break ice in the river to wash the sheets. All things I didn't appreciate as much as Lola and Lucia would have.

~

We like the Ventosa sisters. In the end we spend a couple of hours with them, hearing their stories as they show us around. Lucia takes us to meet the one and only full-time resident, Gabina. She keeps the key to Uncle Domingo's house and will give it to us when we return with a builder to get a quote for the work that needs to be done. Lucia even recommends someone who could do the work on Domingo's house.

Gabina's age is tricky to judge. She could be anywhere between seventy-five and ninety but looks strong and healthy. She would have seen all her friends and neighbours leave to live in town or die of old age. How sad to be the last one left. There are others here occasionally but nobody permanent. Several houses have summer residents, several more are weekenders for people from Madrid or Soria. More recently, agriculturalists have bought up land around the village, built sheds for their tractors and bought a house to live in for a couple of nights a week during busy planting and harvesting times. One such farmer was the man who followed us on that first visit to Ventosa and told us the house was for sale.

Gabina is the height of her local contemporaries. A metre and a half tall, she's a round woman with a grey bun, wearing a practical but ancient apron over a practical but ancient dress. She has a friendly face with deep wrinkles from working outside in all weather. Her gumboots are outside the door to wear in the vegetable garden. She gives Lucia a loving hug before she goes. She would have known her since she was a baby and probably the previous Lucia too. She agrees to hold on to the keys until they are needed again.

As we're driving back to Almazán, Alex mumbles, 'We could do this.'

Could we, I wonder? Consequences, there are always consequences. Not sure that I thought them through before we made this bold move to Spain. What if Alex wants to do different things from what I want to do? What if we buy this house and we start to miss our friends in Australia?

~

The very next day we plan to go to the Ayuntamiento (town hall) responsible for Ventosa and ask some questions about building rules and regulations. I ring them first to make sure they are open today and I'm greeted with a 'Why on earth would we not be open?' As that is the case, we hop in the car to ask some questions face to face.

The council building is prominent in the town, painted in a two-tone red and cream, next to the main square, which is undoubtedly called the Plaza Mayor. There's a distinct lack of variety with street names here. You can bet that there's a Plaza Mayor in each town, a Calle de la Iglesia (Church Street), a Calle de la Fuente (Fountain Street) and so on.

The entrance to the town hall is on the second floor. The desk is unattended but eventually someone shows up. This must be the cheerful character I spoke to on the phone. He's a large man with a hangdog face who looks like the weight of the world is upon him. I tell him that we are interested in buying a house in Ventosa and would like some facts about council regulations. He's reluctant to help and makes it quite obvious. I work as much magic on him as I can muster while talking about sewerage.

'Can we get connected to mains plumbing and what would it cost?'

'No idea,' he declares. 'You must ask the honorary mayor of the town these questions. I will get you his number.'

He comes back some time later with a yellow sticky notepad. It has Arturo written on it with a telephone number.

'This is who you must call,' Hangdog Face tells us. I ask what Arturo's last name is. 'You don't need that,' he answers. 'He will be the one on the telephone when you ring. He must come out to the parcel of land, stand on it with you and answer all your questions.'

Right! As Hangdog Face thaws out a degree or two, he tells us that the council architect will be here next week on Thursday at 10.30am and if we have any more questions we should come then. He also prints something off for us that shows the boundaries and ownership of the parcels of land in the village.

Outside, Alex wants to call Arturo straightaway. He does not appear to be very committed to his role as a voluntary and unpaid mayor. He's in Ventosa a lot, he says, but doesn't know when he's going to be there next. He lives in Soria capital, 30 kilometres away. He can tell us now, though, that the old owner, Domingo, did not want sewerage when it came to Ventosa in 1960.

'He didn't take the water connection that was available at that time either as he was not willing to pay for it. So, therefore, you can't have sewerage now.'

Gee, the council seems to hold a grudge for a long time! Domingo has been in the cemetery for decades but Arturo's still annoyed with him. I ask about a septic tank.

Arturo answers, 'The family who is selling this house know all about it. They should tell you this. You can't have a septic tank because you have a well. Septic tanks can't be placed near wells. The family looked into it some time ago and were told they couldn't have a septic tank.'

Arturo refers us back to the Ayuntamiento, where they will be able to give us all the information we need. I am afraid the predictable Spanish 'pillar to post' thing is developing here.

Having another look at Uncle Domingo's house may give us some answers and maybe a lot more questions too. As we drive into the village, there are five people gathered on a corner of the street having a beer. It looks like maybe they are old residents 'back home' for a few days.

'Stop,' I say to Alex. 'I'm going to have a chat with them. They might know something about sewerage.'

Two older couples and a younger man stare at us in surprise. I introduce us both and tell them we are thinking about buying a house here. They are extremely interested to know why here in particular.

'Alex fell in love with the house at the edge of the village,' I tell them.

They all love that house they say. It has the best views, looking over to the Sierra beyond. One couple, in their early sixties, called

Jose Luis and Carmen, take us for a tour of Ventosa and comment on many of the houses, who owns them and how often they come to visit. The Ventosa community is spread right around Spain but are united in loving their home soil. We end up at their house so we can see their renovations.

Luis tells us, 'Carmen inherited the house from her father and we have fixed the lower floor and built some bedrooms on top.'

Carmen tells us she was born and grew up in Ventosa and still loves it here. 'I now live in Cataluña, but I miss my *pueblo*, my village.'

'I have a daughter and a granddaughter in Cataluña,' she says wistfully.

'How often are you in Ventosa?' I ask.

'When we can. Jose Luis and I spend some time there and some time here. It's not easy.'

As we look around her home, Carmen shows us framed photographs of her daughter and grandchild. She makes the sign of the cross before she puts the photo back, as if to protect them from any harm. I can tell she misses them terribly. It makes me wonder about how Alex and I will manage transitioning between two countries if we do buy a house here. Right now, there are lots of thrills but, in the long term, would we miss our life in Australia? The ongoing dilemma of any migrant. Maybe my sense of place would be even more out of whack than it is now?

Jose Luis and Carmen hope we can buy the house. It has always been a favourite with the villagers, they tell us. They would love to see it restored and would love us to buy it. It's flattering to hear this, but I really want to pick their brains about the practicalities of sewerage! Eventually I front up and ask them.

'No,' they say shaking their heads. 'We don't know anything about sewerage.'

~

I may have been infected with Alex's bug. Meeting Lola, Lucia, Jose Luis, Carmen and Gabina has pushed me over the edge. I can't stop thinking about Uncle Domingo's house. If we buy it, Alex may be too busy looking for the Romans and walking in the Sierra to restore the house. Despite these thoughts I fall asleep with a happy heart, dreaming of saving Spain's abandoned villages one house at a time.

Chapter 13

The River Cottage

While we're waiting for a builder to come and quote on the repairs needed for Uncle Domingo's house, we're off to Bilbao to see the Guggenheim Museum, have a look around and eat Basque food. On our way Alex remembers that we are about to pass a small town he has circled on the map. There's a house for sale there in our price bracket. I didn't know we had a price bracket, but we seem to have one now. Real estate websites list several houses that compare with Uncle Domingo's house in Ventosa. Most cost at least a few thousand euros more. The ruin real estate market is still an unknown quantity to us but we're learning. We've looked at houses for sale in different places now and we're starting to understand a bit more about which conditions add more euros to the price. Proximity to the capital will add value. A roof, all walls standing and connection to sewerage, water and electricity are obviously important but, regardless of those details, a house in a settlement with some permanent inhabitants generally costs more. Not surprisingly, what adds most to the potential asking price is a bar and a bakery. We're doing the homework we've set ourselves before making an offer on Uncle Domingo's house. What can you buy for how much and where? This should help us appreciate if something is value for money or not.

The village Alex circled is not far off the highway, so it won't take long to have a look. A Roman bridge over the river brings us into a picturesque hamlet. The ad reads:

Beautiful plot on the banks of a little river. The house is in poor condition and you would have to replace the roof and reform the house completely. Adjacent is a barn in good condition with a renovated roof. Magnificent village only a couple of hours from Madrid. Euro 25,000.

The house looks abandoned. We sneak into the walled garden through big squeaking metal gates that sound like they belong in a horror movie. The overgrown plot is next to a babbling creek lined with poplar trees and fragrant yellow broom. A plaque above the French doors on the balcony shows a carved stone that spells out 'Ave Maria'.

Alex looks up the symbolism of those words on his iPhone and calls out, 'Christian prayer asking for the intervention of the Blessed Mother in the lives of individuals on Earth.'

'I wonder if and how she intervened. Looks like they've all left a while ago. Maybe the Blessed Mother intervened too much,' I reply.

Another carved stone under the 'Ave Maria' shows the house was built in 1766. The barn does look like it had a new roof not long ago. The timeworn, tiled roof on the house itself looks dubious though. For some reason, this house gets under my skin instantly. I like this place very much. Is this where I find my new self? Or perhaps an old self. It's three storeys tall, the faint blue stucco on one wall falling off in a few places to expose the stone underneath. The other walls are bare stone. A wrought-iron balcony runs the length of the second floor and has French doors with faded blue shutters. There's a sense of timelessness, of lives lived. I imagine a young girl, a hundred years ago, being serenaded by a handsome shepherd in the garden below. I start murmuring my appreciation. Is it my turn to fall in love with a Castilian ruin? Alex looks at me, stunned. We are meant to be looking at other houses for comparative purposes only. For Alex, the point of this exercise is to justify him buying Uncle Domingo's house.

Now it's me saying things like: 'Oh, look at this walled garden. What a perfect place for a barbeque,' and 'What a lovely place. People still live in this village!'

Alex goes silent. This old stone house, in a cobblestoned street, looks impossibly romantic. Perhaps this house should be in the line-up along with Uncle Domingo's. I'm supposed to be the sensible one who makes sure that we spend our money wisely. Now it seems that I'm the one losing her heart to a ruin, except in a different place. Strangely, I feel a sense of belonging here. The house just feels right. I want to dance, hug a stranger and smile from ear to ear. The spell is cast, my whole body tingles with excitement. None of this was planned. We didn't set out to buy a house in Spain and now look at us – somehow there are two houses on the list. This village of San Juan de Soria appeals to me more than Ventosa, although Uncle Domingo's house has wonderful views. Here it's the location next to a river that seems utterly familiar already. We investigate further and find that there are two bars, two butchers (allowing me to pick the least frightening one), two banks and a bakery. There's even a *casa rural* (a country house with self-catering accommodation) and another fancy guesthouse, along with an aged-care home that employs many locals. It's delightful, but the house lacks the views that makes Uncle Domingo's house so exceptional. Even so, this house, this location by the little river, the rolling hills nearby, feels like a place we could make happy memories.

Alex agrees that we should at least try to arrange a look inside, as we've been inside Uncle Domingo's. Via the website I leave a message for the owner, Clara. Not taking any chances, I also ring and leave a message and text both mobile numbers in the ad. I stand in the garden quietly for a minute to let the scene sink in. We'd be crazy not to buy this lovely cottage.

We're ravenous and have to get a move on to find somewhere to eat or we'll miss out on lunch. We get back in the car and head north. La Rioja region borders with northern Soria. The capital, Logroño, has a dubious claim to fame; in the seventeenth century it was the main seat of the Basque witch trials that were part of the Spanish Inquisition. Now this region is famous for its vineyards, which can be seen in all directions. Not as wild as the land around Ventosa, but still attractive scenery with intermingling strands of trees, mountains and cliffs. Winding country roads overhung with pink, sweet-smelling almond blossoms complete the picture.

In the highlands we travel through oaks, beech and pine forests, with pockets of juniper and holly. The valleys are covered with vineyards, whereas the hillsides are used as pastures for livestock such as cattle and sheep. Even though pork is ubiquitous in every restaurant, I have never seen pigs roaming freely on a farm. There are massive sheds from which hog odour emanates, and this is where I assume all the pigs are housed – indoors, no grass, no soil, no natural light. Not much of a life. I feel more guilty each time a plate of *torreznos* appears.

We stop in a town called Islallana to find some lunch. We only recognise the modest bar because a couple of elderly men come out the front door as we pass. We bravely enter and there are a couple more patrons at the counter. The owner is a big-bellied man with greying stubble and a jet-black mop of hair. I'd put money on the fact he's had this same hairstyle since big hair was the fashion in the 1980s. The only thing that may have changed is that he now needs a regular supply of black hair dye.

'Hello, what's for lunch today?' I ask.

Big Hair, surprisingly, replies with the high voice of a choir boy. 'I can do you a bean stew today.'

I look at Alex with raised eyebrows that say, 'Are you game?' He nods back.

'Okay,' I say, and we get ushered to a dilapidated side room with tables and chequered tablecloths that, like his hair, seem to be from another era. Once this bar perhaps had prospects, aspirations of being a vital establishment in Isallana's future. By now it may have accepted its place in the world as a modest, old-fashioned bar in a modest, old-fashioned town. Another couple, a classic-looking Spanish pair, each with the Roman nose to prove it, are already in the dining room. They're ahead of us so we can see what's being brought out before it's our turn. Big Hair, with a big smile, brings us fabulous bread of the chewy variety and a rough red wine. Wine is always included in the *menu del día*, usually a table wine of dubious quality. This wine is often mixed with *gaseosa*, a cheap lemonade. It does improve the wine in this case.

Next comes a plate of thinly sliced fleshy tomatoes, sprinkled with salt and drowned in olive oil. What we would call heritage tomatoes. It's real food. Such a stunningly simple starter and yet mouth-wateringly delicious. After this, Big Hair enters dramatically holding an old porcelain vessel that looks like an heirloom. In it we see a dark substance with things floating inside. The Spanish couple are already eating it, so we're willing to try too. Ladling a couple of spoons into our bowls he wishes us *aproveche* and goes back to serve behind the bar.

It's a black-bean stew with a couple of pork bits that I recognise as chorizo and some pork ribs. The flavour is good. Hearty country food with good country bread. For dessert, we are offered coffee, which comes with a plate of homemade fresh goats' cheese slices.

The total bill for the pleasure of this authentic Basque lunch comes to something we couldn't buy a sandwich for in Sydney.

~

As soon as we enter the Basque lands all signs are in Euskara (the Basque language) first, followed by Castilian Spanish. Spain has four languages and many more dialects derived from these. The language known as 'Spanish' is more precisely Castellano, or Castilian in the English spelling. Castilla y Leon is where the most authentic Castilian is spoken. All other regional languages were banned during the Franco period, but people never stopped speaking their own language at home. The other languages spoken are Euskara (Basque), Catalan and Gallego. Each of these is a separate language with its own vocabulary and grammar rules. I learned to be reasonably fluent in Castellano, the official Spanish that every school child learns. When I lived in Alicante, the locals also spoke Valenciano, a language closely related to Catalan. I never learned Valenciano fluently, as everyone could also speak Castellano. Occasionally I did like to come out with a sentence in Valenciano simply to show off. Speaking Castellano, I find it easier to understand French, Italian or Portuguese than either Basque or Gallego.

The words in Basque are so much longer than the translations in Castilian. I'd love to see a Basque Scrabble game if it exists. They must have an increased number of Xs at least. The X or K, so valuable when playing an English Scrabble game, wouldn't be worth a lot of points in a Basque game.

The Basque landscape is dramatic – big cliffs and rolling fields of verdant green. As we come off the high plateau, it's obvious that lower down and closer to the coast things grow faster. Here all the trees, like poplars and oaks, are in full leaf, whereas only 200 kilometres south, on the mesa, they are still tentatively unfurling their leaves.

Soon we get to Bilbao, a city with some 350,000 inhabitants. Bilbao has won a string of awards for its 'urbanism', whatever that means. Despite the accolades, driving on the wrong side of the road in a strange city is still nerve-wracking. We booked a hotel online in the centre of town. As we traverse the suburbs towards the centre, I call the hotel to get directions to the carpark. Just in time, as we come around the corner, there it is. The hotel is not exceptional but tries to be funky, with bold red and black writing on the walls, and staff in orange T-shirts. The muzak, however, dates from the 1970s and 1980s. This era would have been right up the alley of our 'Big Hair' lunch host today. On the other hand, the hotel is in a good central spot and the staff are especially nice. They even retain their composure when I ask, on Alex's behalf, if he can have another sheet. Alex has an aversion to the hotel custom of making the bed with only a bottom sheet, topped with a doona. He always wants a top sheet too, for enhanced temperature control. Fussy! Anyway, shortly after the request, housekeeping knocks on the door with an extra sheet.

~

We hit town on foot just as the sun is setting, turning the sky a soft pink. The streets are packed, the population seems to be enjoying its 'urbanism' in spades. It's a Saturday night and there are people everywhere. The crowd is made up of all ages and genders. Socialising groups are as likely to be family as they are friends. I love seeing elderly women going out with a couple of friends for a wine on the square. Groups of wine-drinking female octogenarians are not a common sight in many countries, but they are here.

As we wander through the old centre, a band is starting up. There's an accordion, a couple of flutes and a drummer, all amplified above the din of the crowd. We could easily have missed it if we'd passed this square a minute earlier. What happens next is truly mesmerising. As the band begins to play Celtic-type music, the crowd gathers to dance around the square in choreographed paces they all seem to know. They almost dance in a trance as if the steps are so ingrained they don't need to think or concentrate. Feet seem to move of their own accord as if in an age-old ritual and the square gets fuller and fuller. The music makes them pull together tightly towards the middle before they all step back again and expand the circle. Every now and then there's a slight jump; they all know when. The dancers make big piles of coats and bags in the centre where they are safe from pilfering. Joyous, light and cheerful music lifts the spirit of both spectators and dancers. These traditional dances are passed on by one generation to the next. I love how everyone, regardless of their age, knows the steps and is enjoying themselves immensely. After a few minutes literally hundreds of people are dancing. I wish I could join them. Is this what being part of a tribe would feel like? Eyes closed and dancing with kindred spirits. I'm envious of their togetherness.

Eventually, we move on to hunt for the famed *pintxos* everybody talks about. Mention a trip to Bilbao to anyone in Soria and they will tell you about the *pintxos*. They are the Basque version of tapas. Bilbao is a foodie paradise, with the highest concentration of Michelin-starred restaurants in the world. To have a memorable foodie experience you don't have to go to a fancy restaurant though. Some of the tastiest morsels are eaten standing up at a bar. After dark the streets get even more crowded around some of the minute bars serving these delicacies, a good indication we're in the right place. The difference between *pintxos* and tapas appears to be that all *pintxos* have a slice of bread to heap things onto. We spot mouth-watering displays piled high with layers of stuff like giant prawns or fresh salmon. We order some wine and *pintxos* in one bar and then at another, as the locals do. It's a celebrated way to have dinner in Bilbao; simply stop when you've had enough.

We walk back to the hotel through dimly lit streets that looked safe earlier but now feel a bit seedy. At around eleven (Spaniards have only just had dinner) we receive a message via WhatsApp from someone called Xavier, the other owner of the house in San Juan, we presume. Texting back and forth we arrange a visit on Monday morning on our way back to Almazán. We need to pick up the keys before 1pm from someone called Jesus who works at the Ayuntamiento.

~

The next morning on our way to the Guggenheim Museum we traverse a city park. One obvious change I notice from decades ago is that dogs are kept as pets. This was not common here in the 1970s. I had dogs; they were my family and lived inside my house. At that time, this was very strange to most Spaniards. Working dogs were the norm, not family pets. Dogs were either hunting hounds or left at farms and building sites to protect the materials and tools, the more vicious the better to scare potential robbers away. Being a dog lover, I looked after a couple of stray dogs in the village when I lived near Alicante. An old dog called Tommy, who had a bit of Dalmatian in him, lay in front of the supermarket most days. He needed some help with removing ticks from around his eyes. I had my friend, a vet called Jesus (there are a lot of Jesuses in Spain, pronounced Hey Zeus), vaccinate some of the stray dogs against rabies and distemper. I was able to get the drugs at cost price, thanks to Jesus. I bathed and treated some dogs for mange and most of all I tried to get them a forever home. At the time, many Spaniards thought I was quite mad.

Attitudes have changed, along with increased affluence, and people now keep dogs as family pets and companions rather than working animals. There don't seem to be many stray dogs anymore, at least none that I see. There are still a lot of stray cats though. They seem skittish and run away when approached.

On our walk through the park, several owners are out with their dogs. While dog ownership has become more common, dog training doesn't seem to have increased at the same rate. Most owners act surprised if a dog comes when called or obeys the commands of its owner. One woman has a colossal dog that looks a bit like a long-haired galgo, a Spanish breed resembling a greyhound. Once this rambunctious galgo is off the lead, he seems to do whatever he pleases. He comes bounding towards us. His owner calls out to us, 'Don't worry, he's only a puppy.' 'Puppy' comes up to my waist and is at least a year old. His owner regards him with an indulgent, proud smile as he runs off again after slobbering all over me, muddy paws on my trousers, disregarding her completely. I am sure they love each other dearly. Dirty trousers or not, I much prefer to see this free-spirited dog than the sad ones chained and neglected at farm sheds or empty houses.

~

The next puppy we see is covered in flowers, greeting visitors to the Guggenheim Museum. This pup guards the doors of the museum with a changing fur coat of tens of thousands of flowers. This *West Highland white terrier*, created by Jeff Koons, has been welcoming visitors to the museum for nearly two decades.

The building itself has a surreal quality. We circle it on all sides, admiring the spectacular structure made of titanium, glass and limestone. It's truly a stunning statement of innovation and beauty. At the appointed time, we're funnelled through the entry system in quick fashion: security, cloakroom for bags, map of the museum and off we go. We are more impressed by the building than the art inside, although I am quite taken with another one of Jeff Koons' creations, called *Tulips*, a bouquet of multicoloured flowers blown up to a titanic size. They are big, bold and glistening. What's not to like?

After some highbrow culture, the metro takes us to the beach, where locals are drinking, relaxing and generally having a good time on a Sunday. Kids kick a ball around while parents and grandparents carry their glasses outside and sit in the squares and parks to chat. An attractive square festooned with bougainvillea acts like a large balcony above the beach, filled with what seem to be happy families. An enchanting panorama of Bilbao lays before us. A zigzag path takes us from the suburbs overlooking the beach to the bars below. We toast Bilbao and our good fortune, as we contentedly sip a glass of crisp white wine.

There's a funicular to take us back up the hill. The trip is 20 euro cents. Who'd bother walking up a steep hill for that kind of money? The wagon to take us up comes quickly and the operator says farewell as if we are being sent to our imminent deaths. The dodgy contraption on dodgy ropes somehow gets us up the hill.

~

We set the alarm to get to San Juan de Soria on time so we can have a look inside the stone house by the river. My excitement builds as we get closer. Just before one in the afternoon we get to the Ayuntamiento, where Jesus, the council worker, has the key to let us in. We follow Jesus on foot through the cobbled streets from the council building to the cottage. The house looks like an abandoned film set, with a facade of graceful decay. It's secluded, hidden away in a walled garden next to a small river. The grass is knee high and dotted with blood-red poppies and blue cornflowers. No gardening has been done for some time, but the wildflowers look a treat.

Jesus fiddles with the door for a bit to open it.

As we enter the house, a pungent smell hits us in the confined space. At first, I think it must be a dead body in one of the rooms, but soon I detect plenty of rodent shit in the feeble light of my mobile phone. The electricity was cut off years ago, Jesus tells us, and the solid stone walls have small windows that are fully shuttered so no natural light penetrates. Cobwebs caress our faces as we stumble around clutching our phones.

Council Jesus tells us that the last person to live here was an older lady by the name of Soledad. The place still looks as if she just popped out on an errand and will come back any moment. All her furniture, clothes, books and papers are still in the house. Clothes are folded on the bed and would look as if they've just been taken off the line if it wasn't for the deep layers of dust that coat everything. Cobwebs the size of throw rugs cover every window and hang from the ceilings in huge drapes. I feel a little shiver go up my spine. The presence of Soledad is still so strong and I get a slightly creepy feeling walking around the house. It wouldn't surprise me if the locals think this place is haunted. Soledad or any of her relatives could still be hanging about in a spooky kind of way. The darkness inside amplifies this eerie sensation. I wonder if there are as many rodents as I've seen droppings. We scare an insectivorous bat out of its slumber in one of the bedrooms. It leaves through a hole in the roof. In the dark bedroom I get a feeling that any time now I could run into the shrivelled body of the previous owner, perhaps a woman so private that she was not missed until now. I carefully open the shutters on the French doors to a balcony to let some light in. Sparkling dust motes float in the air like powdered light. It feels like being trapped in a time warp.

We realise the house isn't as small as we'd thought from the outside and sits on a fair-sized block of land. What's for sale is a three-storey home, a large stone barn with a vaulted ceiling, a walled garden and a dramatic hunk of derelict stone. This is a ruin at the far end of the garden. It looks like an old barn with a missing roof but it would be perfect as an enclosed patio. The original owners kept their pigs and sheep in the big barn with the new roof, Jesus tells us. This barn is a solid structure, so big we could build a whole house inside it in a *Grand Designs*-style barn conversion. It's full of ancient farming equipment. Handcrafted wooden pitchforks, wooden animal feed troughs, horse harnesses and old leather whips. In the house itself there are three rooms downstairs; one is the entrance, which runs through to the barn, with two rooms to the left. The smaller room was used for tools and drying herbs, and storing a lot of junk, the other is the kitchen. To the right there's a funny little bathroom. A prehistoric wooden staircase leads to three rooms upstairs. There's an attic above that, full of large wooden trunks and more bats. The floorboards upstairs are the widest I've ever seen, about 70 centimetres across at my guess. The trees from which these planks were cut would have been gigantic. Charming as the cottage and its location are, it needs a lot of work. The ceiling is collapsed in one room because of the hole in the roof and there is no real kitchen or a usable bathroom. The space has an enormous hearth, big enough to sit inside. Many generations would have cooked their meals here, and lots of cooking implements still hang on the walls. A solid hook and chain dangle in the middle of the fireplace ready to take a pot of pork stew. Smoke has blackened the wooden beams and the walls in this room. In more recent times a gas bottle and a two-burner stove were added to make life easier. There's a fridge as well but it has a lock on it.

The bathroom is eye-catching in an unusual way. It was built in the late 1960s, when sewerage came to town, Council Jesus tells us. Because the river cottage is built below the road, there was a problem. To avoid pushing shit uphill, a new bathroom was constructed well above the existing floor level, so gravity could do its thing. The result is a functional bathroom but only for people under a metre and a half tall. My tall Dutch genes mean I have to crouch down to cross the floor to use the loo. On the plus side, there is a vast barn with a new roof. I can't get my head around how we'd use this barn, or how to revamp it, but I do love this old cottage and the garden by the river.

A whispering voice tells me we should buy this house. I want to sit in a window seat looking at the river, reading a book or scribbling in my notebook. I want to plant climbing roses in the enchanted garden. Oh no! This is bad. We have a problem. Alex is in love with Uncle Domingo's house and now I'm losing my heart to this cottage by the river. What have we started? It's all Alex's fault of course. He's infected me with his contagious passion for saving a ruin. When we came to Spain there was no plan to buy a house, we were going to rent something in a nice place and now we are faced with a dilemma. Each of us likes a different house. What we do have in common is that it seems that both of us want to immerse ourselves in the project. To save a ruin from collapse, hopefully the same one.

Once we leave San Juan de Soria and Jesus, Alex and I keep talking about where we go from here. We've seen quite a few houses in a similar price range now and all seem to have a collapsing roof or decaying walls, or both. All need heaps of work. We must decide between two money pits! If we go ahead with this, we may have to sell up in Sydney so we can fund this utter folly. Because that's what it comes down to in the end. What are we willing to risk, for what is looking more and more like a shared dream of living in Spain and saving a ruin?

Chapter 14

Cathedrals and a Parador

We arrive back in Almazán and our life slips back into our morning routine, a snappy walk followed by coffee in a bar. By frequenting different bars on different days, we sample all Almazán has to offer in the coffee department. Entering a new bar is lots of fun, as everything goes quiet at first. All the customers turn to look at us and hold their breath to hear our order.

Today there's even more excitement in town. The first bar, one on the Plaza Mayor, has opened its terrace; tables and chairs have been placed outside. We have coffee al fresco in the tentative rays of sunshine, taking in the scenery around us. The palace and adjoining buildings of fading splendour are the setting of a rewarding Castilian scene. We look at each other over our cups and silently nod. Yep, this is good.

~

In the river cottage we saw a postcard of Burgos displayed on the sideboard. Unsent. Bought for the picture of the cathedral perhaps. It inspires us to check it out ourselves. We have a few days before we can ask questions of the council architect about water and sewerage in Ventosa. Time to find out more of this enchanting part of Spain. Burgos, the historic capital of Castile is only a couple of hours away and we're ready for another excursion. This city is inextricably linked to the illustrious figure of El Cid. Half history and half legend, El Cid was a mercenary soldier who lived from 1045 to 1099 (mercenary soldiers don't make old bones). He fought for King Alfonso to liberate parts of northern Spain from the Moors. The city of Burgos commemorates this feat with a humongous statue of the liberator showing his flowing beard and respectable moustache, mounted on an equally humongous horse. Dominating the centre of town, this statue can be glimpsed from all the streets leading to the main square.

Our hotel is in an old palace, right in the middle of town next to the Arlanzón River. There's a lot to see in town, the cathedral being one of the main sights. The largely Gothic thirteenth-century building has everything you'd ever want to see in a house of worship, from gilded arches and pointy spires to priceless artworks. Despite the oversupply of churches, it is impossible not to be impressed by this one. The volume of magnificent art on the walls and ceilings, its carvings, statues and glass leadlights are breathtakingly opulent. Burgos is on the path of the Camino de Santiago pilgrimage and a visit to the cathedral is a must for pilgrims coming through town. Regardless of its obscene riches, the church still wants a bit more of our money and charges a stiff entrance fee. Alex is again appalled at the Catholic Church getting into our pockets. Luckily, he mumbles his displeasure in English so we're safe from being evicted or cursed by the nuns who are selling the tickets.

In addition to an entrance fee and a fee for the guided tour, there's a souvenir shop with every Catholic trinket you may wish to purchase. Rosary beads are a prevalent item, as is Jesus on the cross in every size, Jesus keyrings, religious pictures, postcards and Mary snowdomes, bottles of Lourdes holy water and miraculous medals, although for what purpose I'm not sure. There are thermometers with an image of the Pope for sale right next to the crucifixes. The fridge magnets hold my attention for some time – they show the Virgin Mary, surrounded by angels, beaming out from golden rays of sunshine. I am even more taken with the hologram postcards showing a winking Jesus. I nudge Alex and hold it up for him, moving it about to show Jesus wink. We leave without making a purchase, perhaps to the disappointment of the stern-looking nun behind the counter.

~

The gastronomic delights of Burgos are well known nationally. The town of some 200,000 inhabitants was declared the Gastronomic Capital of Spain in 2013. Maya told us that the one thing we had to do was to eat some *morcillas*. I have not yet shared this description with Alex but *morcillas* are essentially a mixture of pig's blood with rice and some spices, stuffed into either pig or cow intestines. This sounds far from appetising but, trust me, they are delectable. The rich smoky flavour of the sausages is complemented by sweet, roasted red peppers on the side. Perhaps I'll tell Alex about the ingredients later.

We head for a restaurant near the cathedral to have the *menu del día*, which includes a good serving of *morcillas*. There's a busload of school kids on an excursion already occupying most of the tables. The noise is deafening but it is nearly 4pm and most places will stop serving lunch soon. Anyway, as we arrive, they are licking ice-creams, so it can't be too long before they leave. I decide to do the right thing and tell Alex what's in the *morcillas* before we order. He eats them anyway and likes them as much as I do. Traditional Spanish fare includes all parts of an animal, the guts, the tongue, even the tail. Often the cuts people in northern

Europe would turn their nose up at are as celebrated here as the most desirable.

Most bars and restaurants have a *menu del día* to make sure workers can have a wholesome, filling meal in the middle of the day. The *menu del día* always has three courses with several choices of entree, main and dessert, and comes with bread, wine and water, all for a very reasonable sum. The set menu of the day usually only costs about half of what the meal would if one ordered each item separately. This set menu targets the workers stuck in town and away from home around the time the most important meal of the day is eaten: the *comida*. The working hours in Spain continue to reflect the old rural life when everyone worked the land and came home for the main meal in the hottest part of the day. Routinely, a tiny sleep or rest was taken during the siesta before returning to the fields at about five in the afternoon. City workers still have these working hours and often don't get home till nine or ten at night. Workers stuck in town will often have the *menu del día* or alternatively the *plato combinado*. The *plato combinado* is exactly what it promises, a plate with a combination of things such as some fish or chops, chips and a salad. It too is a good choice for an economic lunch.

The city of Burgos is worth a bit of random wandering around. We find surprising plazas with enchanting vistas around many a corner, as well as a few promising-looking alleyways to come to in the evening for tapas and a drink. It is usually in the dark and dingy alleys that light up at night where the best tapas are served. By nine in the evening, work finished for the day, the bars are packed with family and friends catching up. The bars clustered here all seem to do a roaring trade. Nearly all the customers appear to be locals, with only one footsore couple who look to be weary but thirsty pilgrims. As everywhere, the service is good, the wine is good and the food is good.

~

Early in the morning, as we drive towards the south, the sun comes out, and we dawdle along sightseeing. We're impressed with the village of Castrillo Solarana. The residents here take wine profoundly seriously, demonstrated by the fact there are some 150 wine cellars dug into the side of the hill on which the church stands. The Iglesia de San Pedro stands sentinel proudly above its parishioners and their wine cellars. Each of these cellars is a unique creation with a distinctive entrance. Some have a stone bench to sit on, others go straight into the bowels of the hill as far as the eye can see. The story we are told is that, before refrigeration, villagers would come here in the early afternoon to fill up a carafe with lovely cool wine to drink with lunch. Some must have stopped for a sip on the little terrace in front of their wine cave before going home.

'This could be a good village to buy an old house in!' Alex thinks out loud.

Unfortunately, or perhaps fortunately, there's nothing for sale here right now. I'm almost relieved. The last thing we need is another ruin to add to the list of ruins we could throw money at.

~

We stop for the night in Lerma, where we're booked into the ducal castle, now a hotel. Paradores de Turismo de España is a chain of Spanish hotels owned by the government. They're often in historic buildings such as castles, palaces, fortresses, convents, monasteries and the like. They are great for travellers who enjoy heritage tourism, while also providing a future for these historic buildings. The restaurants are usually fantastic, not only serving quality food but offering specialities of the regional gastronomy. The Parador de Lerma is a striking seventeenth-century palace converted into a hotel of infinite charm. It's in the middle of town, in the medieval quarter. We are checked in by a charming young man whose name badge tells us he's called David. He asks me coquettishly to confirm that I had indeed expressed a preference for the 'matrimonial bed', the double rather than twin beds.

'Yes, I still like my husband quite a lot,' I say.

David blushes down to his knees. When looking at said husband I see that after forty years I'm still able to embarrass him too. Points to me all around!

David sees us to our room in person. First a lift, then corridors and more corridors. It appears to be on the top floor. I try to keep up with a sashaying David carrying my colourful daypack. There's more sway on his behind than a Kardashian. He finally delivers us to the last room along the top-floor corridor. I have a strong suspicion that he is worried about noise we might make. Obviously, my request for the matrimonial bed means we should be kept away from the other guests. I can't help another chuckle to myself.

The stately room is furnished in medieval style. Up a few steps, a small window in the thick stone wall looks out over the large plaza, where the market will be held tomorrow, David tells us. How often did the duke, his family or the servants look out of these windows and what did they see back then?

The lavish hall surrounded by columns in the Parador would have been the duke's courtyard. It now has a glass roof. A few guests are having quiet drinks there, including a man we have already dubbed the Major. He's an older Englishman with an impressive handlebar moustache. Tall and bent over he leans on a walking stick and wears a green tweed sportsjacket from the previous century, when both he and the jacket were in their prime. As we were checking in the Major sidled up to the other receptionist.

'Thank you for your help earlier. However, I was rather

disappointed at having only one bidet towel!'

The receptionist cheerfully responds, 'Yes, we only provide one bidet towel!'

Whether they understood each other or not is not clear, but the Major shuffles off in disgust, mumbling, 'Incredible!'

At drinks time, we find the Major and his wife having gin and tonics in the glassed-in courtyard in typical English gentry fashion.

'I wonder which one of them got the bidet towel,' Alex whispers.

'Perhaps they're willing to share,' I suggest.

Dinner is served in one of the big rooms to the side of the courtyard. There are only a few diners, attended by severe-looking waiters.

The Major and his wife, the only other foreigners here tonight, don't come to the dining room. They had a sandwich in the courtyard earlier with their gins. Spanish food and mealtimes may be a step too far for them after 'the bidet towel' affair.

~

Breakfast is served in yet another spectacular room. Spanish breakfast in a good hotel consists of sweet pastries, cheeses, cold meats, sausages and more *morcillas*, the local delicacy. I pilfer enough at the buffet for a picnic later in the day. It's always very satisfying, stealing breakfast for a picnic lunch on the road.

The Major and his wife are at breakfast too. We give thanks to the gods of elderly Brits they have both survived the night. An unlikely feat in some respects. An even more unlikely feat is that the Major has driven himself here in an English right-hand drive. As we are packing up, we spot him shoving a well-worn leather suitcase into the boot of an also aging but rather classy silver Rover. The poor old Major seems reluctant to adapt to change; the bidet towel, the late dinners and suitcases without wheels all mark him as a man struggling in a changed world. How well are we adapting to change now that we have moved to live here?

Chapter 15

Hope and Ángel

Life returns to what we think is our new normal, after the excitement of looking at ruins, the latest fiestas and our trip away to Burgos. On our way to the council offices, to find out more about Uncle Domingo's house, we stop off at a bar we have not yet frequented. Bar Veronica is in a nearby village, the only bar in this hamlet. An older lady is serving as we come in. She wears a worn-out dress matched with a cardigan that's also seen better days. It's held together with strips of sticky tape on the elbows. Business may not be booming here. Her son comes in later and pats her on the bum. They are both unusually tall, making me think they're not from these parts. We vote this the most dismal bar we've been in so far. Everything seems to be in a state of disrepair, even the owners. There are a few customers though. Road workers in hi-vis clothes sheltering from the rain and a middle-aged man with a sadly droopy moustache reading the paper by the window. The coffee is excellent though and cheaper than Almazán. The smaller the town, the cheaper the coffee, it seems.

~

The council secretary, he with the hangdog face, told us to come in at 10.30am on a Thursday, when the architect would be here to answer all our questions. We're right on time but see the secretary and another employee cross the road to the nearest bar. We do the same but leave them alone to have their coffee in peace as we chat with the bartender for a while. As the council employees ready to leave the bar Hangdog sombrely tells us, 'This is the architect. She can answer your questions.' We follow them out of the bar at some distance, but they get caught by other people asking questions too and we get to the Ayuntamiento before them. Sitting in the waiting room, Hangdog comes bustling in to usher us to the council meeting room. It's a large square room with a row of dark wooden tables for the councillors and rows of seats for the general public.

'Those papers I printed out for you the other day,' Hangdog whispers, 'don't show them to her or anybody. I am not supposed to give them to you.'

I manage to nod before the architect comes in. Esperanza (Hope) is a fortyish woman with a curly mop of shoulder-length blonde hair, showing dark roots. She has a nice face with unusually green eyes and green eyeliner. She has a groovy style, dressed in a long jumper with thick tights, quite practical for climbing about building sites. I tell Esperanza we're after information about the possibility of sewerage connection and running water, and what we're allowed to do with the building. I explain that we need this before we can make an offer to buy the property. I also tell her that the local mayor advised us we could not get sewerage because the previous owner had not wanted it when it came to town many decades ago.

'Not true,' says Esperanza. 'Access to sewerage and water is a *right*. You may need to pay to bring it to your house, but you have a right to it. These local mayors often don't know what they're talking about!' She rolls her green eyes dramatically.

Hangdog Face and the architect search for the plan of the

sewerage system in Ventosa, which seems to have disappeared. They give us a form to request a copy of this plan. I guess the idea is that the form will encourage the plan to be found. Esperanza also rings a builder to give us a quote, so we know what we're up for. It turns out to be a man called Ángel from Josh and Maya's village. His name literally means angel, which bodes well perhaps. Esperanza seems very helpful and smart too. She tells us that she's the president of the architect association and, when the time comes, she can recommend a good architect.

'An architect is always needed for these sorts of projects,' she advises.

We leave with the form, which we must bring to council after we've spoken to Ángel, to receive a copy of the sewerage plan, once it is found.

'Now we have Hope and Ángel on our side. Surely a positive sign?' says Alex. He'll clutch at any straw it seems.

I ring Ángel and explain who I am. He already had a heads-up from Esperanza at the council and is very obliging. He's the local mayor of his village, which brings him regular work from council I presume, so he's careful to be on their good side. We agree to meet in Ventosa tomorrow at noon.

'Well, between noon and 1pm,' he qualifies.

'Okay, we will be at the house to meet you there.'

Pinning our hope on Ángel may not be a wise move. Our next step is to ring our contact, Lucia, one of the Ventosa sisters, to ask her if we can get the keys to visit the house with the builder. She says we can, but she strongly suggests we also get a quote from another builder called Ricardo. She knows Ángel and he's not reliable, she hints. She also intimates that Ángel is a distant cousin of hers. I don't want to put her in an awkward position where she has to be more direct about her cousin's crappy building work. I take the hint without further question. Esperanza from council also mentioned that Ángel may not be punctual.

'He may say that he can start the job next Monday, but he may actually start a month later,' she says. 'But he's good with quotes.'

~

On our way home snowflakes dance through the air. A mean wind nearly wrests the car door from my grip when I get out. The snow melts as soon as it lands on the ground; the weather is extremely changeable. Why on earth would we, who live in paradise on the beaches of northern Sydney even consider living here to do battle with council, builders *and* the weather? Any house here needs central heating. We know nothing about these things. Alex seems frustrated at times as I need to interpret for him when he's busting at the seams to ask the questions himself. His Spanish will get better but I worry that his lack of fluency makes him feel isolated and far from his kin. What we do know is that it's all very intriguing. We meet plenty of locals we wouldn't normally get to meet, even during an extended stay in another country. We toggle between terrified, amused, interested and wondering about our sanity. Tomorrow may bring more clarity. Ángel may give us some idea of costs. That could kill the whole thing in no time at all.

~

Darkness is a catalyst for spreading doubt in one's mind. After going to sleep with a happy heart because we may save a ruin, I wake in the middle of the night. My mind starts to race, going over and over the premise of why we think buying a derelict house is a good idea. From there my thoughts take off on a merry ride through the dark recesses of my brain. Why did I think it was a good idea to live in Spain? I've now lived in Australia for decades –

it is home, I have friends, a life. How could I do this to Alex? He has always felt an unease about me having given up my life in Europe so we could be together. Am I taking advantage of Alex's vague guilt to get my way? I finally fall asleep only to wake up early with my heart pounding. I don't want to buy a house. We don't need to buy a house to live in Spain. Our lives here are rather good as they are. We're not bored with each other or with life in general, so why would we seek to complicate our existence? It would be a lot of work. Are we up for that?

The next day my fears and doubt dissipate. In the light of day, everything seems a hoot again. Far from putting the idea to rest, looking around Uncle Domingo's house has set Alex on fire. After my dark thoughts during the night Alex certainly does not act like someone who's only here under some notion of equalising the score regarding what continent we live on. There's a lot to find out about buying a house that needs this much work. He's urging me on to get going, impatient for the day to start.

We're meeting builder Ángel later today so we have plenty of time for our early-morning walk, there are more signs of spring, earthworms this time. They have suddenly arrived everywhere, crawling on the road and in the garden. The bird that seems to have won the earliest breeding award is the European goldfinch. I see one feeding a fledgling. Despite the cold they have managed to raise a baby, no mean feat, as it was snowing only yesterday.

After our walk we have a coffee in bar El Arco, which, unsurprisingly, is right next to one of the stone arches into town. This is the Puerta de Herreros, the Blacksmith's Gate, which is on the border of the new and the old part of town. At this time of the morning there are loads of business types getting their quick fix of caffeine. No lingering over the coffee for them. It's a five-minute turnaround: order, drink, pay and get out. We've not seen anyone order a takeaway here in Spain. In the bigger cities this may be the case but here it's always drunk at the bar. It's a brilliant way to catch up quickly with friends, colleagues and acquaintances, for customers always seem to know someone else in the bar and have a bit of a chat. What sets El Arco apart from the other bars is the almost miraculous appearance of the bartender, who steps out of a dumb waiter behind the bar. Designed to bring food down from the kitchen upstairs, it also disgorges a crouching barmaid who jumps out to help when the bar gets busy.

~

Fortified with caffeine, we navigate our way to Ventosa. Alex comments on the loneliness of the countryside in this part of the peninsula. Although there's a lot of farming and cropping, the surroundings feel isolated. There's a rule against building on rural lands. Farmers must live in town and travel to their plots. This means that the rolling hills are devoid of scattered barns and sheds, and there's no graveyard of cars and tractors by the road. It does mean, however, that there are a lot of tractors travelling on rural roads. Farmers park next to their house overnight and commute to work on their farm vehicles. We see tractors parked at nearby bars as farmers come in for a pick-me-up.

It also means that the region is dotted with picturesque stone villages clinging to hillsides. All roofs uniformly showing the same colour terracotta tiles. I imagine families living with other families for many generations, intermarrying, feuding, bartering and sharing. Perhaps it is that sense of belonging I crave. You probably can't buy that even if you buy a ruin in the village. As we're driving past these villages I get a pang of envy sometimes. I want what they have, that sense of community. If nothing else, this trip helps to clarify my emotions.

Meanwhile, Alex is extremely excited about meeting Ángel,

who is going to give us advice and a quote on repairs. First, we need to pick up the key from Gabina, the last permanent resident of the village. She's the cutest miniature old lady. If Hollywood were on the lookout for a friendly witch, they could do no better than cast Gabina. She reaches my elbow in height, has a scratchy voice, which she uses at an alarmingly high pitch in rapid Spanish. Lucia has asked her to give us the keys and told her at what time we're due to arrive. I grab the heavy knocker and beat the door with it as gently as I can, but she's not there. Some tradesmen are working next door, restoring a house.

When I ask if they know where Gabina is they reply, 'She went to feed the chickens. Should be back any minute.'

I go around the streets looking for signs of chickens or Gabina herself, whichever comes first. She evidently hides her chickens well because I can't find any. Dogs are barking in various places where they have been left to guard a house or an agricultural shed. A bit after noon, we put the car close to the house, where we are due to meet Ángel, so he sees the car and knows we are here. Walking back to Gabina's house after parking, we see her coming around the corner of her street. She's been looking for us.

'I thought I heard a car,' she screeches.

She holds on to the keys firmly until we have a chat.

'What do you like about Domingo's house?' Gabina asks, holding her head on an angle to look up at me. I feel I'm a freakshow standing next to her, as I'm almost twice her height. If she notices it doesn't seem to faze her.

'Ah, we love the view. The position of the house on the edge of the village looking at the Roman garrison is wonderful. It's such a pretty village!'

'Yes, it's a pretty house in a pretty village,' she agrees with a satisfied smile, obviously delighted to know that other people like her village.

'I knew Domingo well,' she adds. 'He's dead now, but I remember him well. He went away to another country but, in the end, he came back here. He was a good man, I liked him a lot.'

'Did he die a long time ago?' I ask.

'Ay, many, many years ago. The house has been empty for a very long time, that's why we still call it Domingo's house. He was the last person to live there.'

After that gratifying chat, Gabina is willing to hand over the keys.

'You can bring the keys back later. I'll be here waiting.'

We're there before the builder and go in to have a look around by ourselves before Ángel gets here. We're excited to get another look at the house. Alex warns me several times to be careful not to lean on things lest they collapse, and to watch my step as floors may be rotten. It's advice he's happily ignoring himself as he scoots around eagerly. We're pleasantly surprised on entering a second time. Perhaps this house *can* be saved. We roam around opening shutters so we can see the light streaming in. The damage looks repairable to our eyes, but not so in Ángel's opinion, who arrives not long after us.

His first words after 'hello' are: '*Hay que tirar lo todo.*' (It all needs to be demolished.) He's made the decision before he's even set foot in the place.

Alex looks shocked as I interpret Ángel's words. He's just been thinking everything was salvageable. Is this the end of his dream?

'It's too far gone. It will cost you more to fix than build a new house. You need to demolish the entire place. Build a new one on the land.'

'But can't we repair the hole in the roof instead of ripping it off and putting a new one on? What about the staircase – can you fix that? Surely you could repair the windows here?'

Ángel reluctantly looks at the things we point out, but

unfortunately he only wants to demolish and start again. And start somewhere else, it seems.

'This is a crap village. I wouldn't want to live here. You should build a nice house somewhere else. Somewhere nicer.'

When I interpret this for Alex he says: 'I wonder what the Ayuntamiento staff would think of that statement? He's an honorary mayor after all.'

This is problematic as we want a quote on repair, not a complete rebuild. The concept that some weirdos like old places to still look old after they have been modernised is novel to him. He tries to convince us to buy something in better condition. I tell him that Alex wants to save a house from being demolished and restore it to its former glory. This is a concept too far for Ángel. He obviously thinks we're peculiar hippie types.

We climb up the hill to find the house closest to Uncle Domingo's house that is connected to the sewerage.

'It would take 60 metres of sewerage pipes and a pump to connect to that,' Ángel states, shaking his head.

He promises to investigate the sewerage issue as this is what the council architect specifically asked him to do. He will also investigate if a septic tank is possible this close to the well or if we can close the well. However, we're not convinced that he's going to do anything at all.

Returning the keys to Gabina, she wants to know how it went.

'The builder said it has no water or sewerage and needs a new roof,' I tell her.

She nods sagely as if she's heard it all before. She tells me that Lucia has told her she's in charge of the keys and she will take good care of them. We say goodbye for now and I tell her that another visit with another builder or architect may be the next thing.

Ángel wants to show us some houses he's working on in nearby villages. The first house he shows us is almost finished. It's an old house with a new roof, new windows, new kitchen, new bathroom, floors and much more. Only the old facade remains. It looks fine, showing good craftsmanship but not the rustic flavour we're after. It's all too new looking. If you don't feel it's an old house when you're inside, then what is the point of buying an old house? He takes us to the next one he's also building, still under construction, but it's the same as the previous one except with blond rather than dark wood. Three walls of the old house remain, nothing else. Nada, zip, nothing.

Ángel will ring us next week about sewerage and plumbing.

'If you don't hear from me by Wednesday give me a call,' he says.

That statement is never a good omen in any language. Tradies have a similar modus operandi the world over. Before he goes, we ask him to give us a figure for a new roof instead of demolishing the house. He rattles off some figures for how many euros it would be per square metre of roof. His estimate for the number of square metres is very generous, at least doubling the roof size. We feel he's a bit dodgy. This may not be our man. Alex is reading more body language than listening to the words but finds him evasive and untrustworthy too. Throughout our conversation he tries to convince us to buy elsewhere, as this village is 'not very nice'. His village is much nicer, he claims. The views are better and it's closer to Soria.

'Well, it's lunch time (*hora de comida*), so I have to go and join my crew. They're in the bar already and I'll miss out if I don't go now!' He nods eagerly in the direction of the bar as he speaks, more animated than we've seen him so far.

~

My heart breaks a little for Alex. He has bought into my dream of living in Spain. Then he too fell in love with a romantic folly only to have his hopes crushed by what may be a dodgy builder. We console ourselves with a lunch in Tardelcuende's Bar Alfonso. As per custom, we say an audible '*Hola, buenos días*' to no one in particular and everybody at once. Some patrons always oblige and respond with a '*buenos días*' of their own. They have sandwiches left for lunch today and we settle for a tortilla with chorizo. A woman who looks to be seventy in the shade is roused from her seat at a table where she's chatting happily. She must be the cook. Indeed, she appears sometime later with two mammoth loaves of bread, which are our 'sandwiches'. Each sandwich could happily feed both of us. We leave making sure we do the reverse of the hello at entry and say '*Adios, hasta luego*' to all and sundry on our way out. They oblige in reply.

Our preferred fountain is in the middle of a pine forest on the way home. This is where every few days we fill up our containers with good drinking water. The water that comes out of the tap is extremely hard and our tea and coffee does not taste like it should. The water from this fountain is lovely and sweet, excellent drinking water. Coming from a dry continent, the urge to turn off the fountain after filling the bottles is almost visceral. It seems so wrong to let all that lovely water run away. The fountain continues to splash as we head for home to contemplate the next move in the Castilian real estate market. I am tired, worn out from trying to get Ángel to understand what we wanted and tired of being looked at as if slightly *loca* (crazy). Although we have Ángel, we have no hope.

Chapter 16

A Renovator's Dream

To keep things on an equal playing field, we need a quote from a builder in San Juan as well. This will help us decide in favour of one charming stone cottage over another. Council Jesus organises a builder to give us a quote to do up the river cottage. We're to meet him in San Juan. We arrive early and do what every Spaniard would do in this situation – go to a bar to pass the time. We end up talking to some patrons and we tell them we're here to see a house that's for sale. A thickset man with a ruddy face and a dicky leg tells us he knows the best house in San Juan to buy.

'I used to spend a lot of time there when I was a kid. I love that old house.'

A few others around the bar pipe in with their comments. They're all talking at once about what houses are for sale in the village.

Ruddy Face turns to me again and adds: 'Natural stone floors. We used to kill and gut the pigs on that floor.'

He seems to think that makes it more attractive. I nod appreciatively. As it turns out it's the house we've come to look at, the river cottage.

Council Jesus finds us in the bar and gives us the keys. We're trusted with the keys and can go explore by ourselves until the builder arrives. We leave the car at the bar and walk to the house. As we pass the church we see massive bird nests on three corners of the bell tower. A stork arrives as we're walking by, his mate already at the nest. As he lands, both birds loudly clack their bills in greeting. We stand and watch them in awe as they display their affection for each other. Any visitor to this part of the country will inevitably see and hear the common stork, *cigüeña* in Spanish. They spend the winter in North Africa and wing it to the Iberian Peninsula to make babies. These birds are such an interest in the landscape. They are loyal to both their mate and the nest site, returning each year to find the same partner in the same spot. Arriving in the early spring, they perform impressive courtship rituals and can be spotted everywhere, from chimneys to churches and telegraph poles. Some church bell towers have a sizeable nest on all four corners.

Alex fiddles with the lock for a while but finally the door springs open and stale air greets us. Paco the builder arrives a couple of minutes after us in the obligatory *furgoneta*, one of those Spanish box-like vans all the tradies drive. He's only ten minutes late, very acceptable by Spanish standards. Paco has a respectable moustache and is probably in his early sixties, but the spark in his eye suggests a younger age. His weathered face looks as if he's constantly on the verge of telling a joke and he swears quite freely. Perhaps he thinks I can't possibly know these words being a foreign woman of a certain age.

He goes around saying things like, 'Shit, I can smell rodent piss!' A while later I hear him shriek, 'Fuck, it's dark in here.'

Despite the dark, the house impresses even more on this second look inside. The stone walls and massive wooden beams make it feel like we're safe and protected. The walls are almost a metre thick, like a fortress. Tiny windows will help keep out the cold in winter and the heat in summer. The height of the ceiling on the lower floor is fine; even tall people won't hit their heads on the beams, except in the bathroom. Calendars on the wall show August 2008. Piles of letters, mostly bills, are unopened on an antique table used as a desk. The house is full of old furniture, wardrobes with moth-eaten coats, cupboards with yellowing linen.

As we're standing in the garden looking up at the eaves, an older woman leaning heavily on a frame walks by slowly. She's dressed in black and has grey hair.

'*Qué haces?*' (What are you doing?) she calls out.

Maybe she's the local vigilante.

'We're thinking about buying it,' I say. 'Do you know who lived here before?'

'It's been empty for some ten years. She got sick and left.' She sounds as if she's in contempt of this person who had the temerity to get sick and leave.

The letters in the house are addressed to Soledad Martinez de Poveda, who we were told about on our first visit. Some are directed to Calle del Huerto Number 6. The house we are told is for sale is Calle del Huerto Number 4, so we're a little confused about the number. *Huerto* means orchard and there is an orchard at the end of the road. It grows lush tomatoes and lettuce, and beans reaching for the sky.

Paco thinks the house is a good buy at 25,000 euros.

'The roof needs fixing but it's got good bones.'

Alex asks a lot of questions and I interpret.

'*Sí*, I'll make you a big window right there so you can see the river. Boom, boom, *sin problema*. I'll also open up some French doors to a terrace. Boom boom.' He does a lively arm movement with each 'boom, boom', presumably illustrating blasting through the walls.

'We also need a bathroom and a kitchen,' I say.

All up he thinks that fixing the house to make it liveable would cost around the ballpark of 50,000 euros. *Boom, boom.*

'You have to draw up plans, submit them to council and, if they approve, I can give you a more detailed quote.'

Paco thinks it's about a two- to three-month project. It's a rough quote but it gives us an idea about the costs involved. We can do a bit of the work ourselves to save money.

The river cottage is now a contender, competing with Uncle Domingo's house that Alex has lost his heart to. Meanwhile, it's obvious we're out of our depth and we'll be easy to cheat. We need to find out as much as we can before we make decisions. How much does a new roof cost? Is Paco a good builder? Do we really want to spend this much money when we could just rent a house? Are we being swept away by the thrill of it all? It sounds like hard work – are we up for that? This is more of a commitment than we had in mind when we decided to live in Spain. Saving a ruin, WTF are we thinking? *Qué haces*, indeed.

~

A week later we're meeting Ricardo, the other builder who works in Ventosa. Josh has organised to meet him at Uncle Domingo's and I have organised to collect the keys from Gabina, the good witch of the village. We have a longer chat with Gabina this time. She's getting friendlier with every visit. I wonder if she would look forward to potentially having more permanent residents in her village. Not being the only and last full-time inhabitant anymore.

We show Josh the house while we wait for Ricardo and talk about what we think we could do with it. The views from the house are stunning. The sky is blue and the sunshine bathes the ruin in a lovely golden light. The German shepherd who has been barking at us on earlier visits is on the loose today and comes over to sniff us out. Evidently we pass her inspection as she wags her tail and lets me pat her.

Ricardo is early, arriving in a *furgoneta* (van) with Ricardo's Construcciones painted on the side. This is the builder recommended by Lucia, Uncle Domingo's niece. Ricardo is a fit-looking man of about sixty, with a face that's seen plenty of sun. He inspires more confidence than Ángel did, but not much. He too thinks the whole roof needs to be replaced.

'It has woodborer and can't be saved,' he states confidently. 'I treat all new wood, so it won't happen again.'

He takes measurements and asks a lot of questions. He listens to the answers and scribbles away. He will give us a quote next week, he says.

After the builder leaves, Alex asks Josh, 'What do you reckon Josh, are we completely bonkers?'

Josh looks at us both in turn, obviously conflicted. He's a nice bloke and doesn't want to hurt our feelings.

Finally, he utters, 'Maybe just a bit.'

~

We continue to wait to hear from everybody who promised to get back to us about Uncle Domingo's house. Alex wants to have another look at the river cottage to see how he feels about it after some reflection. I love that he's getting warmer on the river cottage as it is in an appealing village with real people living in it. Driving into town, we get to the main plaza first, lined with three-storey stone buildings. Most need a lick of paint on the doors and windows but have that delightful patina of Provence or Tuscany. This village has very few ruins. Families have held on to the old homes and kept them in moderate repair, with an enchanting shabby-chic look. The Santa Lucia Church draws our eyes to the end of the square where it looms over the town. It's a handsome Gothic building from the sixteenth century. The storks are sitting on the bell-tower nest. From there the cobblestoned alleyway leads down to the street by the river, where the cottage has been standing for more than 250 years. I am expecting to see a film crew around the corner any moment now. This is the perfect location for a movie set.

We brought a ploughman's lunch of bread, cheese, jamón, boiled eggs and fruit to eat in the overgrown garden of the cottage. There's no one here to object to our presence. It will give us a bit of time to hear, smell and soak up the atmosphere. As soon as we step into the garden, a pitiful little kitten wanders out from under some rocks. The skinny thing starts to follow me around through knee-high weeds as I wander through the garden, meowing pathetically from its tiny lungs. Its eyes are open, but it looks no more than two to three weeks old. It would still be entirely dependent on mum's milk. But where's mum? While eating lunch I fret about the teeny kitten. The old zookeeper in me wants to look after it, make it comfortable and happy. It makes me realise how much I miss the animals in the zoo that were such a big part of my life. Before I can have any pets we need to settle somewhere – another reason to make a home. The little kitten has found me again on the other side of the garden. Last thing we need right now is a kitten. Miniature kitty wedges itself under some rocks and stops calling for a while. We check out the garden thoroughly, looking at this and that. Alex gets quite animated.

'Look at this. There's a pile of slate in that corner. We could use that to pave a barbeque area.'

'But look,' I say, finding the sewerage outlet and pointing to the electricity connection. 'Even better!'

We stand in awe admiring these mod cons as we might a lavish entertainment area or a spectacular ocean view during an Australian real estate inspection.

'I never realised how much I've taken utilities for granted until now!' Alex murmurs as he admires the electricity connection in the street.

Despite the distraction of the kitten, we soak up the atmosphere in the garden, hear the river gurgling below and the birds chirping in the tall poplar trees along the riverbank. A pigeon takes flight and the smell of lavender wafts around from leggy bushes in the ruin. We sit on a stone bench outside the front door warming our faces in the sun, as we fancy the inhabitants of this house have done for more than two centuries. The house faces south, which means it has lovely winter sun (quite the opposite to Australia). I imagine the terrace we could build and the future breakfasts we could have out here.

As we get up to leave, the kitten comes out again, meowing like it did before, with some renewed vigour after a little sleep. I start to despair, thinking I will not be able to leave it here to its own devices. It's obviously been abandoned and will die unless we take it with us. Luckily, just as I bend over to pick it up, I see an adult cat slip under the gate into the walled garden. Mum's back. I gently slip kitty in the same rock crevice I saw Mum disappear into. She makes no audible objection. All must be well; the bub has been accepted by its mother.

After this little feline drama, we go for a drive to see more of the immediate surrounds of the village. The landscape around San Juan is more modified than around Ventosa, less wild but very appealing, nevertheless. Cows with bells, like in the Swiss Alps, are roaming around on gentle green hills dotted with ancient oak trees. There's an understated beauty to this country.

To be on the safe side, before we leave to go back to Almazán, we do a drive-by of the house, but to our relief we find no kittens on the loose in the garden.

~

We liked what we saw when we had that picnic lunch in the garden of the river cottage and have organised to take another look inside. Council Jesus, who has the keys, forgot we were coming but the girl in the Ayuntamiento chases him down. He comes to find us in the bar next to the Ayuntamiento, where we're sipping coffee, to give us the key. He sends us off on our own this time to have a look for as long as we like.

'If the Ayuntamiento is closed, drop the key at the bar,' he suggests.

As we are about to leave the bar, an elderly gentleman shuffles after us as fast as he can.

'I heard in the bar that you are looking to buy a house,' he says. 'I have a house for sale too, right next to the one you are looking at. Would you like to see it?'

'Sure,' we say.

This could be interesting. Julian, as he's called, captures us to see his house first, a large stone building, also next to the river. It turns out to be an interesting shambolic rabbit warren of a place. A labyrinth of rooms connected to each other with complex corridors and narrow, flimsy staircases. Bedrooms lead to other bedrooms. To make something of this house you'd need a fair bit of money. Rubbish removal alone would take quite an effort as all the rooms are chock full of generations of precious objects and plain old rubbish. Every room is packed to the rafters. To get from one place to the next, we climb over disintegrating cardboard boxes, piles of clothes, boots, cooking paraphernalia and loads of unidentified stuff. Perhaps hoarding was a common feature in this village. Over the last couple of centuries, the various inhabitants have added rooms in a rather haphazard way. It's difficult to make sense of any layout in the house. We ask Julian how much he wants for it.

'It belongs to my cousin, who is in the nursing home,' Julian tells us. 'I look after it for him and grow some vegetables in the garden.'

After he thinks about a price for a while, he says, 'My cousin will want 75,000 euros.' We tell him the one next door is 25,000 euros.

'Well, 55,000 euros then,' he counters.

That's a fairly large reduction in a truly short time. The price, in all probability, includes the dead cat we see inside. Not the mother of the kitten we saw next door though. This one is a large ginger male curled up on some cardboard boxes by a window. At first it looks asleep but tufts of fur float up it as we make our way past it and I realise it is truly mummified, not even smelling anymore.

We promise Julian we'll think about his house too and, satisfied with that answer, he goes back to the bar to report to his mates.

~

Alex and I get the chance to look around the river cottage by ourselves. Alex starts to point out what we could do with this room or that. He's in awe of the nearly one-metre-thick walls, the wide floorboards and the piles and piles of interesting things left behind in the house. We open some of the shuttered windows and the French doors to the balcony. The natural light helps us to soak up the ambience and get a feel for the people who lived here. Although layers of dust cover every surface, there's evidence of lives lived. It is obvious that no one has been here for a very long time though. Letters, calendars with reminders scribbled on them, an invitation to a baptism eleven years ago is propped up on the sideboard. A black-and-white photo of a swarthy-looking young man is on the bedside table next to a Bible.

Council Jesus told us before that the elderly woman who last lived here was called Soledad. It very much looks like Soledad was deeply religious. There are prayer cards lying around, statues of Jesus, pictures of Mary on the wall, rosary beads, a holy cross above the bed and postcards of churches and cathedrals. The house is full of religious memorabilia, but very few other decorations are on display under the dust and cobwebs. The decor is a combination of fine antiques and cheap furniture from the 1960s and 1970s. Some of the finer pieces look to be of a similar age to the house itself, more than two hundred years old. Alex strokes a sideboard.

'I think this may be cherry wood. I wonder if we could buy the furniture with the house.'

I smile and nod at him, pleased that the river cottage is growing on him too.

The three bedrooms are reached via a timber staircase, giant tree trunks fashioned into steps, each shaped further by generations of feet. The middle of each step is smoothly concave where the timber is gently worn. The staircase likely dates from 1766, when the house was built. From there, another staircase leads to the third-floor attic where the family treasures are stored. We count seven enormous trunks with keepsakes. Some contain documents written on parchment. Everywhere we look, we see records of the history of this one family in this village in northern Spain. We're both pointing at things, admiring the vast ceiling beams, imagining how the cottage could look with a bit of love and care.

A little later Alex calls from another bedroom, 'Did you see the pink marble-topped washstand? I hope that comes with the house too.'

This is a good development. Alex is starting to like the river house too. I'm intrigued with this place and relieved he is showing some interest. I still feel that I don't want to stand in his way if he continues pursuing Uncle Domingo's house, but I'll be glad if he gives up the idea altogether.

~

Once home, we make lists of the pros and cons of each house again. Renovating the river cottage may be more pragmatic than Uncle Domingo's. Happily, Alex likes the river cottage more and more after seeing inside again. Seeing the cottage today on a lovely mellow day, blue skies and a babbling river makes it an appealing but still adventurous purchase. Alex starts planning some renovations. We calculate what fixing each house might cost, hoping that some or any of this will make sense and help us decide what's next. As we're doing the sums for both places, we consider the unknowns of Ventosa and increasingly it looks like the idea of buying Uncle Domingo's house is dying a slow death. Alex may not have a Roman garrison to look out on with snow-capped mountains beyond but the river cottage has water, electricity and importantly, connected sewerage.

~

Later that evening, sitting in the garden in Almazán, the Northern Hemisphere stars are winking in a clear sky. We're chatting about the ups and downs of buying a ruin in the 'empty Spain'. We're about to drop a good proportion of our savings and more if we are to buy one and make it livable. We're likely to have to sell our house in Sydney to make this happen. That's a big step, not so easy to back out once we do that. We have to give up a lot to follow this dream, this folly, yet it makes us both happy and excited to be alive.

'Both places have been for sale for years. No one else has been stupid enough to buy them, so why should we?' I say, throwing in a bit of negativity to see what reaction I get.

'It's hard to look at any of this rationally. It doesn't make a lot of sense to buy a ruin in a depopulating region. We could have a few nice holidays for that money,' says Alex, pretending to be sensible too.

'You're right, it's probably not a smart financial investment.' Then I add more softly, 'But it's not about that is it? We're not doing this because we want a good return on our investment.' Although I'm not sure what it is that I'm looking for.

'There's nothing wrong with doing something just because it feels right,' Alex says pointedly.

'Bloody hell. This is like a tree-change on steroids,' I mutter. 'If we wanted a renovation challenge we could do this back home, move to the Hunter Valley, Tasmania or the Barossa but, no, you've got to pick a ruin in bloody Castile!' Conveniently, I ignore the fact that I too have fallen in love with a ruin. Conveniently, too, I ignore the fact that I wanted to go back to live in my beloved Spain.

Alex wisely pays no attention to my jibe. 'I wish I could make up my mind about which house to make an offer on, though,' Alex says wistfully. 'I keep thinking about Uncle Domingo's. I love where it is. I just can't get it out of my head. It *feels* right. It's nothing to do with how I think, it just feels like we should buy it. I just need a few more days before I can decide one way or the other.'

To make up for my earlier outburst I use my most compassionate, loving and wise voice to say, 'Doesn't matter, honey. It'll all work out in the long run.'

Alex, gazing back up at the sky, says suddenly, 'Look. A shooting star!' We clink glasses and take another sip of some excellent Rioja wine. Surely it's a sign?

Chapter 17

Distractions

Neither house is going to sell in a hurry as they've been for sale for years. We have time to let things percolate in our heads for a while. Maybe we'll come to our senses. It feels like we're on a holiday as we travel to nearby Pamplona. After arriving in the old centre, dawdling along, Alex and I inevitably talk about the running of the bulls and how this feat of machismo has captured the imagination of many young Australians, Americans and northern Europeans, in particular. The Fiesta of San Fermin is what the running of the bulls is all about. The tourist brochure tells us it goes for nine days with bulls running every day. The distance of the run is only 849 metres, but that is an extreme adrenaline-fuelled 849 metres. The narrow streets of the centre show evidence of this yearly event. Some entrances to houses have what outback Australian cars have, a bull bar. Here they are solid metal gates that look like they could literally stop a bull. Once you've had a bull through the front door, I assume you want to avoid a repeat.

Every town and village has a patron saint and San Fermin is Pamplona's. We read up on San Fermin and find out he's said to have lived in the third century, although his legend may be from the ninth century. Somehow he was forgotten for some six hundred years. He's certainly been making up for that lost time. San Fermin was both a legendary holy man and a martyr, a popular combination in these parts. Legend has it that he was martyred by having his feet tied to a bull and dragged around until he died. Before that death it is claimed he performed the required number of miracles for sainthood. Apparently, after his demise, a sweet odour arose from his grave, the smell causing ice and snow to melt, flowers to grow, the sick to get better and the surrounding trees to incline reverentially toward the saint's resting place. How San Fermin is now honoured by testosterone- and alcohol-fuelled youths running in front of very frightened animals, I'm not sure. Funny how these things happen.

Physically being in a city makes its history and culture come to life. At home I would never read up on the running of the bulls in Pamplona, but now I'm here, it's fascinating. Bull-running is supposed to have started in the fourteenth century in north-eastern Spain. While transporting cattle to the markets, young men would try to hurry up the bulls using tactics of fear and excitement. After some time, this developed into a competition as the men would try to run in front of the bulls and make it to the pens safely without being overtaken by the heavy beasts. The running of the bulls happens in a few towns and cities, but the Pamplona *encierro*, as it's called, is the most famous. Contemporary culture popularised bull-running, particularly Ernest Hemmingway's 1926 novel, *The Sun Also Rises*, which signposted the road to Pamplona. The story portrays American and British expats travelling from Paris to Pamplona to see the Festival of San Fermin, the running of the bulls and the bullfights. Nationally, too, the Pamplona bull-run is well liked and has been shown on live television for over thirty years.

There are rules of course: participants must be eighteen years old and over, run the same way the bulls are running (!) and not be drunk. I'm not sure how the latter is judged. Although there is no formal dress code, the traditional attire most commonly worn is white pants, white shirt with a red scarf around the waist and another red scarf around the neck. Blood, should there be any, shows up nicely on the white. Despite the rules, there are casualties every year. Some fifty to one hundred bull-runners are injured annually and fifteen have died since record-keeping began in 1910. Most of these fatalities were due to being gored by a bull. As the runners and the bulls are funnelled into the bullring there's another risk, that of falling and being trodden on by other runners and big heavy bovines. Most of the runners are male, but in 1974 the prohibition against female runners was lifted and women have run since then. Five women have been gored by bulls during the Pamplona *encierro*. If your idea of amusement is navigating your way through a crowded narrow alley with a stampede of raging bulls, then this event is not to be missed. Alternatively, you can rent a balcony above and watch from a safer distance.

~

Bullfighting and other opportunities for young men to show their toughness continue to be popular in Spain. A few mornings ago, as we walked past the bullring in Almazán, I was shocked to see it was built as recently as 1980, a time when bullfighting was being criticised nationally and internationally as a cruel practice. The aficionados and supporters of bullfighting see it as an essential component of Spanish culture and tradition, the substance on which the nation's patrimony is founded. The love of bullfighting even enters politics. Some hardline right-leaning politicians have added 'support our traditions, hunting and bullfighting' as a condition for forming a more centre-right coalition. Meanwhile, Spaniards on the left side of politics are working with animal welfare advocates to end the tradition. Catalonia banned bullfighting in 2013, the second region to do so after the Canary Islands. No doubt this brutal practice will end at some point in the future as more and more citizens commit to improved animal welfare. I suspect bullfighting will not go down without a fight though. And neither will public displays of Spanish machismo.

~

Strolling through the park in Pamplona, there's a lot to take in. It's a Saturday and obviously a popular day for first holy communions. Many girls between seven and twelve years old are milling about in their white dresses, some with veils. What's with little girls looking like virgin brides? I can't quite put my finger on the emotional reaction I have to seeing these innocent young things portrayed as women to be married off. It makes me feel uneasy, this focus on the virginal, pretty and innocent, committing to a religion that will determine what's right and what's wrong on their behalf. I shake off those feelings as best I can and try to take in what I see without further judgement or reading too much into it.

Literally dozens of different groups are in the park opposite the big cathedral taking photos of family groups around cute little girls in white dresses. I can't see any boys dressed up for communion. Perhaps they do communion on another day. Everyone is dressed to kill. This seems to be where fashion designers make their money, perfect families of beautifully dressed people. Nothing 'off the rack' here, and it seems no money is spared for these celebrations. Younger generations don't go to church that often anymore, and even fewer attend mass weekly like they used to in the old days. But the communion is still a rite of passage for Spanish boys and girls. All fiestas and rituals, such as weddings and funerals, continue to be steeped in Catholic tradition. As soon as there's a fiesta, a celebration or a tradition, a priest will be involved in some way. In stark contrast, I notice a couple of Goths taking pictures of each other in front of the arches of the fort. They're dressed all in black, their hair, clothes, fingernails and lipstick. I'm struck again by the juxtaposition of the old and new Spain.

~

We buy some lottery tickets in a Pamplona bar while we're there. Lottery tickets are sold in bars, on the streets and in shops in Spain. The selling of government lottery tickets is reserved for persons with disability. I have vivid memories of the blind lottery seller in Alicante nearly twisting his head right off ogling my friend Mimi wearing hot pants in the 1970s. Obviously, vision impaired or not, he liked what he saw.

Spain is obsessed with lotteries and in particular El Gordo. The official title is the Spanish Christmas Lottery, but its nickname is El Gordo, the fat one. It has been running since 1812, making it a strong Christmas tradition. The winning numbers are broadcast live on radio and TV, often sung by young, high voices that ring out from TVs through open doors and windows across neighbourhoods all day long on 22 December each year. This job was formerly reserved for orphans of public servants but now the pupils of the San Ildefonso School draw the numbers and corresponding prizes, delivering the results in song. Our lottery tickets are the common weekly variety, not El Gordo. We fantasise about winning the one-million-euro prize. Only a few months ago we'd have spent it on more travel. Now all we can think of is that it would buy a new roof for either of our two desirable ruins.

~

We leave Pamplona to stay in a rural hotel. Once we settle in the late afternoon with a glass of wine, we ring Ángel. He promised to find out about sewerage and septic tanks as well as give us a quote for a complete restoration of Uncle Domingo's house. Ángel ignored our calls last week but picks up this time. His advice is interesting and somewhat controversial.

'It's stupid to buy this house in Ventosa,' he says. Bang, no beating around the bush. 'There are better places to buy. I happen to have a block of land you can buy and I can build you a house on it. It will be closer to your nephew. Surely you want to be close to family in preference to anywhere else?'

I can't get a word in. He's been saving up this little rant for us it seems. He's even trying a bit of emotional blackmail by mentioning closeness to family. To drive the knife of disillusionment in a bit further, Ángel also mentions that getting electricity connected will mean several new electricity poles in the street that will cost 6000 euro each.

'It's not sensible nor possible' is his final verdict, delivered with great passion.

He's not made a single enquiry about sewerage or septic tanks and we're about as far from any answer on that as we were a couple of weeks ago. 'His village is better than Ventosa' is all he has to say and he happens to have a block of land he can sell to us. We look at each other, wondering what to do next.

'I'm not sure what to believe,' says Alex deflated by this latest 'advice' from Ángel. 'I'm not sure he's right on anything. We have to investigate these electricity pole estimates ourselves.'

At almost the same time we get a text from Xavier, the owner of the river cottage, asking if we have been to see it with a builder.

I text back: 'Yes, we're still looking into a few costs. Will know more next week.'

We're silent for a minute or two, taking in where we are. A

terrace bar in a Basque village. Someone is walking the milking cows home through the narrow streets.

Alex cheers up and comments, 'It's all surreal. None of this feels like it's actually happening. It's almost a sideshow to a great holiday!'

We spend dinner that evening trying to compare the pros and cons of each ruin against the other but find it impossible. One has impressive views of mountains, ancient Roman sites and the last remaining resident, the cuter-than-cute Gabina. Whereas the other is a 250-year-old charmer next to a river in a village with two bars. We need to have at least the key facts straight on both houses to understand what's feasible and the costs involved. Even for us romantic fools this seems essential.

Chapter 18

Pillar to Post

We don't trust Ángel's advice, and as soon as we're back home we start to look into things ourselves. We understand that the road to be dug up for the sewerage line belongs to the regional government, the Diputación. They have an office in an old palace in the centre of Soria.

We climb the stairs to the second floor, follow long corridors until we come to a sign that reads Carreteras y Obras (Roads and Works). A woman in her mid-thirties comes to the counter to ask how she can help.

'We want to buy a house in Ventosa, but it has no wastewater outlet. We want to know if the sewerage line can be extended if it means digging up the road.'

Rebeca, as she's called, thinks it's a *barbaridad* (barbarity) that we should have to pay for this.

'It is your right to have this service,' she says. 'Council elections are coming up. Put pressure on the politicians,' she advises. 'They should pay to promote house renovation in the village. They must think you are rich!' she informs us.

She shows a copy of the Cadastre map, and we work out where Uncle Domingo's house is. Rebeca promises to speak with the engineer in charge of these things.

'I will speak to him and email you what it will cost to connect to the sewerage system.' Rebeca is very sympathetic to our troubles. She also wants to know a few more things. 'Why are you here, why in Soria? Why here in this part of Spain all the way from Australia?'

This is still a good question. We're still not sure exactly why. We mumble something about 'authentic Spain, unspoiled nature and all that'. We should be good at answering this by now as we're asked the same thing everywhere we go. The subject is closely related to our search for a good life and my late-life crisis. Meanwhile, the answer remains somewhat elusive. Rebeca is very friendly and she seems genuinely concerned about us and the lack of response we've had from the authorities. Unfortunately, we never hear from Rebeca again.

~

I wish Alex were a bit more interested in the river cottage. It already has sewerage, water and an electricity connection and it would make our life so much easier. However, I'm just grateful we're here, living in Spain. The least I can do is to let him follow his dream about a house with a view of a Roman garrison.

I ring builder Ricardo to ask when he could give us the building quote for Uncle Domingo's house.

'Waiting for prices on the wood for the roof,' he says. 'Should have that next Saturday.'

~

Trying to work out how to get a handle on the cost of getting electricity to an abandoned house is our next step. Ángel said we needed several poles to bring electricity to the house and every pole is 6000 euros. The house and land are only 18,000 euros so that's a big extra investment in the scheme of things. There are different electricity providers in different states. Who do we need to ask? Soria province is not listed on the scroll-down options of a website I've found. Finally, we work out there is a customer-service office for an electricity provider right here in Almazán. They must be the suppliers then. They're in the new part of town, in walking distance.

The woman at the counter is into customer service big time and shows us how to apply online for advice on the cost of connection. She can deal with us once we're ready to be connected but is willing to help in the meantime. The request for information online is free of charge and it will give us the costs and a photo of the spot where they will put the meter on the house. That usually means a big hole in a lovely age-old stone wall.

On the return journey we pass a *fontanería* – a place that sells everything to do with plumbing. Maybe they know about septic tanks and what the regulations are? A young, bearded man called Carlos is helpful. He tells us it is better to connect to sewerage if we can, because of the high yearly cost of pumping out septic tanks. Although he sells septic tanks, he doesn't know how close to a well you can have one. Carlos tells us that most people put in a septic tank illegally, such as for farmland shacks that are not meant to be lived in permanently. He takes our email address and will let us know what he can find out. Already he has been more helpful than the Alcalde del Barrio, the voluntary mayor. By late afternoon he's emailed us with information on costs and recommends a big septic tank, so we don't have the expense of emptying it every year. There's no news on the distance it needs to be from a well though. He also gives us the news that we can't put in a septic tank if we are able to have a sewerage connection. How hard can it be to get accurate advice about these issues? Ridiculously hard it seems!

Once home, I scrutinise the forms from the electricity providers. They look complex. I hope my Spanish stretches this far. I have used up most of my Spanish words for one day. I'll leave it for tomorrow.

~

The next day is extremely windy. Big dust storms carry away the ploughed fields. It makes me sad to see fertile soil blowing away. Alex is keen to check on Ventosa to see how it's going in the wind, particularly as its name means windy one. Is Uncle Domingo's *casa* engulfed in a heavy dust cloud? Alex is partially hoping it is so he can put to rest his infatuation with this house. He keeps saying he's trying to *get over it*, as if his obsession with Uncle Domingo's house needs an antidote. I too am willing to go and check on 'the windy one' but, as it's lunch time, I'm starving by now.

Bar Veronica, where mother and son run the show, is on the way to Ventosa. From the outside we see mother through the window, wearing the same cardigan with the sticky tape on the holes at the elbows. A different son is behind the bar this time. He has long, dark hair on a balding head and his glasses are filled with thick lenses making his eyes unrealistically big. He struggles to understand me as I ask in good Spanish, '*Qué podrías hacernos de comer?*' (What could you make us for lunch?) He seems to be stunned that we have the power of speech, being foreign and all that. Mum hovers nearby and smiles at me. She seems pleased by the fact that the foreigners have come for a feed at her bar for a second time.

'I can do fried eggs with ham or with chorizo,' she tells us as she pushes her stunned son out of the way.

Terrific. After consulting with Alex, we go for the chorizo. The other patrons in the bar are fascinated by us. We take a table at the window with a view of the street. Our table is right under the television, which is blaring from a corner of the room. They can have a good look at us while pretending to watch TV. Every time I glance over, their eyes are rigidly fixed on us. From the moment we walked in we've been stared at, analysed and talked about by the drinkers at the bar. So much for thinking that we could blend in, being just like the locals. They, too, seemed quite stunned that strangers who do not live in the village could simply come in and ask for food. The food comes steaming on a plate swimming in olive oil. We gobble it up in no time, mopping the plate with fresh bread. We're getting used to a glass of wine at lunch time. How long does it take to become an alcoholic? Not long I assume.

Most people don't quite believe we can understand what they say, so they talk openly about what we may be up to here in this non-tourist part of the peninsula.

'What would they be doing here?' asks the fat man with the big moustache to his companions at the bar.

'*Guiris* (grey nomads) like the beaches. They do know there's no beach here?' They all have a little laugh.

'They're lost,' suggests the skinny bloke in high-vis.

As we leave, we say a friendly *adios* and Alex adds, '*Vamos a la playa.*' (We're off to the beach now!)

~

There's no dust storm in Ventosa and Alex isn't cured of his affection for Uncle Domingo's house. At home I try filling out the online form for the electricity connection. A lot of the questions I can handle but when they get to things like 'potency requested' and 'level of tension', I get lost. Really? Would they ask the customer what level of tension is needed on the wire? Every time I fudge some numbers it tells me they are wrong. Continuing to the next page is not possible without full marks for the previous page. It's like a bloody online exam. The simplest option is to go back into town to ask for more help from the nice woman in customer service. When we get there she's on the phone but helpful lady number two is also willing and able. She scribbles some numbers on a form and tells us to scan it and send it electronically with a map showing the house's location and a photo of the front of the property. Within minutes we have the whole lot photographed and sent off. We'll see. Maybe I am of little faith and I should have more trust in email communications. (It turns out my suspicions are correct. We never hear from the electricity company.)

I am starting to seriously question the merits of pursuing Uncle Domingo's house when we also have the option of the river cottage. It has water, sewerage and an electricity connection. With Uncle Domingo's house we're spending a lot of time chasing our tails, being sent from pillar to post. I suppose we could always call the house 'Pillar to Post' if it's the one we buy in the end. I'm trying to be patient because Alex should be able to pursue his favourite ruin. After all, he's willing to live here to indulge my love of Spain and my existential crisis. We should be buying the ruin he'd be most happy with. I tell myself I should only see the river cottage as Plan B if Uncle Domingo's falls through. Meanwhile, I am worried we may be on a wild goose chase. There seems to be a lot of delays, waiting for officials, bureaucrats and tradesmen who have promised to investigate things, only to be sent to someone else who says the first person should have given you that information. It feels like we've been going around in circles for weeks, making enquiries here, there and everywhere. Yet, we're still no closer to knowing if we can have basic utilities in Uncle Domingo's place. I'm wondering how long Alex is willing to play this game.

Chapter 19

Deadlines and a Fair

Meanwhile life goes on in Almazán. The fair is in town. We're locked out of the Arboleda park, our preferred morning walk. They're setting up for events happening the coming weekend. The street next to the bridge is full of wagons and trucks for the *feria*. Looks like we are getting all sorts of rides, as well as an agricultural fair to follow. The closure of our usual walking track leads to the discovery of another track along the Rio Duero on the other side of the bridge. We pass some old houses and pig sheds. The sight of the pig sheds continues to worry me. I looked up the government figures for the average annual consumption of pork. It sits at just over 20 kilos per Spaniard. The number of pigs slaughtered in Spain each year outnumbers the entire Spanish population. Improvements in animal welfare are happening but change is slow. Meanwhile, the terrain is dotted with the long, low buildings that house pigs. Presumably, life in these sheds could be improved significantly. The more pig sheds I see, the more I question why I still eat pork. But am I strong enough to give up the *torreznos*?

It's cold again this morning, barely eight degrees by nine o'clock but with clear blue skies and sunshine. If you can find a spot out of the wind it's quite pleasant. We go to Bar Tirso de Molino on the Palace Square. It's been closed for repairs for a week or more.

The woman who runs the bar greets us with the question: '*Dos cortados?*'

'*Sí, por favor!*'

~

For a small town there's a lot going on in Almazán all the time. I'm still getting over the Easter processions with Jesus and Mary going about the streets on a regular basis, the incessant drumming, music and food. And now we find ourselves in the middle of yet another fiesta. After Easter we missed something that looked like a farm animal sale in the Arboleda. We saw the pens being erected, went away to Burgos for a few days and when we got back they were raking up the soiled hay and dismantling everything. It's impossible to see all the fiestas and events, even in one town. The big agricultural fair is the next thing happening. Posters are being put up, tents and marquees erected and supply vans filling the park. There are more tractors, harvesters, irrigators, ploughs, diggers and graders than I've ever seen in one place. They're all shiny new and mostly red. Is this the colour most loved by farming folk?

On the other side of the bridge the rides for kids are being set up. They are still packed in tarpaulins, so the full effects won't be seen until tomorrow. One van is open, the Churrería. Churros are a sort of long fried donut rolled in crunchy sugar. They're Spain's traditional hangover food. After a night on the town, one goes out for a thick hot chocolate with sweet comforting churros. When I say hot chocolate, this is more like melted chocolate than a drinking chocolate. The churros are used to scoop it up. The Churrería is open and has churros but no chocolate dip until tomorrow. We buy a dozen to share anyway, sitting in the pale morning sun on the edge of the stone bridge. Life is good.

~

Alex is getting impatient with the lack of progress on the house buying. We agree to set a deadline and decide at the end of the week. I ring Mari-Paz, the actual owner of Uncle Domingo's house, to give her a deadline. I'm still a bit daunted having to do this on the phone in Spanish. On the phone, gestures and facial expressions don't work, so I need to be more precise with my diction. The way the Spanish answer the telephone is very off-putting for a start. The normal answer is *Diga* (Say) or *Dime* (Tell me) or even a short punchy *Sí?* This command 'Say' puts me on edge straightaway. It sounds like the person on the other end is too busy to put up with my crap in their already hectic day. Until now I have not spoken with Mari-Paz, only with her two sisters, Lola and Lucia, but they do not own the house.

Mari-Paz answers the phone: '*Diga*.'

'*Hola*, I am the foreigner who is interested in your Uncle Domingo's house.'

I tell her our story of the many roadblocks we've experienced. I'm on a roll with the lingo but still nervous, hoping she can understand me.

'Your Spanish is good, I can understand everything you say.'

Emboldened I continue. 'As we are not the owners, authorities don't give us much help. Everybody tells us that getting water, sewerage and electricity is possible, but no one can tell us how much it's going to cost. We can't buy the house without knowing that.'

Then Mari-Paz mentions a new piece of information that may change things considerably.

'Do you know the building is registered as a barn, not a house? That might be an additional issue.'

'Can a barn be connected to the essential services? We're keen to make an offer but can you, as the owner, get the information we need?'

'I need to consult various government departments. That could take a bit of time.'

'The rental of the house we're living in runs out in a couple of months so we will need to make a decision soon.'

Mari-Paz is silent for a moment and then replies: 'I'll try to get back to you in a week, but it may take longer to find things out properly.'

At least we have a deadline, of sorts. But the news about the property being registered as a barn could be a major stumbling block. I break the news to Alex gently. He's a bit shocked that his love interest turns out to have a hidden secret.

~

Today our postal vote forms for the Australian elections arrive. Alex is thrilled. He assumed that any mail from the other side of the planet would be subject to the mysteries of planetary alignment at least. The paper is long and cascades down the table. We are firm in our favourites and take great delight in studying who's who so we can put some parties in the very last place, the pleasures of utilising our democratic voice. We need a witness to our vote and they must be Australian and enrolled to vote. It does not say anywhere that this person can't be your wife or husband, so we use each other as a witness. To be sure our vote will arrive in time, we go to post it straightaway. The line-up in the post office is long and after a *Buenos días* Alex asks, '*Quién es el último.*' It seems the right thing to do here, too, just like at the markets. I hear later arrivals do the same. We follow a man in a red jacket who said he was the last one before we arrived. The postal employee sees the Australian Government logo on the envelope and notices the word 'election'.

'Ah, you have elections now too!' he says importantly.

Spain had its elections a couple of weeks ago, European, state, regional and provincial all at once.

'In the end,' he adds, 'we will still elect a politician.' We share a joke about politicians being the same everywhere.

~

After the postal voting, the late afternoon seems like a perfect time for a visit to the agricultural fair. The whole town must be here, it's throbbing with activity. I'm drawn by invisible forces to the cheese, *embutidos* (cured meats) and ham hall. Producers from all around Spain are selling and promoting their wares. Cheese, salami and the likes are sliced up for tasting before selecting. We marvel at the varieties of cheeses. We could have bought so much but restrain ourselves to a kilo of sheep cheese from la Extremadura, a province bordering Portugal. The cheese is advertised as being from 'spring milk' and cured for one year. I haven't heard the expression 'spring milk' before but the cheese is extremely smooth and spicy at the same time. Perhaps this is the first milk after the ewes go out to grass again after having been locked in the barn all winter. Whatever it is, it's a winner of a cheese.

A couple of nuns ahead of us get the royal treatment at every stall. Not for them the miserly free offerings. They get generous slices to eat. It's obvious that respect for the holy orders in Spain is still compelling. People may not go to church in the numbers they once did, but their reverence for men and women of the cloth appears undiminished. The nuns make their selections at various stalls and leave with quite a booty of cheese and sausages to share with their convent sisters, one presumes. The nuns buy some chorizo at a stall from Navarra. We follow their lead because we like the look of the stallholder, who is dressed in traditional attire.

I'm not sure how practical this would have been as work clobber as he's wearing an embroidered bolero jacket with glossy blue knickerbocker trousers. This must be his fancy outfit for fiestas and dances. He looks very dapper though as he wraps up our chorizo.

Some dried fruits from Andalucía are our next purchase. A very shaky old man carefully wraps his hand in the plastic bag to use as a scoop. We take a quarter kilo of figs. He's overestimated the amount needed and grabs the surplus with his bare fingers to throw them back. Not a mistake either, he employs the same technique with the dates next. You're given the illusion of hygienic handling with the plastic bag but, for those that come after you, it's tough luck.

Bars have been set up throughout the fair to quench thirst and catch up with family and friends. After viewing the massive machinery, the stalls with produce from every region, leatherware, knick-knacks and handcrafted jewellery, we are ready for a drink. As we settle on the ubiquitous white plastic chairs (are they in every country now?) we notice a crowd has gathered nearby. A mammoth pig is being roasted by a team of men in black T-shirts. The man in charge is all shiny with pig fat or sweat, maybe both. The pig looks like a gigantic boar and has been split and opened like I've seen done with a chicken. We've never seen a pig as big as this being roasted. The roasting is nearly complete, and the team is having their photo taken by the press and their families. Family albums will be full of blokes with proud smiles celebrating their pig-roasting prowess. After numerous selfies they seem ready to serve. This looks like the council's promotion of homegrown Sorian products. The black T-shirts have white writing that proclaims 'Soria's produce is grand!' The need for the army of black T-shirts becomes clear as the roasted pork is distributed to the waiting masses. Slices of roast pork are handed out on fresh bread to catch the dripping.

It strikes me again, as the whole town is gathered here to celebrate, that there's a strong genetic resemblance among the people of this region. The Sorians appear to have had few new genes added to the gene pool from marauding armies since they dispatched the Moors in the 1200s. Their unifying feature appears to be short, stocky bodies that can toil in the fields and bring home the bacon. The local obsession with pork is catching. I'm tucking into some delicious roasted boar when I realise that my tastebuds have, once again, got the better of my principles.

Chapter 20

A Fiesta for a Dancing Saint

Today we're riding our pushbikes further into pig-farming territory. It's windy but the smell of hogs is overlaid with lavender, which is in full bloom and strong in the air. The mauve and purple hues in the fields and by the roadside make me weak at the knees. I'd almost forgotten the smell of these wild blooms from my youth. Years of suppressed homesickness bubbles up as the fragrance tickles my nostrils. Memories buried under a mountain of silence come to the surface. It's hard to describe the emotion I feel, somewhere between happiness and the sweet pain of nostalgia. Mostly, though, I feel gratitude to be here again.

There are lots of storks in the fields, frantically trying to find enough food to feed their growing babies. Now, in late spring, the young birds are getting ready to take flight. They are almost as big as the adults, but their beaks are black, not the bright red of their parents. They stand on the edge of the nest flapping away like mad, exercising and building up their flight muscles. They are preening frenetically too, getting their brand-new flight feathers ready for take-off. Hopefully, the wind will not lift them out of the nest before they are ready to fly.

~

It's a quiet Sunday morning and there aren't many people about, even at 10am. The square is being hosed with a powerful fire hose. A beer-bellied man, somewhat unbalanced by his unfortunate weight distribution, is pointing the hose, directing the spray, while the woman we see cleaning the streets most mornings is carrying the heavy hose behind him. She does not get to do the spraying, just the lifting.

Streets in Spain are still commonly cleaned daily, which does not help to discourage the habit of throwing bits and pieces on the ground. Despite that, I have noticed a big improvement in the amount of garbage in the bushes and along the roads. There's much less rubbish about than a few decades ago; some environmental consciousness is evident.

As we're sipping yet another excellent coffee on the Plaza Mayor, contemplating waste-management practices, the black-bobbed head of the woman from the Tourism Office comes into view. She stops for a chat, to see how we're going, what we've done lately and how much longer we're staying in Almazán. This is an opportunity to ask why the square is getting the royal treatment today. Is something happening later?

'Cleaning up after yesterday's party,' she says. The *verbena* (fiesta with dancing) was on from midnight to 4am. Did you not hear it?'

We must have slept right through that, although the music from the fair on the other side of town did waft through the house until midnight or so. This town has music galore. Since we've been here there have been drums and marching bands for weeks, for one fiesta or another, all accompanied by music and, in most cases, church bells and fireworks. There will be another *verbena* as part of the Fiesta de San Pascual Bailón – one session for the youngsters from 8.30pm to 10.30pm and another from midnight to 4am for the adults.

'The fiesta of San Pascual Bailón and the Zarrón is of significant tourism interest,' she assures us importantly. 'You must not miss it!' she exclaims as she rushes off to open the Tourism Office.

~

Each year on 17 May, the town of Almazán relives a much-loved ritual. The Brotherhood of San Pascual Bailón, a brotherhood formed in 1816 and is still going strong, is responsible for organising this in the saint's name. Originally the members of the Brotherhood were herders and cattlemen who chose San Pascual Bailón as their patron saint. Apparently, San Pascual was a joyful character who would regularly burst out in dance. A dancing saint is of course perfect for a fiesta dedicated in his name. Not being a single-issue man, he's also the saint of cooks, preventing stove accidents and fires in the kitchen. The party to honour San Pascual, who was a shepherd in his childhood, is held on his birthday in May each year.

A statue on the Plaza Mayor in Almazán depicts a figure called El Zarrón, who is now synonymous with this fiesta. El Zarrón is a cute fellow in a herder's outfit with a hat full of big, long feathers. It is this symbol of the shepherd that has become more and more prominent in the celebrations. The character of El Zarrón is now the star of the show. His original purpose was to control young ones who disrupted the brothers in the procession. He is now more celebrated than the saint himself.

I'm intrigued to see how this will play out. The fiesta's website states that it is 'a celebration with pastoral symbolism in which eight couples dressed in traditional costume perform the dances of the XVIII century'. At the same time, two outlandish figures with foxtail hats flog spectators. I'm not sure how they build a whole weekend of festivities around this theme, but I am looking forward to seeing it. Before it starts there's a mass, of course, after which the dancers perform, while the Zarrón, enemy of the devil, distributes blows left and right in the square. After the second round of dancing and flogging there is a mixture of wine, sugar, cinnamon and wet bread called *soparra* that will be served at the house of someone known as 'the butler'. I'm utterly fascinated: the *soparra* is apparently served in handcrafted wooden bowls but who gets it and where the butler lives is unclear. The website I find is short on detail. I guess the locals are in the know and that's the point.

On another website I find some words about lollies and teenagers. I can't wait to see how this all pans out. Not surprisingly, the formal council website warns that the elderly and young children must avoid the flogging zone for their own wellbeing. I can barely conceive how the proposal for this festival was handled by council: a party on the streets with adult men dressed in strange outfits luring teenage boys with lollies and then flogging them if they get too close. Additionally, people will come and watch this and cheer. It seems totally inappropriate. But, if it's traditional, then that's different. Traditions must be maintained, after all.

It begins as all fiestas tend to do, with a holy mass in one of the several churches in town. At the end of mass, a priest emerges from the church carrying a tall silver cross, followed by another priest carrying a flag. Lots of excited kids in traditional costume fill the first rows in the procession. The chattering is deafening. They've been sampling the lollies already and the sugar high makes them noisy. The girls, as cute as can be, have the same outfits as the adult women: big red skirts, an embroidered shawl, white stockings and black lacquered shoes. The boys and men have long white socks with black knickerbocker trousers, a white shirt and a black vest. There are also many dapper-looking young boys dressed up as El

Zarrón. The figure of El Zarrón is very cool and lots of boys want to be him. After all, he gets to do the flogging. He wears brown leather pants and a jacket, coupled with the hat with long feathers tucked into the band. From a distance it looks like a tall crown.

The crowd follows the priests to the Plaza Mayor and the marching band arrives from a side street followed by eight pairs of dancers. The marching band plays sweet cheerful tunes. We spot our neighbour Lorenzo in the band, as we have for every procession to date. The dancers go around and around the Plaza Mayor, swirling to the melodies of the traditional eighteenth-century dance music. In the gap between the band and the dancers, two Zarrónes come out swinging their truncheons made of a leather water carrier but filled with sand for this occasion. Spectators throw lots of lollies onto the ground (the lolly shop is open so throwers can buy their own in addition to what council provides). Teenage boys run to scoop up handfuls of sweets whilst the Zarrónes try to hit them. Surely this is a good contest for young boys needing to display their toughness. No bulls have to be maimed in the process. The band, the dancers and the floggers all seem to work around each other. Dancers don't get hit; only the teen boys do. There are a couple of ambulances on standby. One rather grown-up young man gets flogged powerfully, I assume by mistake. I see him go down clutching his right eyebrow. As he lays in the gutter the Zarrón who hit him is the first to check if he's okay. It seems he is because he's back in the fray a few minutes later.

The festival is a bizarre and incongruous spectacle. I'm simultaneously impressed and bewildered. I can't even begin to imagine how this tradition evolved. But everybody seems to have had so much fun and that's all you want from a fiesta. We never do find out where the butler's house is or get to try the *soparra* but we go home thoroughly entertained by what we've seen.

Chapter 21

A Birthday to Remember

My birthday closely follows El Zarrón's and our house has been filling up with guests. It's been many decades since I had a birthday surrounded by my blood relatives. Yesterday, my sister, Elsa, and her partner, Manuel, arrived. Elsa moved to Spain, with her then-young son Josh, after I settled here in the 1970s and still lives in Alicante, some six hours drive away. Our friends Dave and Alison have come from Australia to join us for a while. Josh and Maya are here too.

'Hey, do you want to know what we've been up to lately?' I casually ask Elsa and Alison as we're sitting on the terrace after breakfast.

'What?' Elsa asks.

'Ok, what?' echoes Alison.

'We're thinking about buying an old, dilapidated house around here.'

They both look at me quizzically, heads cocked to the side, wondering if they heard me correctly. They, like me, thought we were going to rent a house in a lovely village and enjoy life.

'We just stumbled across some places for sale and then we got caught up in the thrill of it all.'

Next the iPad comes out and I'm showing photos of both places. Elsa and Alison laugh and exclaim ooohs and aaahs, loudly, which brings the rest of the family to have a look too.

'We're confused, though. Alex likes one place and I like another better. We're both in love with a different house.'

Everybody has something to say, and after a while the cross-chatter dies down and I can hear individual sentences.

'How much do they want for that one?' 'Can the roof be fixed?' 'What's the village like?' 'Is there a shop?' They're all talking and asking questions.

So far nobody has declared us *loco*. Well, maybe Manuel. He's always been the serious one. Elsa is delighted. 'I'd love you to buy a house here, that's more permanent than renting.'

Dave wants to come and help us renovate the cottage. Alison has always wanted to learn how to build stone walls and this seems a good opportunity.

'There's still the issue of deciding which house though,' Alex reminds everyone.

Wisely, nobody expresses an opinion on which is the better buy. It's the concept that's got them all excited. The choosing is still up to us.

~

Alison, Elsa and I go to the markets and the butcher to buy everything we need for a big birthday nosh-up. Brightly coloured fruits and vegetables are piled up and laid out to show off their luscious freshness. The butcher is very animated today. He speaks some English to Alison. He's clearly proud of his language skills.

'Learned on the beaches down south to impress the tourist girls,' he says.

He impresses the elderly matrons in the shop too. They look at him with motherly pride as he speaks in a foreign tongue. The shop looks almost indecent with its fleshy displays. I see Alison looking around and follow her gaze, eyeing off sausages of every size and colour, stuffed like chubby fingers hanging from the ceiling. Buttocks of ham dangle from hooks above our heads. We buy way too much food, of course. We carry the veggies, ribs, sausages, chops and *morcillas* up the hill to the house and fluff about for hours getting everything ready.

We laugh and chat as we prepare the communal meal. Later we gather on the top terrace for celebratory drinks before the festive barbeque. I'm grateful to be surrounded by family today; it hasn't happened for such a long time. Being in the warm embrace of kin and good friends is all I want for this day. Then Alex comes up the steps singing 'Happy Birthday' in Spanish. He hands me a glass of wine and an envelope. His grin tells me this is no ordinary present. He holds his breath as I tear the envelope open to reveal a card.

The card shows a picture of the river cottage. His gift is a house in Spain! For days he's been saying that he can't give up on the idea of Uncle Domingo's house in Ventosa, but all this time he's been planning to give me the river cottage. The words on the card read:

> For your birthday. I am the luckiest person in the whole wide world! Not only a cottage by the river but a partner who is just as willing as I am to have a crazy adventure.

Before I know it, I feel a little tear slip down my cheek. It's me who is the lucky one. This blue-eyed surfer coming into my life has been the greatest gift of all. Little did I know when I met this penniless Aussie backpacker here almost forty years ago that he'd one day give me a house in Spain. Everyone is excited about Alex's exceptional gift. He appears to have been able to keep it a secret from everybody. Alex seems to be genuinely pleased, both for me and himself. His ear-to-ear grin shows how Spain holds a special place in his heart too. Here we are, about to embark on some crazy adventure. Alex wraps his arms around me in some silent acknowledgement that we're in this together.

The barbeque is an old-fashioned wood burner. For several hours it's had the attention of every male in the house as wood has been chopped and a fire stoked into having just the right kind of coals for the meat. The order of what goes on first also gets a solid discussion, with compromises made, and finally everything is ready. The table is loaded with the butcher's finest cuts and sausages, salads, a potato bake and my favourite, alioli, Spain's best garlic sauce.

'*Aproveche.*'

Enjoy your meal, indeed.

I tear the first bit of meat off a pork rib and find it too big. I want to spit it out but that seems such a rude thing to do at the table. So I make a most regrettable decision and swallow it. As soon as I do, I know that I've made a mistake. The lump is stuck halfway down my throat and does not move from there. A slight panic washes over me. I can still breathe but it's definitely stuck and it feels sharp. I knew I should have given up eating pork. Not making a stand against all those inhumane pig barns is now sticking in my throat, literally!

I wave my arms about and point at my throat. 'There's a bone in there,' I tell my now anxious family. They stare at me in horror.

'Eat some bread,' Alison suggests, 'that will move it.'

(Later we find out that's what one does with fish bones but not with meat.)

'If you relax it will probably go down,' Elsa advises.

'Okay.' I drink a big glass of wine. That should relax me. I can still swallow liquid, so that's a good sign. But *relaxing* is pretty hard to do when you know you've got a rather large lump of pig stuck in your throat.

There is no doctor in Almazán, so eventually it's off to the emergency department in Soria. How to spoil your own birthday party? Just ask me.

The hospital in Santa Barbara is half an hour away. The admission process is not too bad. I give the details of my Australian travel insurance and that seems enough.

'Please take a seat in the triage room.'

Josh tries to speed things up by telling staff that his aunt can't breathe very well. That's a white lie since the bone is in my oesophagus rather than my windpipe. The triage nurse looks over the top of her glasses, sees I'm breathing, and promptly ignores us. Finally, after what seems like hours (I guess time goes slower with a bone in your throat), someone comes to take me into an examination room.

'Open wide.' A female doctor stands on her tippy toes to look down my throat but can't see far enough. She sends me back to triage, where I sit and wait some more. Eventually I get sent for an x-ray. These show there is indeed a bone stuck in my throat. Bugger. The ear, nose and throat specialist comes in to stick a scope down through my nose.

'Yep,' he confirms, looking at the camera's findings. 'There it is. Would you like a look?' he asks the female doctor.

'Yes, I would,' she replies enthusiastically.

Sure. Let's invite a few more people from the waiting room to have a peer down my throat.

'I can't do anything until the morning,' the ear, nose and throat guy says as he pulls the scope back up. 'You'll have to stay here overnight and we'll get it out in the morning. As you can breathe there's no urgency.'

My throat feels like it's swelling by now, the bone digging in painfully, but there is nothing for it, I have to wait. A male nurse comes to put in an intravenous line and finally hits a vein after blowing up a few in my left hand. Thankfully, he shoots up some painkillers after that. I am driven to a waiting room in a wheelchair. I am now confirmed as a patient and get parked among the other waiting patients. I send my loved ones home to continue celebrating my special day without me. There's nothing they can do here anyway.

Finally, some hours later, I get a bed in a ward and a pair of fetching red-striped unisex pajamas. It's a mixed ward and most of the other patients are very elderly. It's going to be a challenging night as some of the dementia patients are restless. Felix in Bed 6 is a persistent whisperer. He repeats the same words, *auxilio, oiga* (help, listen), again and again. A nurse talks to him softly, telling him to keep his clothes on. It's not exactly conducive to sleep knowing there's a potential ninety-year-old streaker lying next to you. I'm glad she's onto him.

'Do you have pain anywhere?' she asks him.

'No,' he whispers in response.

I am pleased he at least knows to whisper rather than speak loudly.

There's also the 'mother from hell' in the other bed next to me. Dementia again, probably, as she's giving her son an awfully tough time.

'Words are easy, but I am living this hell. I am desperate I tell you and all you have are words. I want them to do something.'

'What do you want Mama?' he asks kindly.

She shrieks, 'I want this to stop. Make it stop.'

'What is it?' he asks.

'You know what it is. You ignore it!' And on she continues, seemingly without drawing breath. She's had a fall and the scan will confirm if she has cracked her skull. The doctor comes to give her the results.

'There are no cracks, purely bruising, you can go home,' he tells her. Poor son. An ambulance is arranged to take her, I'm not sure where. I hope for the son's sake it's a secure ward in a nursing home and not home with him.

I get more drugs down the intravenous line for pain, some fluids and antibiotics. A nurse comes to take some blood and then every few hours my blood pressure, temperature and oxygen saturation are measured, just to make sure sleep is entirely impossible. For someone who started out having a lovely day with family and friends, the evening hasn't quite turned out as I'd hoped. Still, the drugs are good and I got a house in Spain for my birthday. How can I grumble?

~

Morning finally comes. I am sending messages to Alex, who's keen to know how it's going. They are going to 'fit me in when they can' I am told. Yesterday's doctor told me I would need a full anaesthetic and then an endoscope procedure to extract the bit of pork. When I get to the operating theatre, however, the surgeon there tells me that unfortunately the bone is located close to the trachea and there is a risk that it may go down my windpipe as they pull it up. The only way to get it out is by coughing and they need me conscious for that. Bloody hell. This is more serious than I thought.

I get rolled on my side and a nurse holds my head. Firmly. A nurse sticks a round plastic guard in my mouth to keep it wide open. Another nurse lays across me under the pretext of holding my hand but in reality I suspect she's pinning me down. They chose a hefty nurse to do this job – more weight to hold me down. My sense of powerlessness is overwhelming. A young female surgeon (under the encouraging words of who I believe is her supervisor) is going to insert the endoscope. Looks like I get the apprentice on top of everything. Lovely – glad to help the teaching process. A tube goes down my throat, I gag, and the hand-holder pinning me down urges me to breathe through my nose. What did she think I was using, my arsehole? The nurses are quite sweet though, saying, 'You're doing very well,' 'Nearly done now,' and calling me *Maja*, a term of endearment in Soria province. The surgeon grabs the meaty bone and pulls it up. It hurts like hell and feels as if she is tearing my oesophagus on the way up. But finally it's out. What a relief. It's all over.

Then they say: 'We have to go down once more to make sure we've got it all.'

Fair enough, but crikey. They might have warned me. I gag and choke as before, but that will teach me to chew my food better in future. Finally it's done. All over. The tube comes out, the round mouthguard is removed and I can breathe freely. The surgeon comes over and shows me the bone. They have cleaned the lump of meat off it to check that they have it all. It's over two centimetres long. Bloody hell.

'Would you like to keep it?' he asks.

They put it in a specimen jar for me to show the folks at home. I get wheeled to my bed to wait for another doctor to discharge me. I take the bone out of the container so I can hold it up to the light, photograph it and send it to the family to impress them. Impress it does. I get lots of messages exclaiming how big it is. Josh texts to ask if it's too early to organise another barbeque.

A surly doctor visits half an hour later to say I can go home if I can eat and drink okay. He watches me eat some yoghurt and as that goes down alright, he discharges me. I have to be on soft food for one week because there is a tiny wound in my throat. No very hot or very cold food. Okay, I think I can manage that.

I call Elsa and Manuel, who had to go home to Alicante to attend to business, and assure them I'm all well and minus pork bone. Alex, with friends Alison and Dave, collect me in the patient pick-up bay outside. I'm so relieved to have the bone out of my throat and I had no anaesthetic so I'm feeling quite well. I'm rather hungry, in fact, by the time I get home. I'm certainly not interested in any barbeque leftovers but I can manage a poached egg.

I'm struck by the irony of getting a pig bone stuck in my throat. Since we arrived, we've been joking about the imagined conspiracy to get us to eat more pork. I've been concerned about the hog barns in the fields, where the welfare of the animals doesn't look great. Now I've literally had pork stuck in my throat, and on my birthday of all days.

Chapter 22

The Iron Lady Gets an Identity and So Do We

In Parque de la Arboleda this morning, the smell of lavender in the air is stronger than the smell of hog. Just as well. I'm pretty much over pigs for a while. Walking the same track regularly is great for observing the transformations that happen as the weather slowly changes. It's late May now and it's warming up. Every day during this part of spring there is something we see, hear or smell for the first time. The vegetation, still mostly bare only weeks ago, is so thick now that the view from one side of the park to the other is completely obscured by trees in full leaf. The bar in the park has all the chairs and tables outside under large leafy trees. Goodbye winter, hello spring!

One of the things I missed living in Sydney is the changing seasons. In northern Europe the seasons are so defined. The pleasure of spring arriving after a long winter, summers that seem too good to be true (in some years), colourful autumns with moody windstorms and winters to cosy up at home. As much as I loved living in subtropical climes, nostalgia about the seasons is inevitable. Reliving the excitement now as we experience winter changing into a tentative spring is almost as painful as it's beautiful. This feeling of nostalgia makes me meditate on this search for belonging

I seem to be on. Is it just nostalgia I'm experiencing, but feel it as a longing for belonging? More to ponder over as we traipse about along the river.

~

Ricardo rang us the day before my birthday to give us the quote we'd been waiting for. This seems to have further convinced Alex that Uncle Domingo's house was no longer a serious contender. After I'm released from hospital, I dial the phone number for Mari-Paz, the owner of Uncle Domingo's house. There's a short pause before the distant ringing starts. I hate having to make this call, but we have to let her know it's all off before she spends more time and effort trying to find things out.

'Ricardo the builder finally came up with a quote for the roof repair. It will cost twice as much as the house itself,' I lament. 'I'm so sorry but we can't go ahead. The repairs are too expensive and there are too many other problems to solve.'

Her voice is kindly when she replies, 'I fully understand.'

We liked the Ventosa sisters, Lola and Lucia, very much. Mari-Paz sounds lovely too. And we'll miss having the opportunity to get to know Gabina better, the friendly witch of Ventosa.

'I'm sorry too, that we won't be in your natal village now,' I tell her.

Mari-Paz agrees and adds, 'I hope your life is blessed, wherever you may be.'

~

Now that we are buying a house we need to apply for our National Identificación de Extranjeros, or NIE – the national registration card for foreigners. One can't buy or sell a house in Spain or open a bank account or even buy a car without this number. It functions a bit like a tax identification number. So, we have to go back to the Iron Lady for our NIE.

She's not in her best mood as we arrive. The gravel-voiced man who allocates people to various officials tries to tell her we want an NIE (pronounced *neehe* in Spanish).

'Don't tell me what they want. I know what they want. They were here a few weeks ago.'

She already has a tall graceful African man sitting before her, but she shoos him towards the official on the desk next to her. I finally convince her that we're here about an NIE, not about the visa extension. Iron Lady gives us some papers and tells us we need to pay our processing fees for this application at any bank. We can use this paperwork to open a bank account if we wish. The Iron Lady stands up abruptly. It's now a quarter past two and she's worked overtime into her lunch break. She dismisses us without looking up from her computer to say goodbye. The banks are now closed for the siesta.

~

Today we also have our first meeting with our *notario*, who is a gyrocopter pilot as well as a notary. His office has a gold statue of a gyrocopter on the meeting table and the walls are adorned with paintings of the flying machine in the air. The *notario* is the legal person who does the real estate contracts in Spain. Alejandro is a handsome middle-aged man who obviously likes flying a lot more than he likes being a *notario* by the look of his office. He comes highly recommended by Josh, so we have faith in his ability to help us wade through the bureaucracy.

Alejandro has a mellifluous voice in beautifully enunciated Spanish and explains what it is we, as foreigners, must do to buy a house in Spain. He reads out every bit of paper that is of relevance. He explains that we can do a Contrato de Arras (an intention to buy contract) and pay a 10 per cent deposit, then sign the final contract a month later and pay the rest. We're pleased with the advice we're getting and have the confidence to go ahead.

The notary will continue to do his official searches to make sure everything is legal with the house purchase before we pay a deposit. We can still change our mind, throw on our backpacks and go hiking about the countryside.

~

A new day, a new challenge. Today's challenge is opening a bank account. The cheque to pay for the house must come from a Spanish bank, the *notario* has told us. How hard can it be to open a bank account? Extremely hard, it seems. First we pay the fees for the application to get the all-important NIE. The bank woman who attends to us is called Lourdes. She's nice and really wants to help. She asks the name of the *notario* who will handle the house purchase. She knows him well, she tells us. It's not such a coincidence, given there are only two *notarios* in Soria. The bank has rules though and without proof that we pay tax in Australia we can't open a bank account in case we're laundering dirty money or the proceeds of crime. We need to work out what can be used as evidence to prove we pay tax in Australia. Once we have that, Lourdes will help us open an account. We need to sort out all these legal hurdles before we can make an official offer on the river cottage.

~

Back to the Policía de Extranjeros. The reception officer, Gravel Voice, makes us wait.

Paloma, as we hear the Iron Lady is called, comes out a few minutes later and beckons for us to come into the inner sanctum. Once seated, she hands us a couple of bits of paper. We both get our NIE. It feels like a bit of a let-down, this simple piece of paper. I was thinking it would be like a driver's licence with a photo and stamps, but no, it's just a slip of paper with a number on it. But this little number means we can now buy a house in Spain. With lots of *gracias* we bid Paloma goodbye.

We now have the last bits of evidence we think we need to open a bank account. The lovely Lourdes is there again to help us. We have our NIE and our Australian tax statements sent by our accountant in Sydney.

'Come in and sit down,' Lourdes beckons us.

She needs to ring HQ several times for advice. Nothing is quite as easy as it seems but, after the hoops we've jumped through, walking out with a bank account feels as close to having citizenship or an extended visa.

~

Now that we know we are in a legal position to buy a house I call Xavier, who I think is the owner of the river cottage, to tell him we want to buy it.

'I'm not actually the owner of the house,' he says to my dismay.

'Who is then?' I ask.

My heart begins to race. I'm shocked to hear this, but Xavier assures me there's no *problema*.

'My wife and her two sisters inherited the house from their grandmother. There are still some issues to resolve about the will, but it can all be sorted quickly.'

He tells me a complicated story of the inheritance going to three sisters, one of whom is his wife, Clara. He is the spokesperson for his wife and her sisters. I have trouble understanding his rapid-fire Spanish and he also speaks with an accent I'm not familiar with. He's from la Extremadura, a region a good six hours drive from here.

He then casually mentions that there are no deeds, but the property is registered in the *cadastre* as owned by the family.

'It's a common story in this part of the world to have no deeds,' he says. 'In 1766 when the house was built there was no registration of ownership. In 1912 the house was registered in the *cadastre* by the ancestors of my wife, but no deeds were ever produced.'

This is my bloody birthday present you're talking about buddy. I would have hoped for more positive news.

I take a deep breath and swallow the lump in my throat as I say, 'Okay, well let's take it from here. Our notary can look into all this on our behalf and, as soon as he is satisfied with the details, we're willing to sign a Contrato de Arras.' I've only just learned about these 'Contracts of Intention to Buy' but make it sound like I know what I'm talking about.

'The contract will have some clauses stating that, if there are any other inheritance claims on the house or any outstanding debts, these will be the responsibility of the vendors, not us, the purchasers. Is that agreed?' I state confidently.

'Fair enough,' he says. 'Don't worry, it will all be fine.'

It's easy for him to say not to worry, but for me it's rather a dampener on the excitement of the birthday gift.

~

We steel ourselves for another interaction with the authorities today. It's time to request the visa extension as advised, so we return to the Oficina de Extranjería. Paloma does not want to see us. We are no longer the concern of the 'Foreigners' Police'. We must deal with immigration, she tells us, waving her arms around. She literally shoos us away as she points to a tall woman dressed in khakis. This may be the moment we stop being pesky tourists and start being immigrants. Ms Khaki examines the *papeleo* (paperwork) we've brought, which includes bank statements and travel insurance. Next she allocates us to a different person – another woman, but this time one who is entirely unremarkable, pleasant looking, with a soft gentle voice and measured confident gestures. She looks dignified in her neat blue pantsuit and is the first person we've seen who looks like a role model for the universal public servant. She may well be the only sane person in this building.

How did she get a job here? Somehow, she gets us through the molasses of immigration bureaucracy in under half an hour. Today has been one of progress.

~

Two days later we're back at Extranjeros, to pick up the papers for Alex's visa extension. Ms Khaki has our papers. These we now need to take to a bank to pay the charges then come back with proof of payment so she can give us other papers.

It's interesting that public servants in Spain don't seem to be allowed to handle money. To pay anything you must go to the bank and show proof of payment to the authorities. It's half past one now and the bank closes at two. We rush to the nearest bank, where only a couple of nuns and one other woman are ahead of us. This may just work. The nuns are quick but then the next in line wants to take out money from various accounts, her own and those of her children, and at 20 euros here and there this is taking time. Finally, she moves off, with a fist full of euros. It's quarter to two. The teller is quick and we run out with the receipts with only ten minutes to spare to see Ms Khaki before she shuts up shop for the day. Alex will become an illegal immigrant in a couple of days unless we get this done.

Ms Khaki processes the receipt and hands over a bit of paper with words and stamps on it.

'Is that all?' I ask.

'Yes,' she says, 'that's all. Later we will send you a *tarjeta* (card) to your nominated address.'

'Not so quick,' a voice pipes up from across the room. It's the Iron Lady. 'Once they have the *tarjeta* they must come back to me. I will need to take his passport away to the Comisaria and stamp it with a date for departure.'

Ah, Paloma. She couldn't help herself. She had to have the last word.

The papers state that the government has six months to consider the request for an extension of Alex's tourist visa. This is not the end of the process then! However, Alex is legal in the country while they consider, at least.

Once outside, clutching the all-important scrap of paper, we do a little happy dance, hoping the Iron Lady is not looking out the window and see these *guiris* behaving like wayward teenagers. She may change her mind.

Chapter 23

One Step at a Time

_____

We wait for the *notario* to get back to us with his advice about the inheritance issues and the missing deeds for the river cottage before we can go ahead and exchange contracts. Meanwhile, we plan a hike to Vea, an abandoned village. Josh tells us that the Spanish countryside has hundreds of ghost villages like Vea, many in the province of Soria. About 53 per cent of Spain has a population density of fewer than twelve inhabitants per square kilometre, one of the lowest rates in western Europe. The original inhabitants move to larger towns for work, leaving behind the homelands where their family lived and farmed the land for generations, growing wheat, tending to cows, sheep or pigs. Villages empty, left to crumble. This ghost-village phenomenon, as it's known, is likely to continue in Spain.

Vea is seven kilometres from San Pedro de Manrique, a lively market town with a wide main street lined with plane trees. There's no road and Vea can only be reached by following a mule path along the river Linares through a spectacular rocky escarpment. The track is lined with ancient stones and carefully constructed stone walls and bridges. Along the path several ruined water mills add to the desolate atmosphere. The backdrop looks inhospitable but has a strangely evocative beauty.

Clambering through an old mill wakes up a small colony of insectivorous bats. They have taken advantage of the abandoned building for protection from the elements. The ceiling beams in the old building still show signs of being hand hewn from big logs.

After a couple of hours, we cross the river to reach the hamlet. Shoes off, braving the painfully icy water to navigate the slippery stones. There are six of us on this intrepid walk, each finding a different way to cross. Dave uses an old flying fox that hangs over the river. Maya carries Maxi the dog. Alex finds a log to balance on further up the river. Josh takes a shortcut rock hopping. Alison and I wade through the cold water hanging on to each other for support, but all of us eventually make it to the other side carrying dry shoes and socks.

Around the settlement there are many stone terraces with old fruit and olive trees, resisting the invasion of the oak forest. The village reveals itself slowly, nestled in old gardens on steep, hilly ground. More water mills, a church and many, many houses. In the end, its inaccessibility became too much to bear and in the 1960s the original inhabitants left to find somewhere else to live, on a road and with television reception.

We're like kids let loose in a playground, scattering in different directions to uncover the melancholic magic of Vea. Some things are best experienced alone and silently. Looking inside the buildings, many things have been left behind. A single iron bed stands in a blue-painted room, a child's bedroom. The walls have drawings and pencil lines documenting the growth chart of a child. The last record was made in 1962 and the height of the child is 1 metre and 22 centimetres. I wonder where he or she is now. The owners of this home and the child would have left Vea during the 1960s sometime, when the lure of the city became too strong.

The church, which I imagine was the centre of Vea's public life only decades ago, is slowly and sadly disintegrating. For centuries, the parishioners would have volunteered their time and effort to keep this lovely building in tip-top shape. Now, it's left to withstand the elements without human help. Eventually, after exploring the old houses, I am the first to arrive at what may have been the main square, now a flat grassy patch of land surrounded by houses and the church. We brought a picnic lunch to have in this idyllic-looking place, the plan being for all of us to meet back here. As I sit down waiting for the others I hear barking. A door creaks open and a dog comes running out as fast as it can on three legs. So, Vea is not a ghost village after all. The dog, a lovely black, white and tan border collie mix, greets me enthusiastically. She wants pats, not fights. Above all she wants a stick to be thrown. Moments later, a bearded young man in his mid-twenties looms above me on a rock ledge.

'*Bien venido a Vea,*' he greets me quite formally in Spanish. 'Do you need anything? Water maybe?'

'We're fine, thanks,' I tell him. But my interest has been piqued. What's such a young guy and his dog doing in the middle of a ghost town?

'Do you live here?' I ask.

'Yes, I've been here for a year and three months now with my girlfriend. She's not here today.'

I notice that some houses nearby have new windows and doors. Perhaps adventurers, new-age hippies, loners or the homeless are using this place to live a cheap, sustainable life. There's no electricity or running water other than the river below.

'My name is Erna. What's yours?' It feels surreal to be doing formal introductions in the centre of a ghost town.

'I'm Javier and my dog is Rosa.'

'Do you grow everything you need here?' I'm bursting with curiosity.

Javier looks like a starry-eyed dreamer from a bygone era. I imagine him writing poetry and playing the Spanish guitar in the stone house behind him.

'Yes, we live from the land around us. There are old orchards we've revived and we grow our vegetables. We get some supplies from town and barter for the things we need with our extra fruit. Sometimes we can sell our vegetables at the markets.'

'It's a long way to town. How do you take your produce to the markets?'

Javier smiles. 'Apart from Rosa, we have a mule, a horse and a donkey. The donkey won't cross the river so he's no use for getting supplies to town, but the horse and the mule are good.'

It sounds like a blissful lifestyle. It makes me wonder why more unemployed or homeless people don't live in these villages. The living would be hard here but quite cheap and in beautiful surroundings.

'How long does it take to visit the town on horseback?' I'm keen to know more.

'Only half an hour if we can cross the river. Sometimes we're flooded in.'

Eventually, everyone arrives at the square after a good look around and they too get to meet the dreamy figure on the rock ledge above us. Reluctantly we say goodbye. But perhaps Javier's glad to go back to writing love sonnets for his girlfriend or whatever romantic pursuit he was engaged in before we disturbed the peace.

We have a picnic lunch on the grass with the bread we brought, a couple of bottles of red wine, cheese, ham, chorizo, fruit and boiled eggs. We talk about all the things we saw, contemplating if we'd like to live here if our circumstances were different. Perhaps we would if we were penniless uni students, but then the university is a couple of hours away. There's no electricity, so you couldn't have a laptop. Idyllic and practical, we decide, are often far apart.

The walking is quite strenuous, rough terrain, up and down. Any notions of how good it would be to live in Vea are soon forgotten on the track back to town. We deserve a drink in San Pedro de Manrique, where we've left the car. The bar lady can see we're pretty buggered and asks if we walked to the ghost village.

'Yes, we did. What a beautiful place!' exclaims Maya with her usual enthusiasm.

'Did you see anybody?' she asks. 'There are about twelve people living in Vea permanently or semi-permanently. They come into town to buy food and barter.' We tell her we met Javier. 'They're no bother to anyone,' she adds. 'They started coming to live here during the global financial crisis, more than ten years ago.'

I remember Spain was one of the worst-affected countries at that time. There was huge unemployment and the country is still recovering from that even now.

The bar lady adds: 'Spaniards were losing their homes because they couldn't pay the mortgage or the rent. The abandoned villages often have some good houses left standing and plenty of firewood nearby.'

It's not a bad option when you think about it. The old vegetable plots and orchards can be revitalised with a bit of arduous work and a simple living can be eked out. An idealist's life in a picturesque place next to a running stream. A fire to keep you warm. There's a lot I like about that if only the walk into town was easier.

~

When we were checking out the real estate market for ruins, we came across many abandoned villages. We're keen to know more about this phenomenon. Alex does a bit of research about depopulation. We learn that there are some 1500 abandoned hamlets. Many of these are being put up for sale as councils require owners to maintain their properties, which many can't afford to do. The countryside is dotted with entire villages that are being sold after their owners abandon them. Adventurous foreigners and enterprising Spaniards are part of the solution as they buy some of these settlements, taking advantage of bargain prices.

Half of Spain's municipalities have fewer than 1000 inhabitants and are at risk of complete depopulation. Although urbanisation is emptying rural lands across Europe, the drift is dramatic in Spain. The depopulation in the rural areas leads to people moving to the bigger cities like Madrid, Barcelona and Valencia, which in turn become less liveable because of increased pollution, traffic jams and lack of infrastructure.

Spain's 'endangered' villages are mostly inland from the coast. They tend to be a long way from the beaches, along narrow, winding roads making access to supermarkets or schools impractical for daily living. However, this usually also means they are peaceful and scenic, have clean air and are surrounded by nature, ideal for those seeking a quiet weekend or holiday retreat, but not practical for those needing a good internet connection and mobile phone coverage. Telecommunication companies are not setting up networks in these remote areas, as the low number of connections is not worth the investment. This leaves the older generation isolated. They will eventually die or move somewhere they can get medical attention, home help and access to shops.

It makes me think about the river cottage. All the bother and complications of the past weeks investigating Uncle Domingo's house seems to pale alongside the sadness I feel at Spain's loss of these historic villages. We can only save one abandoned house, not a whole village, though that was the thought that first inspired us in this venture.

~

Meanwhile, there's not much we can do to move things along while the *notario* does his searches, so we do some touring with Dave and Alison. We want to show them the Basque kingdom of Navarra (Navarre in Basque). Alex and I were here a month ago and we want to share our discoveries with our friends.

Country roads take us to Ochagavía. We have two rooms booked on the first floor of a hotel looking out over the river, which has multiple curved stone bridges along it. The people here are decidedly different from those in Soria, being mostly tall and large boned. Even the dress code is different. Most men wear the pancake flat Basque hats either in black or bright red. Alison stalks several of them to get a photo without them noticing.

'Bugger, they are just too fast for me,' she bemoans as she runs to catch up with us. The medieval village looks stark. Despite the cold, the front doors are partially open to allow a peek inside the entrance rooms. The floors here are traditionally paved in intricate patterns with river pebbles, dark and severe but hauntingly beautiful.

We're having a drink and arguing about where to go for dinner when I hear the owner of the hotel say, 'I just got the first wild mushrooms of the season. Four kilos of wild fungus!'

I share the big news and Dave suggests, 'There's our answer. We'll have kilos of fungus for dinner.'

This region is renowned for its wild mushrooms. Whole tourism ventures are based on other Spaniards coming here to savour the mushrooms. Some town councils, eager to promote the *micología* of the area, place statues of mushrooms on the road into town. These are unfortunately difficult to distinguish from a bunch of penises, but no one seems to mind. There are even carved wooden 'cocks' on the top of the bar today. Alison looks sceptically at them but curiosity wins and we decide to have dinner here.

'You're the one with the best Spanish; you do the ordering,' Alex suggests.

After a big lunch we don't need much for dinner, so I order some *raciones*. *Raciones* are larger portions than tapas and good for sharing. The down side of me ordering is that I am keen to share all my culinary memories and my eyes are way bigger than our combined stomachs.

I ask the waitress to bring us scrambled eggs with wild mushrooms, the signature dish of the day, but also some *croquetas de jamón*, sheep cheese and *patatas bravas*. *Patatas bravas* are cheap and filling and make a good snack to share. Essentially, they're fried cubed potatoes with either a traditional homemade spicy tomato sauce or a more modern-day mayonnaise. These days you often get both at the same time. With crusty bread and a bottle of red, it's more than plenty for dinner. Lucky we don't have far to go to our rooms, because we're uncomfortably full. I've ordered way too much food, again!

~

The following morning the hotel serves my favourite Spanish breakfast of toasted baguettes smeared with olive oil and loaded with freshly grated tomato, served with freshly squeezed orange juice and good strong coffee. Fortified, we make our way from Ochagavía to Espinal to get to the beginning of the Camino de Santiago (the Way of Saint James).

'Let's go,' says Dave, wiping the last crumbs of bread out of his beard. 'It's time to hit the Camino.'

'You bet,' Alex replies and gets up so quickly, he knocks a chair over.

The whole Camino pilgrimage thing came about because in the ninth century a religious hermit followed a shiny star (as you do!) and came across the tomb of the apostle James. The bishop at the time agreed that it was indeed the remains of Saint James. Lots of time has passed since that discovery and the Camino is now more popular than ever. In Spain, the journey starts in the town of Roncesvalles and spans 738 kilometres to Santiago de Compostela, on the other side of the country, in Galicia. There are many routes to the final destination at the cathedral in Santiago, but the one starting from Roncesvalles is well known and the busiest.

Tonight, we'll sleep in a *casa rural* in a village called Espinal (Aurizberri in Basque). Our landlady, Milagros (Miracles), welcomes us warmly. Milagros is not an uncommon name here. I love the way babies in Spain are given names so full of parental expectations, although perhaps it was gratitude in this case, a longed-for child? The house is cavernous and a big wide staircase with corridors at least 4 metres wide lead to our rooms. Along the corridor walls there are pompous chairs at regular intervals, as if a formal dinner is about to take place. There's a shared bathroom so big you could comfortably throw a party in it, too.

'Settle in, make yourselves comfortable and, when you're ready, come back to me with your passports,' Milagros suggests.

We all line up with our passports half an hour later so she can fill out the official paperwork. What a hotel or a *casa rural* wants for paperwork varies quite a lot. Some want only to scan one passport, whereas others want everyone's, along with the car number plate, my mobile phone number and the promise that I'll name my first-born son after them (well, almost anyway).

'What are they for?' Alison asks Milagros, pointing to a spray of thistle flowers on the front door. 'I've noticed these on most houses here.'

'They're for good luck. We burn them on 23 June to dispel evil spirits. The next day, the day of San Juan, we go to the *campo* (fields) to collect a new one. This brings good luck to the household for the whole of the next year,' Milagros explains.

~

Two years ago, I walked the final 220 kilometres of the Camino with Alex, Dave and Alison, and now we're back and ready to experience the beginning of this eminent journey. We're not above a little cheating though. The first thing we do is organise a taxi to take us to Roncesvalles at the so-called Spanish start of the Camino. The taxi takes us on a beautiful road jaunt through landscapes that look more Swiss than Spanish. I picture Heidi coming out yodelling at any minute, on her way to see her grandfather with a loaf of bread and a hunk of cheese. Towns along the way all have illustrious names like Jaurrieta, Abaurea Alta, Garaloa, Aribe, Garralda, Auritz. They're all full of medieval stone buildings. The taxi driver takes us to the border between France and Spain, where we start our short Camino walk for old times' sake. It was only two years ago but we all loved it and being so close to the start means we can at least relive it for one day.

'Do you get a lot of work from pilgrims?' I ask the taxi driver.

'*Si*,' he replies. 'There are lots of pilgrims who take a break from walking, so I make a good business out of lazy walkers. Or maybe tired ones.' He has a little chuckle. 'I also transport backpacks from one hotel to another, so people can move about without a heavy bag.'

The taxi drops us next to a green paddock. The track starts here. There are several other groups, some Japanese, some Germans, a couple of French and our ragtag bunch of Aussies with one almost-Aussie. The walking is easy, undulating paths crossing green hills, some kilometres through the oak forests. These forests are where some of the best known witches' covens of the sixteenth century would meet. The covens were much feared, which led to nine women being taken and burned at the stake in these parts. The white cross, a symbol of divine protection now, lines the path to keep us safe from witches. It must be working because we see none.

~

The Camino started as a European medieval pilgrimage. Today 'pilgrims' walk it for all sorts of reasons: religious, spiritual, and because it's a magnificent long-distance journey passing through diverse scenery. I suspect our group does not have a deeper, meaningful reason for being on a pilgrimage walk, but I've never asked.

For a while Alison and I keep the same pace. After walking silently for a while, she looks across at me with such a happy face that I wonder out loud, 'Why do you love the Camino, Ally?'

'I love it because life takes on such simplicity when you're walking here. There are no commitments, and I have no ambition other than one foot in front of the other. That's all I have to do.'

For a while we move together in silent companionship, the wind in the trees and the sound of our boots on the path. We are overtaken by some other walkers occasionally, wishing us the standard Camino greeting, *Buen Camino!*, literally 'Have a good path', but it really means 'I wish you a wonderful life'. Do I believe in the transformational aspect of the Camino as many do? For some, this is an inner journey as well as a physical one.

I try to put my feelings into words and tell Alison: 'I like the meet-and-greet, the fleeting relationships you have with strangers on the track, the way you get a peek into their lives, and then they're gone, never to be seen again. That's what focuses me on appreciating the moment because that moment does not come again.'

'I remember a conversation I had on the Camino two years ago,' Alison says thoughtfully. 'This man, he was from Finland I think, told me he'd walked the Camino five times already. Every time he walked, he felt like he was getting closer to his true self.'

I think about that for a while as we follow in the footsteps of pilgrims before us. I feel I'm coming to terms with my identity, finally realising that I am not my job title. I am me and that's enough. I'm a Dutch-Australian with an enduring passion for Spain, I am loved and I am healthy. I have an entire future to invent. Everything can change, except Alex. He's my constant.

'Modern city life is so hectic and noisy that there's a great benefit from walking in nature. Spending time in your own head may help to accept who you are and where you're at,' I say, getting philosophical after all.

With only daypacks carrying a bit of water, a jumper, a raincoat and not much else, the walking is easy. We feel like cheats, everyone else is just beginning the long journey and we are doing this for only one day. Once going I don't want to stop. I would love to do the full length of the Camino. Just walking, day after day, until I get there. The Camino in a way is akin to joining a tribe. For the duration of the pilgrimage, you're part of something greater than your individuality.

The Camino takes us on winding roads, through forests and fields, passing settlements and farmhouses along the way. Each village is subtly different from the next in architecture, cuisine, crops and climate. It's such a divine way to travel. As is characteristic in this part of the world, we never have to go far before there's another bar for a drink or a restaurant for lunch. On one hilltop, where the Camino crosses the road, an enterprising young woman has set up a mobile bar in a caravan, serving coffee and snacks to the already hungry walkers.

'Come and have a look,' Alex calls after he's wandered off the track in the middle of an oak forest for a private wee. When we get to where he is, some 30 metres into the forest, he points at a memorial. A pair of hiking stocks and some old boots are on the ground with an engraved plaque that reads, 'In memory of Anita's favourite hike'. The four of us stand quietly in front of Anita's memorial, paying our respects to this unknown woman.

'What was her story, eh?' Alison ponders.

'Whatever it was, she'd probably rather still be in those boots,' Dave adds laconically.

Quite a few people must have told loved ones that they would like to be remembered here or have their ashes scattered along the route, as we spot a few other memorials along the way.

~

It would be fantastic to keep going and going, one step at a time, all the way to Santiago de Compostela but I remind myself we're buying a house instead.

After a good sleep in Milagros' beds, we wake refreshed and ready for another day. We head for Pamplona by car, and we arrive by midday. We leave Dave and Alison here to go on with their travels without us. It's been lovely to share some of our time here with them, as well as useful to bounce our house-buying dilemmas off good friends who know us well. David and Alison think we're a little barmy, but not certifiably mad, which is a relief. I'm looking forward to them coming back to spend more holidays with us, perhaps next time in our own Spanish house.

Chapter 24

Contracts and Chorizo

———————

I wake up in a panic this morning, thinking, 'Oh my god, why are we doing this, we don't need to buy a house in Soria. What the fuck are we doing?' It's a brief moment of utter terror. Why does the night spread such doubt? This is all my fault. I dragged Alex over here and now we're going to be the owners of a ruin that needs hard labour and a lot of money. By the afternoon it feels like great entertainment again. I'm up and down like a bloody yo-yo. Alex goes through the same emotions, but fortunately we don't do the big doubt thing at the same time. One of us is shit scared while the other is hot to trot. We seem to take it in turns.

The *notario* has given us the all-clear and we can now ring Xavier and discuss our purchase in detail. Now is the time to take the plunge, this news makes up our collective minds. We take a deep breath, dismiss any lingering worries and jump in, ready to enjoy a journey into the world of Castilian ruins. Xavier, the husband of one of the sisters and their spokesperson, is our contact. This little fantasy we've been playing with is about to get real. We want to keep all the contents of the house, which the sisters do not seem to value or care about. The old family belongings will be wonderful to decorate and furnish the house.

However, we're still to agree on a price that includes the contents so the *notario* can add this to the contract. I may need some Dutch courage to make the call.

I have a few trepidations about ringing Xavier, but it's got to be done. The thing is, this has been going on for weeks now and at no point have we discussed a final price or made an actual offer. All our conversations have been around the legal issues to do with the inheritance and the lack of deeds. I am sure he's assumed that we agree with the asking price. After all, it's only 25,000 euros for a house and a barn next to a river on a block of 400 square metres. That's not a bad price. Anyway, we talk about the timeline for signing the contract and exchange. Xavier tells me he can come any time because he has not worked in two years.

'Not because I am retired,' he says. 'I am still too young to retire, but there is no work in La Extremadura.'

Poor man. Now I feel even worse that I'm about to try to beat him down on the price. We continue to talk about what the *notario* said and he tells me what his *abogado* (lawyer) said. Then I broach the subject.

'Well, we've never actually agreed on a price,' I say in a chirpy way. 'We'd like to offer 23,000.' I throw this sentence quickly down the phone line.

Xavier sternly replies, 'It's advertised for 25,000 and that is the price.'

Our brief venture into understanding the real value of a ruin does not give me a lot of confidence. We still have no real understanding of the prices for a house with a hole in the roof. Maybe the price is what it is because nobody else is bidding. I begin to talk about contents. Xavier says they don't want much.

'We'll throw it all out,' he says. 'Except for a few small things.'

'Tell me what those small things are,' I say. 'We need to list this in the contract. We can use what is in there because we don't have a house in Spain and it will help us get started.'

'Okay,' he replies, 'we'll take the table that's upstairs and some bedside tables that match. You can have the rest.'

'In that case,' I say, 'we will meet your asking price of 25,000.'

I haven't exactly demonstrated great negotiation skills. We agree on the price and I promise to tell him what happens at the *notario* on Monday when we sign the initial contract. We'll pay the deposit by *talon conformado*, as Xavier requests. No idea what that means but I assume it's a guaranteed bank cheque. Not from our private account, which may or may not have the euros to cover it, but underwritten by the bank itself, so the money is secured. I will also let him know the time and date the *notario* will set aside for final settlement, as both parties have to sign at the same time in the same place, as Spanish law requires.

Once I get off the phone with Xavier, Alex grabs me around the waist and spins me around the room. We are bouncing around like a pair of school kids on a sugar high, laughing hysterically at what we've done. To celebrate we open a bottle of Ribera del Duero, a regional wine we've become very fond of. Under the circumstances it tastes like the most delicious wine we've had here to date.

~

Our money arrives in our Spanish bank account from Australia on time to pay the deposit. The delays we used to have with international transfers may be a thing of the past. We get a bank cheque for the deposit, which we hand to the *notario*, and sign the initial contract. I ring Xavier immediately and tell him it's done. We set a date for signing the final papers together for settlement. Xavier and his wife will come from La Extremadura, where they live, so they will plan to stay the night.

~

We take Maya to see the river cottage for the first time after the contract is signed. As we pick up the keys from the bar, the barman asks if we have bought the house.

'Yes, we've paid the deposit,' I say and a cheer goes up in the bar. They must have been listening to the conversation.

Several voices call out, '*Bien venido*!' (Welcome to the village.)

The patrons are toasting us and speaking excitedly among themselves. I hear the word *extranjeros* (foreigners) quite a bit as they talk about us. We leave quickly as we're keen to get to the house. We roam around inside with Maya, looking at this and that. She seems to love the charm of the cottage and the garden too. The sound of the cuckoo rings out over the garden. When we're on the first floor, we hear a human voice calling out too. We look down from the balcony to see a woman standing in the middle of the garden holding up a chorizo sausage. A woman in her fifties with a wide smile and shining brown eyes. She heard in the bar that we've bought the house and has come to welcome us with a gift. A chorizo made in this village. What a lovely thing to do. She has heard that I am Dutch and Alex is Australian. She swoons over the Australia bit and says there has never been an Australian in the village. She tells us how much she loves Australia.

'I'm your neighbour. I live near the square and can tell you a lot about the house and the family who lived here,' she says. 'I spent a lot of time here as my friend grew up in this house.'

She disappears as quickly as she appeared, calling over her shoulder, 'I don't want to hold you up. You have things to get on with.'

Her name is Mari-Carmen. She will always be known to us as 'Mari-Carmen of the Chorizo'. Is a chorizo the Castilian equivalent of a neighbourly cake when people move in next door? I can't seem

210

to be able to get away from pork, even though being welcomed by Mari-Carmen is very touching. I've had to overcome my fear of eating pork after the rib incident in favour of continuing to sample the Castilian delights.

~

The day of house settlement finally arrives. We're up early to make sure everything goes smoothly with drawing the bank cheque to pay for the house. This is the first time Alex and I have bought a house without a mortgage. But, then again, the asking price was considerably lower than Sydney house prices. Again, it's Lourdes who helps us. When we leave, cheque in hand, she blows us a kiss. I blow one back.

'Buena suerte!' (Good luck!) We have bonded with her over the endless filling out of forms to open a foreigner's bank account.

~

The rest of the week will be a fiesta in Soria (again) and all the offices will be closed. If we can organise to get the electricity connected before they close, we'll be days ahead. Unfortunately, the woman at the desk can't find the house in the system. There is some confusion over the street number. It's a common problem here – at some stage the street numbers were changed by council, but other businesses kept using the old ones. It seems that Number 4 already has electricity connected but that is not us. She finally finds the name of Soledad Martinez de Poveda, the last inhabitant of the house. She is listed at Number 10. However, there is no Number 10 in the street. The house itself also has a faint Number 6 written on it above the front door. When we were in the house, I noted mail on the table for Number 8 also. It seems there's ample potential for confusion. Now the electricity woman has found 'our' house at Number 10, she finds that it's been empty for eleven years. This means it needs a qualified electrician to update the meter and the connection box inside the house. That won't be an easy task to arrange with yet more fiestas approaching. The electricity woman kindly gives us the card of a highly recommended electrician. We'll try Electrician Enrique later to see if we can entice him to help us out before everything closes for the big fiesta in Soria.

~

At five we rush to meet Xavier and his wife, Clara, at the *notario*'s office. We're ushered into the same large meeting room where we met the *notario* before. The sellers are already there with their *abogado*, a smug-looking character who does not utter a word throughout the proceedings. Although all conversations have been with Xavier, we are actually buying the house from Clara and her two sisters. It was left to them by their grandmother in Calatayud. This grandmother was the sister Soledad was visiting when she fell ill and did not come home.

Xavier is a fussy-looking man in his late fifties, neat and respectable on first impression. He tells us in excessive detail how he's changed the locks for us. He mentioned this on the phone a while ago too. He's proud of his efforts and states that he is quite *manitas* (handy). To further emphasise the point, he raises his bony hands above the table and wiggles his fingers. For some reason this haunts me. I will think of his *manitas* every time I open the door with that key. Clara, or Clarita as Xavier calls her affectionately, is a very petite woman. Obviously, she has the diminutive Sorian genes. She's neat as a pin to match her husband and seems genuinely pleased to meet us.

Alejandro, the notary, comes in and goes through the contract verbally, making sure all parties understand what they are signing. We're 15,000 kilometres from home and about to drop our savings in exchange for a ruin with a hole in the roof. Alex and I look at each other. He winks. We then all sign the contracts in Alejandro's presence and the cheque changes hands, as do the keys to the house. After the show Xavier has made of changing the lock, the keys look unassuming. There's a keyring that was a freebie from a bank, holding one key for the front door and another for the big steel gate.

When we leave the office, Alex gives me a reassuring hug and says it's all going to be alright. We stroll over the square to the nearest bar to have coffee and something sweet to get my blood sugar up. We share some pastry made with *cabello de ángel* (angels' hair), which is a preserve made with the thready pulp inside a pumpkin.

~

This is our first full day as the owners of Calle del Huerto, Number 4, 6, 8 or 10. The *papeleo* shows we've bought Number 4, so we'll sort out the confusion later. We wander through the house in awe. We can hardly believe we own this place! This has been a family's home for over 250 years and it's a treasure trove of antiquity. Soledad's possessions are everywhere. Her name means solitude. Was her life a happy one? There are so many memories here, memories that belong to a person we've never known. Do her possessions hold a memory of the woman who owned them? Slowly Soledad's life will unfold before us as we go through the belongings in the house to sort out what to keep, what to donate and what to throw out. Already we know that Soledad was a very pious woman. The house is full of religious paraphernalia.

There is a Jesus or a Maria on every wall. Every flat space is covered with something holy, multiple Bibles, saintly ornaments, church calendars and prayer cards lined up on the sideboard, all covered in ancient spider webs. The sideboard has a glass top and underneath it, through the layers of dust, Alex spots a black-and-white photograph of a stern-looking couple in their fifties. We'll have to find out from the locals who they are. Mari-Carmen of the Chorizo will know.

Council Jesus arrives first thing to connect the water. Impressive service! Although we'll only have cold water in the bathroom it will be extremely useful to wash hands, flush the toilet and draw water for a cuppa. Bathrooms in Spain have not changed much from when I lived here decades ago. Poor plumbing always leaves a pong in the bathroom and beyond.

There is no evidence that a washing machine has ever been connected. There is one of those old stone sinks with a built-in washboard. Many villages still have their old washhouses as a memorial to the laundry days of yore. This communal place was where women gathered to air dirty linen (that of others!), often next to the river where water was rerouted to the washhouse. Most likely these places were the centre of all rumour, gossip and possibly even real news. When I arrived in Spain for the first time in the early 1970s there were ads on TV advertising washing machines with tantalising slogans like 'washes almost as good as your own hands'. Pride in their handiwork obviously made housewives think that a machine could only be second best to elbow grease. These days not many would prefer to do the sheets and towels by hand. Soledad was from an era when everyone did their washing by hand. The linen we find in her cupboards and trunks is impeccable, superbly laundered and ironed, although now yellowing on the folds.

I ask Council Jesus about the confusion with house numbers.

He explains that the house numbers are often all over the place, with different providers of electricity or Wi-Fi.

'Just put the electrics on at Number 10 if they think that's where you are and you can change that later, after you are connected. If you try to do it now, it will delay the connection.'

Okay, whatever house number they want to give us is fine as long as we get some light.

~

Xavier and Clara arrive mid-morning to collect the things they have set aside to take back to the Extremadura. We don't mention there's a bit more lined up than agreed.

'I'd like to keep one of the keys to the front door,' Xavier says. 'It's to give to our cousin so he can pick up that antique table.'

I interpret for Alex. We look at each other and I can see Alex is not in favour either.

'Sorry, Xavier, but all our private things will be here soon and we're not comfortable with a stranger having a key. Can you ask your cousin to give us a call when he wants to pick it up?'

Xavier looks decidedly uncomfortable now, as does Clarita. He mumbles something about how his cousin is very trustworthy but then the truth comes out.

'Well, he's not actually my cousin as such. He's the owner of the big *casa rural* around the corner. I've sold the table to him.'

So not a cousin getting a family heirloom, but Xavier making some extra cash. Perhaps he's not so upstanding after all. Still, this small fib is no big deal.

'The man who bought the table is in Madrid and I will ask him to contact you next week. His name is Jesus.'

It's getting a bit confusing with more than one Jesus about. He may have to be 'Jesus of the Table'.

Xavier and Clarita leave very soon after these revelations. They are obviously embarrassed by the little lie about the table. We farewell them warmly. We don't want them to feel bad, they may need the money for all we know.

~

Electrician Enrique comes as promised and on time. He shows us how to connect and use the electricity illegally until he can do all the legal paperwork. What a treasure! He also explains that the old electricity was 120 volts and therefore any lightbulbs still screwed in will blow rather quickly. Josh and Maya come and help us for a while. Maya and I start sorting through the first of Soledad's many wardrobes. What to donate to charity and what to throw out? Soledad had some very stylish outfits and was evidently a well-dressed lady. It's interesting as the house she lived in is so remarkably simple and basic, yet she dressed like a wealthy person. She would have washed these lovely dresses by hand in the old stone washbasin we found.

In Soria town we order a new mattress so we can start sleeping in our house as soon as we have cleaned some space. The man in the shop promises to deliver in three days, although Soria is in fiesta. He says the factory is in Madrid and as there is no fiesta there he can get the mattress delivered to Soria. He will then deliver it to us himself as he lives in a nearby village.

After lunch we empty an old wardrobe without doors that for some reason is in the kitchen. Inside it, under some newspapers, Alex finds a pistol. It looks old, is heavy and above all seems to be genuine! What do we do now? Maya emails photos of the pistol to her brother in the military police in Las Canarias. He's an authority on weapons.

'It's the same gun used by James Bond in his movies,' his text tells us. 'Undoubtedly from the Spanish Civil War in the 1930s.'

He tells us that under Spanish law we must hand the pistol to the Guardia Civil. There is a Guardia Civil post down the road, but it does not seem like a good idea to walk through the streets with what may turn out to be a loaded pistol. They may arrest us as they confiscate the weapon. The Guardia Civil is duly called and a while later two serious-looking officers arrive. They are young, handsome and look like identical twins. About mid-twenties, dark hair and both with neatly trimmed beards. I have trouble telling them apart. These are the new-look *guardias*, out to win our hearts and minds.

'Could you please show us exactly where you found it?' Twin One asks politely.

'Here, in the bottom of this wardrobe under some old newspapers,' I reply while pointing at the daggy old wardrobe without doors.

'Who exactly found it?' asks Twin Two.

'My husband, Alex,' I say pointing at said husband. 'He doesn't speak as much Spanish as I do,' I add.

At least not enough to explain the possession of an illegal weapon, I think.

'Passports please,' asks Twin One. He smiles and for a moment I consider turning on a transistor radio and trying to find a station that plays flamenco because here's a *guardia* I wouldn't mind a dance with! Alas, I fear I'm forty years too late.

As the house is still dark and we have no electricity, the *guardia* wanders off with the pistol to the barn where a shard of sunlight hits the ground.

'Would you please have a plastic bag we could put this in?' Twin Two asks. Well, I think it's Twin Two. Now they've moved about I'm not sure who's who.

They open the pistol's ammunition cartridge. There are no

bullets. Satisfied with our answers and having recorded our passport details, they take the pistol away.

'If it's not illegal, like a fake or something, can we have it back?'

They nod politely, in unison, but we get no receipt, so I think it might be the last we see of the old gun.

Chapter 25

We Bought a House in Castile

We leave the house in Almazán for the last time this morning. We have such fond memories of our time here. This very house, renovated by our absent landlady, Renske, inspired Alex to save a ruin too. We give the garden one last good soaking before we go. Renske will arrive in a few days to enjoy seeing it in full summer bloom. Neighbours Constanza and Lorenzo are out. We leave a fluffy toy koala climbing up the pot plant on their front step, bearing a note to thank them for their kindness. Almazán feels remarkably familiar now.

We've loved living in Almazán and discovering all it had to offer. It's another goodbye. I should be used to them but they are always bittersweet. Our new village is yet to reveal its secrets. We're excited about moving into our own river cottage. The roads in and out of Soria are dead straight, and according to local folklore they were originally Roman built so the army could march in straight lines. It does not take long to get to our new village via the highway following a Roman road.

We've been cleaning for a few days now and today we start with a good scrub of the bedroom so we can sleep here after the new mattress arrives this afternoon. After a short while we are both festooned with ancient spider webs. There are armies of spiders, entire ecosystems occupying every corner in every room. The poor spiders don't know what's hit them. They've had the place to themselves for eleven years and now all this commotion.

We're not set up for making food yet, so for lunch we head up the hill to the bar in the middle of town, which seems to have changed ownership since we first came here. An older bloke was running it then and it was pretty much a traditional bar with a traditional type of menu. We hear that he's run off with both the money from the sale and the barmaid, leaving his wife bereft and destitute. This topic is providing some conversation at the bar. Some say they could see it coming, that there was something going on with the barmaid for some time. Others say it took them by surprise.

The new barman shows off some of his high-school English. He's not bad either. This will come in handy when friends from Australia come to visit. His wife is lovely too and welcomes us warmly.

'*Simpáticos* like you are a welcome addition to our society.' She adds, 'We also looked at buying the river cottage. We liked the garden for our three dogs. We were going to keep the barn and bulldoze the house.'

This seems to be what we are expected to do too. They may be surprised!

~

It's a balmy day again today – we are well into summer now. The heat makes me feel a little lethargic. The news talks about a heatwave all over Europe. It was already 27 degrees at eight o'clock this morning. Inside it's lovely and cool within the thick stone walls. Even though it's climbed to 35 degrees outside, the thermometer inside shows only 22 degrees.

In the coolness of the house, I go on with getting the bedroom clean and in some order. I'm curious about the extraordinary amount of new linen stored in various trunks, all good quality and lovingly embroidered and edged with lace. Maria, the older lady who often walks by, may know why this is the case. I stop her for a chat to find out if she knows why there's so much bed linen in the house. Maria tells me that Soledad hand-embroidered linen to earn a little money.

'People would ask her to embroider the names of a couple on some sheets and then they'd give them as a wedding present,' Maria explains.

We've been told that Soledad had a son called Leonardo. There's a photo of a young lad in a white communion suit on Soledad's table in the bedroom she used as a desk. I ask her what Soledad's husband's name was. We only ever hear Soledad and Leonardo mentioned. She shakes her head and wanders off. I go back inside and continue with sorting the personal effects in the wardrobes so we can use the empty closets to put our things in. I look forward to filling the empty wardrobes with the contents of our backpacks. We've been taking loads of Soledad's clothes to the Humanidad charity bin. Some of her possessions are hard to part with. I very much like the white embroidered nightgowns. I fancy myself wearing this as I dramatically open the bedroom doors to the balcony, like a heroine from a bygone era.

As we meet the locals, they tell us more things about Soledad. It seems she was quite poor. There is no mention of a husband. I've asked a few neighbours now and the answers are evasive. It seems she was supported by her neighbourhood. Some have told us they gave Soledad things like clothes and furniture. Isabela, when passing by with her little dog, points at some rugs I've hung up to air and says, 'I gave her those.' She probably gave her some of the smart dresses too. Several villagers have now told us Soledad was the recipient of charity. A life full of hand-me-downs. The house may be overly full of junk because she couldn't afford to turn any gifts down.

~

I finish cleaning the bedroom and the room next to it so we can move in and have somewhere clean to put our bags as well. A little dirt-free haven amid the rubbish. Some of the sheets I find are still wrapped in plastic and are brand new. They will come in handy when the new mattress arrives. It looks like we'll be sleeping on the bedsheets intended as a wedding gift for Daniel and Lupe. How come no one picked up these sheets? Was the wedding cancelled or did they not get a chance to collect them before Soledad got sick? Maybe we'll meet a couple called Daniel and Lupe one day in the bar and we can tell them we're sleeping on their wedding linen.

There's also a bed we can use with the new mattress. Not sure how old it is, but we guess from around the 1920s. It's made of lovely silver metal in flowing lines, in what looks like an Art Deco style. Alex fashions some wood supports under the sagging spirals and we'll be good to go with a clean mattress. A baptism certificate for a girl called Maria Ximena hangs on the wall above the bed. It's dated 1885. I don't think it has moved in that time as the wall underneath it is discoloured in the shape of the picture frame. Who was she and why is it still here? Maybe Soledad's grandmother?

Before lunchtime I ring the mattress shop to confirm delivery this afternoon. A woman answers, not the man we ordered from.

'Ah,' she says. 'He mentioned he had a delivery to San Juan for Tuesday.'

'Nope, we agreed on Friday,' I say, trying to sound firm.

I hear her ringing him on another line while I wait. Unsolicited by me she tells him, 'The clients say that if they can't have it delivered today, they don't want it.'

She sounds like she's used to the shenanigans of the delivery man and knows exactly what to say. I wonder how much more efficient Spain would be with more female bosses like her? He rings a few minutes later to say that he will deliver today at four.

~

Josh has put the electrics on like Enrique, the electrician, showed us. Enrique deliberately slowed his actions down so we could get an exceptionally good view of what he did. Now with illegal electricity, we can use the vacuum cleaner we bought in town the other day.

While Josh helps Alex carrying some heavy furniture, I amble to the bakery to buy food before they close for the siesta. Walking out from 'our' house I pinch myself that this is really happening. I am not watching a movie about this, I'm doing it!

I go up through the village, passing the gorgeous stone house that belongs to Mari-Carmen of the Chorizo. Opposite Mari-Carmen lives a man we've met too, whose name is also Jesus. He'll be Jesus of the Square. I notice a specific fragrance in the air. It smells like pine trees today. Real ones, not chemicals in a bottle. Almazán always smells like the nearby pig farms, so this is a step up. I reach the next bigger square with the church, where the old men follow the shade on different benches as they chat. I have seen one fellow every time I've been in town. He's in a wheelchair and I've spotted him in front of the old people's home a few times too. I assume he's a resident there. He has an unusual way of moving about. While sitting in his wheelchair he uses his legs to move himself to where he wants to go. It looks odd but at least he's mobile.

Cristina in the *panadería* wants to know all about us. They still bake fresh bread in a massive wood-fired oven every day, and it's good country bread, seven days a week. In return, giving her some information is the first thing I can do for this community. They are bursting with curiosity. I understand that her role in passing news to the villagers is imperative and give her a few facts: our nationalities, that we're retired and love the village. She'll be able to share the news with her regulars.

'Why are you here, in this village?' is her next question. We're getting used to this enquiry and more prepared to answer it. I have been thinking a lot about why we are here. 'I'm confused, searching for something – what, I don't know – having a good time though' may not be what to say to practical strangers.

'Because it's close to many beautiful natural areas. We also love that there is a *panadería* and two bars. It's a lively village and close to the capital. We think we're really lucky to have found it!'

This village looks like it may have a reasonable future. The primary school has a full playground of screaming children, there are two banks, two butchers, two bars, a pharmacy and Cristina's *panadería,* which also sells a few groceries, fresh fruit, vegetables and good local wines. I get some freshly baked bread, some pastries, wine and cheese for later, as well as some garbage bags.

'I don't have a price on these,' Cristina says, pointing at the garbage bags. 'You can pay for them tomorrow.'

Wow, I haven't even slept here and already have credit in the shop.

~

The bar is a great place to hear stories about the old inhabitants of our home, as well as gossip and local myths. First and foremost, they all agree that the house is probably haunted. It's no good to have a house standing empty for too long.

The old bloke who drove to the bar in his tractor tells us, 'Those who lived there come back as ghosts, particularly if they did not get the last rites before they died.'

There's a lot of nodding around the bar as they all agree. We're interested in the more recent residents and encourage stories by buying a few rounds for the bar.

'Tell us about the family that lived there last?' I ask. 'Did you all know them?'

Another farmer with a round belly and a twitching eye, as if he's winking, makes himself comfortable on the bar stool. He's ready to hold forth.

'The property belonged to the Martinez family. The people everybody knows were Raul and Esmeralda, their daughter Soledad and her son, Leonardo. The last person to live here was Soledad.'

A third short fat bloke with a baked-in-the-sun look takes over the narrative from here: 'Her parents died and Leonardo moved out in the 1980s. She was there on her own after that.'

Winking Eye cuts back in, his voice strong and determined to hold the floor.

'Some eleven years ago, Soledad went to visit her sister in Calatayud, fell ill and ended up in a nursing home over there.'

'Everything shows that she was planning to come home. Beds made, clean washing folded on the bed, shoes lined up under the wardrobe, trinkets and custom jewellery on the bedside table. It's like someone left briefly and is due to come home any minute,' I contribute to the conversation.

Except it was left to be covered by spider webs and dust. It is heartbreaking to think none of her loved ones came to tidy up and look after her things. Possibly, some came and took what they wanted but left the rest. I'm saddened to think nobody honoured Soledad's memory by treating her precious possessions with respect.

'What about Leonardo? Is he dead too?'

The three short fat blokes all have something to say. Nobody says so outright, but it is alluded that Leonardo was a disappointment to his mother.

'He was very promising, clever in school and destined for a big future,' says the tractor driver, shaking his head mournfully.

No doubt we will find out a bit more one day, but all signs are that Leonardo went off the rails and did not become the success he was meant to be.

One patron who is not in our original group at the bar comes over and tells us: 'He was all take and no give, only came to see his mama when he needed money.'

Poor Soledad! We are determined to give her memory the regard she deserves. Everything points to a devout, impeccably dressed lady. The place is full of her memories. It looks like she filled her time with embroidery, baptisms, weddings, funerals and the holy mass. She would have gone up the hill every day to hear mass in the Church of Santa Lucia.

~

Alex and I have dinner at home in the garden just as the sun is setting. It's cool under the tree, with a little breeze. It's just bread, cheese, wine and some fruit. This is the moment I want to remember forever. Just sitting here together watching the sun go down after a hard day's work. I realise that I'm starting to come closer to what it is I'm looking for. Alex and I working together to follow a dream. A crazy dream of rescuing a ruin in Spain, but a shared dream.

'I'm happy,' I say to Alex and the world at large. 'I can't quite believe it,' I add, 'but this is our house.'

'Look at the sky,' Alex adds. 'The north star is right above us.'

The river babbles, some birds are calling as they settle for the night. Altogether it's been a thoroughly satisfying day. We go inside as night falls over the walled garden. The bedroom is now vacuumed and ready for sleeping. Inside the stone walls it's pleasantly cool with the French doors open to the balcony to let in a gentle little breeze. The mattress was delivered as promised and we're about to sleep our first night here. I guess we'll find out if it's haunted like everybody says.

Chapter 26

Soledad's Shame

After all our scrubbing and cleaning we dropped into bed exhausted last night. The bedroom, now free of spider webs, looks a treat. It's perhaps my best loved room in the house for now, with its low ceiling beams, whitewashed walls and wooden shutters on the French doors. The floorboards are wider than a dining table, and the bed, freshly made with clean, embroidered and lacy sheets, looks very romantic. Lying in bed you can look out through the French doors to the balcony, over our garden, the ruin and then the terracotta-tiled roofs beyond.

During the night there was no sign of Soledad or any other ghostly occupants. If there is a ghost, we didn't hear or see a thing. Today it's time to get back into a walk around the village before breakfast. We've been too occupied getting things ready to move in to have walks as well.

The village is delightful, with the main square and most of the old part on relatively flat ground. We're in the low part of town by the river so there's a short climb up to the main square through meandering, cobbled streets. All buildings in this part of town are made of stone like ours. The plaza is surrounded by three-storey homes in various stages of elegant decay. Once these would have been the stately homes of relatively well-off people. Very few are now in good condition. Paint is expensive and not a lot is left on many windows and doors. The look of gracious decline in the village is quite enchanting. About a third of the houses appear to be closed permanently, window shutters done up firmly, snow screens still in the doors, even though it's summer. Others show some signs of life, like washing drying on a line or a chair on the balcony. Some residents sit outside in the early morning sun and scrutinise us closely. By now everyone in town knows that some foreigners have bought the old place by the river. We say *buenos días* to all we encounter and friendly greetings are returned.

As we get back to our street, we notice that a neighbour is pruning an old olive tree in the garden to our left. The tree is in the front yard of an old handsomely restored mill house, likely to be the same age as our place. We stroll over to introduce ourselves as the new kids in town. Our neighbour is Virgilio and, on hearing voices, his wife, Ada, comes out too. The family lives in Logroño and this is the weekender shared between various family members. They tell us that the mill used to be a flourmill. There were many mills along the river, mostly for flour and timber. Ada mentions that it's their matriarch's eighty-fifth birthday today and we're invited to come and share a coffee after lunch to meet the rest of the family and help Mother Antonia celebrate her birthday.

We get some more cleaning done and spruce up a bit before Ada comes to get us after lunch. Caffeine quickly changes to alcohol. Gin and tonics all round as we get to know one another. Ada's full name is Inmaculada (the immaculate). Women are often given the names of some virtue or other. There are many Inmaculadas, Purificaciones (purification), and Marias de la Paz (Maria of the Peace) and so on. It makes me wonder why Soledad's parents thought solitude or loneliness was a good name for their baby daughter. From what we can gather, it is exactly what happened to poor Soledad after her parents died and her son left: she was alone and possibly lonely.

Birthdays (*cumpleaños*), as well as Patron Saint's Day (Santo, or Día del Santo) are both still celebrated. Spain is still very much a Catholic nation, at least in its traditions, and saints are still a big deal in most families. There are lists of saints and martyrs to choose from on several websites. For example, if someone is called Carmen, then the date that the Virgen del Carmen is commemorated, 16 July, is the day to wish Carmen a happy Día del Santo. Traditionally, many parents named their child after whatever saint was commemorated on the day the child was born. In the past, presents were only given to someone on their Patron Saint's Day. Now it's more customary to give gifts on their birthday only, although often the two still coincide. When I first lived in Spain during the 1970s, nobody partied on their birthday, only on their saint's day. There was no saint for most northern European names, so we all made one up so we could still have a party.

Our neighbours appear to be the classic extended Spanish family that hangs out together. There are three generations: the birthday matriarch, her two daughters and their husbands, and the combined teenage children. There's lots of teasing, lots of laughter, singing and celebrating the special birthday. Somewhere in the middle of the celebrations we get the tour of the mill house and Alex takes mental notes of how things have been renovated. Virgilio and his brother-in-law have done all the work themselves and are quite handy.

The old mill is enormous, renovated tastefully and with heaps of bedrooms to accommodate everybody. The features of the old mill machinery are carefully retained and visible behind glass. Birthday girl Antonia was born and grew up in the mill house, which has been in her family for generations. Her family and Soledad's have been neighbours for centuries. Antonia left home to work in the big city, Logroño, to the north, married there and stayed. She loves her village though and is grateful for the opportunity to spend time here with the whole family. She knew Soledad well, although she was a couple of years older. Antonia realises we're interested in the family who lived in the river cottage and begins to tell the story of the people she knew as a girl.

'Raul and Esmeralda were the adults in the house. Raul, a farmer, had fields around the village. He grew oats, wheat and corn like nearly all the farmers around here. He also kept a couple of milking cows, sheep and pigs. The couple had two daughters, Soledad and Catalina. Soledad was the eldest.'

Ada softly interrupts to say, 'They had other children too, didn't they Mum?'

'Yes. Sadly, Raul and Esmeralda had other children, but they died very young. They're all in the Martinez family grave in the cemetery.' Antonia shakes her head sadly as she shares this information.

'How many children did they lose?' I ask as sensitively as I can. I don't want to appear morbid.

Antonia looks up to the ceiling as if she may find the answer written there somewhere. Her brow furrows. It's all so long ago, she only heard the stories from her parents as this all happened before she was born.

'I don't remember exactly but I think there were three babies who died, two boys and a girl,' she finally states.

'When Soledad and Catalina were born in the late 1930s, Raul and Esmeralda were already in their late thirties. Knowing how precious life can be, they doted on their daughters. They did have to do chores though, like all children those days. The family kept a couple of milking cows in the dairy at the end of the garden,' Antonia says, pointing in the vague direction of the ruin in our garden, which apparently was the milking shed.

Antonia remembers the sisters taking the cows out to graze in the fields during the day after they'd done the milking in the morning. They'd then fetch them again in the late afternoon to spend the night in the dairy.

'You could hear the cows mooing at my place when they were ready to be milked in the morning,' Ada says, her eyes glazing at the memory.

Antonia enjoys her role as the storyteller and we're more than happy to hear her. I'm fascinated and want to pick her brains about everything she remembers of our new home, but I respect the fact that memories from long ago can't be rushed. Alex does tentatively ask about Leonardo. To our surprise, Antonia clamps her lips together, falling immediately silent. We won't get any more of the past out of her today. We're not sure what we've done wrong.

'It's alright,' her other daughter, Celia, tells us. 'Mama doesn't like to talk much about it ...'

Celia carries on telling the story.

'Poor Soledad fell pregnant out of wedlock in the early 1950s. It was a terrible shame on the family. There were lots of rumours at the time, but one persistent story was that her own uncle, her father's brother, got her with child.'

In those days and even now in Catholic countries, abortions are considered a mortal sin, graver than almost anything.

'Soledad gave birth to Leonardo when she was sixteen years old, an event that marked her for life,' Ada continues. She was fortunate in that her parents did not throw her out. She and her son lived with them until their deaths, some time in the 1970s. He did well in school, always coming first in the class. He redeemed his mother's shame by being such a good son. Leonardo later studied economics and became a teacher.'

We tell them about all the books on economics we found. We thought the books might have been his.

Antonia is willing to pick up the story again from here. 'Leonardo was clever, very clever. He was his mother's pride and joy.'

'Sadly, he went off the rails when he grew up. He became an alcoholic and brought new shame on his poor mother. He deceived others in town, borrowing money and not paying them back. He was even suspected of breaking and entering properties in the village, but that was never proven,' Antonia adds.

It's getting late and I fear we've overstayed the invitation for a coffee after lunch. We bid our new neighbours *adios*.

'Poor Soledad,' Alex says as we leave the mill house. 'She had some crosses to bear.'

These stories have made Soledad come alive for us. As she becomes more familiar to us, our empathy for this woman increases. When we stroll the few metres to our new home, past the ruin of the old dairy, we can almost hear her cows mooing.

~

Breakfast in the garden is fast becoming one of our favourite times. The mornings are crisp, with no sign yet of the heat to come. In the entrance room, where light from the front door shines on a big table, we've set up a rudimentary kitchen. On our rickety gas burner, we manage to toast yesterday's bread and coach the stove-top espresso maker into action. Every day we clean and scrub and haul junk from the attic. But for now, we sit under the linden tree, with coffee and toast, enjoying the still before the cleaning storm begins again.

The garden is an overgrown jungle where I work early each morning before it gets too hot. The front door is almost hidden in blackberry brambles, making getting in and out of the house a perilously scratchy journey. I'm slowly clearing the tumbling blackberries away from the stone wall of the garden and I unearth an area near the gate that is paved with huge flat stones. Everything is overgrown and the paving is covered with 10 centimetres of soil, growing blackberries and weeds on top. I've no idea how far the paving goes but I slowly work away at it. It looks like we have a good, well-advanced plum tree in the garden. I rediscover not only paving stones but muscles that have lain dormant for years. They take a little to warm up in the morning. My body may not be up for this but my mind is determined to keep going. Good hard physical work may be exactly what I need. Something to look back on at the end of the day and feel useful in some way.

Being in the garden gives me a chance to meet some locals. The house is only a few hundred metres from the main square, but at the same time it's on the edge of town, more like a farmhouse than a village house. This street would not normally see a lot of through traffic but, now there's an attraction, many saunter by to have a look at the foreigners who have bought the old pile of stones by the river. Early this morning I meet another inhabitant. His arrival at the garden gate gives me a chance to get up and stretch my aching back. Jacinto returned to his ancestral village after a lifetime in Barcelona. He's now retired and living in the square above us in a restored building that once belonged to his father. From his porch he can see the walled garden of Soledad's house. Jacinto has an impish grin and looks like a cheerful character. Many of the men we've met so far seem to have names starting with 'J'. We have met a Julian, a Javier, three Jesuses, a Jacinto, several Juans and two Juan Carloses to date.

Meanwhile, Alex is two levels up and continues to vacuum up pigeon poo and other animal droppings in the attic. The poor bastard is doing the worst job. He's swearing a lot. Luckily, the neighbours are some distance away and, if they are walking past, I don't think they'd understand the English expletives coming out of the roof. They may get the tone but hopefully not the meaning.

I've started cleaning the old kitchen, accumulating bags with old bread and loads of other food that's never been thrown out by the family. In the eleven years the house has been empty, the foodstuffs are nearly fossilised. The fridge opens eventually and, while there's no dead body inside, I find an eleven-year-old sausage and some cheese still inside. The fridge works now we have electricity, and I scrub the living daylights out of it while I daydream of the farmhouse-style kitchen we can have here, a place where I plan to create signature dishes to spoil old and new friends and family when they visit. Maybe a fine kitchen will miraculously make me a superb cook and friends will flock to Spain for our fabulous hospitality. I'm dreaming while cleaning but, after all, that's why we bought the house here, dreaming about what may be.

In my real life, I have a decrepit two-burner gas stove that can either go full bore or barely on, nothing in between, and frankly scares the hell out of me. We've bought a few plates, some cutlery, a bread knife, a sharp knife, a stove-top espresso coffee maker, wine glasses, a frying pan and a saucepan. Nothing yet to produce any culinary highlights, but I can still dream. I look forward to this stone cottage by the river making some sweet memories of sharing food and ideas with friends and family.

Meanwhile, I fill all the garbage and recycling bins in town to half full, leaving some space for others in the village. We do several trips to the tip for the bigger rubbish and reward ourselves with a cold drink in the bar.

Cristina in the *panadería* tells me that the summer residents have started to arrive for the long holidays. The week-long fiesta in Soria marks the start of summer. It will be a busy time soon with all the former residents escaping their respective cities for the slightly cooler mountain air, except that right now there's a heatwave all over Europe, including here. The big news is that the *panadería* will extend its hours to open after the siesta during the summer period.

~

As fixing the roof has the highest urgency, Alex continues to clean out the attic to give the builders clear access. The mountain of animal droppings may end up being traipsed everywhere unless we get rid of it now. Alex has a mask and goggles, to avoid catching any disease from years of wildlife happily pooing in the attic. This man is such a hard worker. Apart from animal droppings, the attic is a treasure trove of possessions from several generations. There are seven trunks up there, each full of family heirlooms. A peek inside one shows lots of incredibly old-looking documents. It will be too distracting to sort through these tempting papers now. We're working around them before we start to investigate the contents in detail. There's also a magnificent ceramic bowl in the attic. It looks old. Only a few days later we conclude that its position was strategic rather than coincidence, being used to collect rainwater leaking through the roof.

We're still camping rather than 'living' here. I clean the bathroom while Alex goes on with the never-ending job of cleaning the attic. When I say bathroom, I mean a bathroom of sorts. It's the unusual addition constructed when sewerage first came to town. As the river cottage is built below the road, the toilet had to be built at elevation. Several steps lead to the entrance of the bathroom, which is on a platform some 40 centimetres above the rest of the floor. There's a petite bath, one of those with a shelf to sit on, a sink and a toilet. They all seem to be in working order since Council Jesus turned the water on. What is trickier is the height of the room. When the floor was raised, the ceiling was not. This probably wasn't a problem for Soledad. Her clothes and her penchant for high heels tells me she was a shorty. But we can only enter with reverentially bowed heads and bent knees. We can't stand up straight and there's only cold water, but in the middle of a heatwave who cares? At the end of the day, we have a clean bathroom.

~

We need to register with the Ayuntamiento so they can bill us for water and council rates. We're attended by a young woman called Reina (Queen), an appropriate name as she appears to be the queen of the council office. I mess up the form and joke that it's because the bar is closed today and I've had no coffee yet. Reina says the local bars are closed because of the fiestas in Soria, and the closest bar open is a couple of kilometres away. Ah, that's near the *punto limpio* (rubbish tip), I say. We have to go there anyway as we've got things to throw out. We do at least two expeditions to the *punto limpio* every day, in addition to full carloads to the clothing charity containers in Soria town.

After the tip we go to the next village for a coffee in the bar Reina told us is open today. It's full of men in high-vis gear and some Guardia Civil in uniform. The bearded barman asks if we've been to the Ayuntamiento this morning.

'Yes?' I reply surprised, wondering if perhaps this is the barman's quirky opening line, rather than 'What can I get you?'

I'm about to share that we've also been to the tip in case that too is of interest.

The barman says, 'Reina called here to say there's one more form, and could you go back to the Ayuntamiento to fill out the form for the *diputación* (a type of land tax).'

As we're sipping our coffee, a man comes in who looks like Paco, the builder we consulted before we made an offer on the river cottage. When I get to the bar to pay, he recognises me too.

'Aren't you the one who wanted to buy the house by the river?' he asks.

'Yes, and we did buy it!' I reply with a cheery smile. 'Your advice gave us the confidence to make an offer.'

The entire bar has fallen silent as Paco and I talk to each other. Everyone is very keen to hear what's happening.

'In fact, I'm glad to run into you here because we'd really like a quote for the roof repair.'

Paco always seems to look like he's about to tell a joke, so I'm not quite sure about him when he says, 'Sure I can give you a quote. If you're there later today, I'll come around and do that.'

~

After our coffee in the bar, Alex, with a dust mask on, is in the attic again bringing down box after box of trunk contents for me to sort through. More possessions, particularly shoes. How many shoes can one person have? Soledad must have had some eighty pairs, since we started the clean-up we've come across box after box of high-heeled shoes. There are also more clothes, corsets, long johns and the like, some of it incredibly old. The amount of paper in the loft is overwhelming. Never was a piece of paper thrown out by this family. Magazines dating to the 1950s, 60s and 70s. Brigitte Bardot is on the cover of one, looking about eighteen years old. We store some of these in the barn to have a good look at later, while we fill up every paper-recycling container in walking distance with old newspapers.

Apart from loads of paper for recycling, and shoes and corsets, Alex also brings down some exquisite finds. Antique water jugs, a washbowl with a 1920s stand, and much more. After cleaning the more precious items outside, we store all we want to keep in the barn for now. We're slowly filling the barn with treasures to use in the future.

The reward of our labour is a glass of wine in the garden, admiring our progress as we clean this hoarder's house. It's lots of work but so worth it for the treasures we unearth. If we'd hired people to clean it out, everything would have been thrown out, whereas we are able to sift through the junk. We've found many gems to refurbish the cottage with once we renovate. We move up to the bedroom early. It's not dark yet and the room has a soft twilight shimmer. The electric light in the bedroom doesn't work but the candlelight is charming. Alex brings up another glass of wine as we sit and look out through the French doors over our garden and the roofs of the neighbouring homes. It's remarkably private. Slow raindrops, silver in the evening light, drift unhurriedly down onto the terracotta tiles. This scene is close to the magic of fairytales. I'm overwhelmed with gratitude that this is now our own piece of my beloved Spain. A glorious realisation that we are here, still together after nearly forty years, in our home in a quaint cobblestoned Spanish village.

Chapter 27

Poco a Poco

We start the day with a cuppa in bed, looking at the daytime view over the garden. We had no dinner last night and there's no breakfast this morning, so after the cup of tea we go to a bar for something more substantial to eat. They have freshly made tortilla with some slices of baguette – heavenly. The boy behind the bar with his scrawny beard is slowly warming to us and becoming more talkative. We have lunch here most days as we're still not set up for anything more than scrambled eggs with chorizo or a simple omelette with a salad at home. After breakfast there's more cleaning and gardening. Regular walkers pass by every day. Walking must be what the doctors in the entire nation have agreed to advise their geriatric patients. It's quite common to see an older person with a cane or even a walking frame a couple of kilometres out of town. They don't seem to go anywhere in particular, just ambling along the road out of town. We don't see any young ones doing this. Like youngsters in all progressive countries, they go to the local gym rather than go for a walk. Isabela, an older woman with a set of large yellow teeth, comes by twice daily as she walks her elderly dog. Maria who lives at the end of our street, grey haired, elderly and walking with a stick, takes her daily constitutional past our house too. Alex chats with her when he's in the garden, quickly reaching the limit of his Spanish.

The locals are fascinated by the resurrection of the garden. Lots of villagers come past the house only to see what's happening, I suspect. Jacinto, Mari-Carmen and many more ask how it's going. They stop at the gate and call out, '*Como van las cosas?*' At the end of the conversation all say, '*Ah, poco a poco*' (little by little). We agree with that!

Today I meet Guadalupe, who lives higher up in town. She's possibly a cleaner as she is carrying a tote of cleaning materials.

Guadalupe tells me to call her Lupe and states: 'I bet the house is full of useless old stuff!'

'Well, yes, there is a lot of stuff in the house,' I reply, slightly evasively.

'All the old women are like that here,' she adds. 'Never throw anything out as it may come in handy later.'

She's right of course. Soledad and those before her never discarded anything. We're not merely cleaning up after one hoarder but several generations of them. That's potentially why the price of the house was so good. Nobody wanted to empty it out.

Alex has been attacking the attic for days now. Trash and treasure keeps coming down the timeworn steps. Another jaunt to the *punto limpio* is in order and yet another load of treasures goes to the barn for safekeeping. He finds copper cooking pots that have been mended beautifully, oversized wine or olive-oil bottles, and books, books and more books. The archaic-looking tomes are all about economics and accounting, textbooks that are decades out of date. They're likely to have been Leonardo's. I'm not sure what use they would be to anyone now.

Meanwhile in the garden, I weed around the dry stone wall separating the garden from the steep incline to the little river. Below runs the canal to the mill house at the end of the road. Lichens and lush mosses decorate the stones that were placed in this spot hundreds of years earlier. I cut back some more grasses and wash some windows while I wait for Alex to bring down more trash or treasure to be cleaned and sorted.

~

Paco, the builder, didn't come yesterday and I ask at the Ayuntamiento if they have his phone number. I assume they do as we've been told he's married to the mayoress of the town.

'Sorry, I forgot,' he says when I call. 'I called Jesus from the Ayuntamiento to see if he had your number.' He promises to come later today.

I also ring the *fontanero* (plumber) recommended by the Ayuntamiento to see if we can have hot water and a tap in the garden. Fernando the plumber says he will come between twelve and one.

Before we hang up, I confirm, 'So we'll see you between twelve and one?'

'Yeah, something like that.' I can almost see the shoulder shrug he must be doing through the telephone line.

Fernando arrives, together with Paco the builder, at 1.30pm, only half an hour later and actually on the agreed day. Not bad. Fernando, the *fontanero*, can do a tap in the garden but he's not sure about the gas cooker and hot water.

'It's not even worth checking either as the gear is old and probably unsafe,' he says.

Meanwhile, Paco goes up in the roof and measures outside. Most beams are fine, the boards under the eaves need replacing on the street side but only one board on the side of the garden. He will give us his quote this week. Fernando says he will come on Thursday to do the tap. He says this so reluctantly that I have a hard time believing him.

~

On our next visit to the *punto limpio* we meet Rafael. He's a tall flamboyant man in his late forties or early fifties who wears an endearingly daggy yellow terry towelling hat. He's a painter and sculptor, he tells us, and also runs a *casa rural* on the main square. He's very chatty but has no English other than, 'One pint of Guinness, please,' he tells us. He'll drop around if he may, as he's heard about the stone floor in the barn. Both the barn and the *trastero* (junk room) indeed have a stone floor laid with round river pebbles. He also says he will cook us a meal one day. He seems to love our house. He waxes lyrical about the shape of the roof and its location next to the river. He wanted to buy it but had no money. He also raves about the width of the floorboards. These are indeed amazing.

We chat for so long at the waste-recycling centre that I have to run to the *panadería* before it closes to buy some bread for lunch. I make it in time to buy a fresh baguette before Cristina shuts up shop for the siesta.

~

As I hang out some old blankets to air on the balcony, an old four-wheel drive slows down outside. I recognise a familiar figure from the bar. It's the ruddy-faced, dicky-legged man who told us he came to the river cottage as a young boy to help with the *matanza*, the slaughter of the pigs. He stops the car and tells us how happy he is that we have bought the house.

'Anything I can do, just ask me!'

'I don't know your name!' I call out as he's about to drive off.

'Jesus,' he replies.

Surprise, surprise. We have a full set of Jesuses now. Dicky Leg

Jesus is a regular at the bar in the middle of town, often as we're having a coffee. We have a little chat every now and then. I like how he arrives in his tractor most of the time. One day when he walked in, he saw us and walked right out again. He came back a minute later with a dozen eggs.

'*Regalo de mis gallinas*,' he says, smiling. (A present from my chickens.) 'Welcome to San Juan.'

Meanwhile, Alex carries more and more things down from the attic. He's at it all day and reminds me of the Eveready Bunny from the battery advertisements. He just keeps on going and seems to have the energy of several young blokes. Meanwhile, I am totally buggered – my body's not willing anymore. The novelty of house cleaning wore off a few hours ago. It doesn't take me long to convince Alex to join me for a glass of wine in the garden. He's satisfied with his work in the attic today. His exciting finds among the trash and treasure include a sausage maker and an implement to cork bottles. We too can make our own wine and sausages one day. These people had so many useful skills.

We talk about how we may landscape the garden. I dream of something lovely and colourful surrounded by the historic stone walls. Alex thinks it needs a grapevine if we're going to make wine and use the corker. Someone in the bar will know what type of grapevine will work in this climate. Alex points here and there to old stone terraces and neglected garden beds. Meanwhile, we sit in the garden, exhausted but satisfied with the day's work. Another villager comes to say hello. The locals are curious about these *guiris* and enjoy watching us go about life in the old Martinez house. Felipe lives in the house at the end of our street opposite the family in the mill house. He's worked and lived in Madrid most of his adult life, he tells us, leaving here at sixteen to find work. He's now returned in retirement to restore an old barn next to his ancestral home.

'I was born in the house opposite the ruin at the end of your garden,' he tells us.

That building, like our ruin, is now missing its entire roof. He owns that ruin together with some *primas* (cousins) who also live in the village.

'I've been in your house many times,' he says. 'You step down to get into the kitchen.'

We mention we've found some envelopes full of black-and-white images. Could he tell us who they are?

Felipe thoughtfully gets his reading glasses from his shirt pocket. He recognises several faces in the photographs.

'That's Raul and Esmeralda, taken here in the garden! It would have been in the 1950s.'

A small black-and-white picture with a scalloped white edge shows a couple standing, stone-faced, next to the front door.

Felipe adds, 'Esmeralda and Raul died maybe some twenty-five years after this photo was taken.'

We put the photos back in the envelope and Felipe asks if we're making progress cleaning out the house.

'*Si*,' Alex replies, '*poco a poco*.' Felipe agrees that's how it's done. Their smiles overcome any language or cultural differences.

Chapter 28

Dining with the Locals

Once more, our life finds a new rhythm in our new home. A cup of tea in bed is becoming a bit of an early-morning ritual. Our bedroom is surprisingly private given that we are on the edge of a village. After that, we have breakfast in the garden or in a bar after a walk. Today it's in the next village, only fifteen minutes' walk away. We have coffee and *madalenas* – miniature cakes eaten for breakfast that are a bit like a plain muffin. Our mission here is checking out garden and courtyard designs for inspiration. It looks like most traditional houses have a courtyard paved with natural stone.

On our way back we see a large lad on a ride-on mower disappearing in the distance. We need our grass mowed as neighbours are warning us about snakes in the long grass because we're next to the river. A gentleman in a T-shirt with green writing sees us looking and points, saying, 'He's gone over there.' He walks with us to show us exactly. Not surprisingly, T-shirt man has heard we bought Soledad's house and come from Australia. The ride-on mower stops near us and I explain we need someone to mow our garden. Jorge is the gardener's name.

'My dad will come around in an hour,' Jorge says.

A couple of hours later, Jorge Senior arrives with Jorge Junior in tow. Dad is a large man too with a white beard and a floppy hat.

'I used to do this garden for Soledad many years ago,' he tells me. 'The boys and I can come and do this for you.'

He walks around and asks what needs to be done. He will cut the grass, take rubbish away, cut down a 'bad' tree in the ruin and pull the tall weeds. Unfortunately, the 'bad' tree is a lovely chestnut that's sprouted too close to the wall of the ruin. It will push the wall over if we let it grow. We accept his exorbitant quote, knowing we need to have this done and we don't know anybody else who can do it for us. It must take more time than we think.

'I'll be back to do it tomorrow,' Jorge Senior assures us as he leaves.

~

While we're working away in the house, the fiestas in Soria have continued. Today there is a procession from the town hall through the main street and the vast park. We don't want to miss this, so we down tools and get ready. We've laundered our clothes with cold water in the old washboard sink like Soledad would have done. A cold shower in the middle of a heatwave is not too distressing, although washing spider webs out of my hair takes a while. We clean ourselves up as best we can.

We get a good spot in the park to see the parade. For an hour and a half people promenade in fancy outfits representing their *Peña*. A *Peña* is a grassroots community group where popular folklore, usually music, dancing and other artistic expressions, are showcased, all accompanied by food and drink, of course. All ages are represented in the procession, from tiny tots to the very old. Everyone struts their stuff in traditional costume, women showing off gorgeous, embroidered shawls in deep reds and greens, long black skirts and white stockings, while men wear black knickerbockers and vests. Many couples promenade arm in arm, their free arm poised defiantly in a hands-on-hip gesture. Some couples have a child by the hand, while others march in groups of mixed ages and genders. What they all have in common is the obvious pride in what they are representing. The expressions of the participants says it all: overwhelming delight and gratification. Tradition still counts for so much here. It's amazing how long this human caravan goes on. This is not a few weirdos who like to dress up. This is an important ritual with all of Soria out on the streets today. Marchers get together in their *Peña* regularly throughout the year to rehearse their marching and their music. Each *Peña* has its own band. Again, we see our old neighbour Lorenzo from Almazán in the procession with his band.

The last several hundred people in the procession are running in a snake-like fashion rather than walking. They zigzag across the road holding hands, but for what reason we do not know. We ask some other spectators what this represents, but nobody is any the wiser. It doesn't seem to matter though. All are dressed in white pants and T-shirts with a bolero of a bright colour, either green, blue, yellow or whatever colour represents their *Peña*. A coloured handkerchief is tied around the neck, too. All the blues hold hands and run together, as do all the yellows and so on. As it's so hot today, spectators cool the runners down using spray guns and by throwing water over them from their bottles. It's great fun to watch.

Tomorrow is apparently the 'day of dancing', we're told. Protagonists will dance from the centre of Soria to the Ermita of San Saturio on the outskirts of the town. I'm not sure why there's dancing and when I ask several onlookers they don't seem to know either. Different *Peñas* organise it. That's all we manage to find out.

~

This evening we're invited for dinner by Rafael del Punto Limpio (Rafael of the Tip). At about ten o'clock in the evening, just as the sun is going down, we toddle to what we believe is his house, right next to one of the bars. We find some others we have met before, neighbours Ada and Celia, with their husbands, Virgilio and Mateo, already on the terrace of the bar. They too have been invited to Rafael's. They tell us to have a drink here first as it's too early to go for dinner. More guests soon arrive. After a drink, we enter Rafael's yard through colossal imposing gates. There are some twenty of us for dinner. The sun has just set and the light is waning. Behind the house, on the paved courtyard, one long table is set up ready for dinner.

We dine outside on the enormous patio, lined with grapevines. Soft lighting comes from standing lamps that have been brought outside. The food is exquisite and memorable. For starters there are yabbies Mateo caught by hand in the river below our house. They are cooked in a tomato and garlic sauce, which we scoop up with the village bread. There are *empanadas* stuffed with tomatoes and tuna made by Victoria, a new acquaintance, along with a variety of cheeses and *embutidos* (cured meats). Rafael, apparently the Renaissance man, has cooked the next dish, *pulpo en su tinto* (octopus in its ink). It's possibly the best octopus I have ever tasted and is served with timbales of rice.

There's been singing throughout the evening, traditional ballads known by most. Our host has an impressive tenor but the main singers are Mari-Carmen, Ada and Celia, with others joining in when they know the words. These are the folksongs dedicated to the fiestas of Soria. They praise the bravery of the bull, who is then promptly eaten. The beef dish made by Susanna, another new acquaintance, is made of bull that she bought in Soria. After the fiestas, the bull fights and the killing of the bulls, the meat is sold at auction. It's succulent and flavoursome, despite the unpleasant end the animal must have suffered. As a foreigner you may have different animal-welfare standards but you can't offend your host or his guests. I can't deny the dish was delicious though.

Each fiesta day has its own composition and must be sung many times that day. Mari-Carmen has a beautiful voice and knows most of the words to the songs.

The next courses are desserts, a *flan* (egg custard) made by Mari-Carmen of the Chorizo. These custards are still made the traditional way with egg yolks and cream, cooked in the oven. Drinks flow freely and empty wine bottles line up on both sides of the patio. There's also Basque cider, served via a contraption that makes extra bubbles. No one is drunk but we're all merry. Rafael made sangria to go with the entrees and, later, mojitos with sugar, lime, ice, white rum and lemonade. Rafael makes Alex come with him to the garden to select the *hierba buena* (mint) for the mojitos, pointing out the stars in the northern skies. The Milky Way is right over our heads, like a van Gogh painting. They are all speaking Spanish, including Alex. The cider, sangria and the mojitos have pushed his inhibitions about grammar away and he's chatting freely. Friendships have always come Alex's way effortlessly.

Suddenly, everybody is up and taking things into the house. Tables are dismantled and carried around the back. Rafael shows us some of his sculptures and paintings. He's exceptionally good. He lovingly strokes the sensuous statues as he shares where each of the marbles came from. Murcia, Alicante, Galicia. He has an impressive number of sculptures called *Woman Waiting for Her Lover*. They are exuberant sculptures of women with generous bosoms. He strokes each cold breast lovingly before he moves to the next.

As we stagger home from Rafael's house at 2am, the *verbena* (dance) is in full swing. The fiestas in our village have started now that Soria is finishing theirs. A massive truck arrived earlier today at the square by the church. It has a slide-out podium attached to it where the band performs. The square is softly lit, with the old Church of Santa Lucia illuminated like an exclamation mark. There are three stork nests on the four-cornered bell tower. The storks are home and don't seem too concerned by the lights. Some two hundred youths hang around on the square, some dancing. It looks like they have brought their own booze as the bar is closed. The music of the *verbena* stops soon after we get home, or maybe we don't hear it after the various concoctions we've consumed. I get the feeling that having Rafael as a neighbour might be bad for my liver, though it might be extremely helpful if we want to get to sleep on fiesta nights.

~

We wake up a little late after our night of partying, although we're still up before nine, as we're expecting the gardeners. This inability to stay in bed may never make us good Spaniards. At least we should try to master the siesta. A gardening crew of four, led by Jorge Senior, arrives just on nine o'clock. Holy crap, they are on time, that's a surprise. They get right into it, flinging grass about with a whipper-snipper. There's something gung-ho about Jorge the Elder. He does not inspire trust, either in his horticultural ability or honesty. As soon as I think this, he starts up a chainsaw to take down the newly found plum tree we were so pleased to find. I run down to ask him to leave that one please. After forty-five minutes of rushed activity, Jorge the Younger says they are going to the tip to take the first load. I'm not sure why all four are going. I assume it's morning tea time. Only two of them return some time later. They finish not long after that.

'How much do I owe you?' I ask as they're packing up the truck to leave, thinking I must have misheard the quote he gave yesterday.

Jorge the Elder repeats the exorbitant figure he quoted.

'You're shitting me, right?' I say in rather good colloquial lingo to make him think he's not dealing with a naive tourist. As they've done the job in a very short time, it may be hard for him to justify the quoted fee. Jorge the Elder has no such qualms. He insists that this little fortune he charges for the work is a fair price. I guess we'll learn soon enough what the going rate is. Meanwhile we're probably ripped off, even if it is good to get the garden tidied up.

~

Jesus of the Table is the next appointment for the day. He comes to collect the table he bought from Xavier, the previous owner. It's a beautiful antique that took pride of place in Soledad's bedroom. She used it as a desk, proudly displaying a photo of what we assume is Leonardo as a young boy, in his communion outfit. It would have been a special day for the family. Although many people have hinted that Leonardo was not a good son, Soledad would have still loved him with all her heart. It's sad to think he never came here after her death to take care of her affairs. Now strangers from the other side of the world are bundling up her possessions, handling her private things. If there's an afterlife, as we think Soledad vehemently believed there was, I hope she knows we're doing this with love in our heart for her, this unknown woman.

There were lots of unopened bills piled on top of this table when we first saw the house. We've cleaned the table up and emptied a draw full of broken pencils, rusty paperclips and broken rubber bands so it's ready to be collected. Jesus arrives close to the appointed time, dressed like the archetypical *pijo*, a preppy Spaniard, in his chinos, polo shirt with a turned-up collar. This continues to be the look of the arch conservative classes in Spain. The old upper-class families often still smart over the end of the dictatorship and I'm still always a little wary of them, but Jesus seems nice enough. We help him lower the table over the balcony and carry it through the garden to his car. It doesn't fit and he says he'll return with someone to help him remove it. For the next hour I joke about the second coming of Jesus, which I think is hilarious, but Alex tires of my joke quickly. Finally, Jesus does show up with his wife. She drives the car while he walks, supporting the table, which rests precariously on the car's rear end. In the olden days he would have had minions doing the lifting, I'm sure. How things have changed. I do hope they get it home in one piece though.

~

I often think about Soledad as I'm sorting through her things: as we carry out the table she sat at every night; as I get the bed linen she hand-embroidered to put on our bed; as I decide which of her clothes to throw out and which to donate. At some moments I feel like an intruder, like some Goldilocks, sleeping in a bed that's not mine, in a house that's not mine. Did she know she wasn't going to inherit the house, but her younger sister was? Why would that have been the case? Was this done to make sure Leonardo, the good-for-nothing son, did not get his hands on it? Someone will tell us one day.

~

Renske comes for lunch today so I pick up a few bits and pieces at the *panadería*. We'll have a seafood salad, cheeses and cold cuts with the freshly baked bread. The lovely bottle of red wine our guest brings completes the lunch. Having lived in Renske's house, we feel quite close to her, probably closer to her than she feels to us as we lived among her things, read her books and ate from her plates. We enjoyed the lovely garden she grew, which kept surprising us with new flowers as the weather warmed up.

We have a coffee outside where the now-mown garden looks like a set for a fancy fashion shoot with a ruin in the background. A linden tree in the middle of the garden shades us from the hot sun. We sit at a big round table we found in the barn, now covered with a white tablecloth and a vase of tall white and purple wildflowers. We were lucky to have found some old mismatched chairs in the barn as well. I imagine having new friends and family visit while we have lengthy lunches on long tables in this rustic garden.

Renske loves Soledad's house too. There's lots to be done but it has great potential, she agrees. She, more than anyone we've met so far, understands an obsession with old stone houses in a foreign country. She's been there and done it.

We chat about everything from home restorations to politics in various countries and the things we've done in our lives. We go for a drink on the square. As we pass the swimming pool, a load of walkers come down from the hills. One hiker must really be feeling the heat, as he strips off, butt naked, splashing water on himself with a garden hose in the park – a chubby middle-aged man with a proud beer belly who seems quite happy to show himself off. Oh Spain, how you have changed with regard to sexuality. Uptight and decades behind in the 1970s, Spain now seems on par with progressive northern Europe. A couple of generations ago, girls had to be home by 10pm and were only allowed out with a chaperone. Now they're out dancing in the streets in high-cut shorts until five in the morning. Nobody bats an eye at the naked man, as if there's one in the park all the time.

A good example of the changing times is the story of Amparo. Forty years ago, Amparo used to babysit my nephew Josh when he was a young boy. She was seventeen and had a boyfriend who wanted to marry her. Hanging out with independent northern

European women, Amparo wisely did not want to get tied down at a young age. The boyfriend didn't take no for an answer and kidnapped her, driving her to the mountains and keeping her in his car overnight. When they came back to the village the following morning, the parents on both sides had already organised the wedding. Poor Amparo had no choice and was married the following weekend. No white wedding dress for her, as she was spoiled goods now. In her baby-blue dress she was walked to the church by her father. He did not even bother with a tie, looking nonchalant in a rumpled suit and an open-necked shirt, walking with his face to the ground, looking ashamed. The events during the wedding reception are even more memorable. During the cutting of the cake, feisty Amparo was still so angry about the whole situation she threw a handful of cake at her new husband rather than cutting it in the customary way. This enraged his family and, before we knew it, both sides of the family were throwing cake and punches at each other. Wedding guests were rolling on the floor, covered in cake and hitting one another.

Amparo was divorced as soon as the divorce laws in Spain were enacted after the death of the dictator Franco on 20 November 1975. He appointed one of the royals, King Juan Carlos, as his successor, and the king gently transformed Spain into the modern democracy it is today. Divorce laws were enacted a few years later. Now Spanish girls of seventeen have the same freedoms as those in the rest of Europe. These changes happened in just a couple of generations. Memories and more memories float back by just being here.

~

The days are long and it's still light when Renske leaves for Almazán. We promise to keep in touch as our homes are relatively close. We go to bed earlier tonight after all our socialising in the last couple of days. It's not long after the summer solstice and it's light until nearly eleven in the evening. Soon after dark, we're between Soledad's sheets in her old bed. It's a little weird I must admit. Lights out (well, candles) by midnight.

I lie awake for a while thinking about how the house may look when Paco the builder fixes things up. I fall asleep designing a new bathroom with a claw bath and rustic tiles. As I drift off, a thunderstorm that's been brewing for hours finally gets going. Rain begins to fall, softly at first, and my sleepy mind combines my dream with reality and I think I'm in the claw bath. I eventually wake up sopping wet. It turns out that the leaks in the roof are quite substantial, with solid drips hitting us and the new mattress. Alex is still fast asleep.

'Alex, the rain! We're getting wet!'

He jumps up, looking dazed and shaking his head, trying to work out what's happening.

Before long we're both racing around to find materials to solve the problem. The enormous plastic bag the mattress was delivered in has the potential to save the situation. We pin the bag to a ceiling beam and it makes an improvised tent over the bed. Water runs off to the floor, through the cracks in the floorboards down to the ground below. The surface downstairs is stone, so that's not a problem. A few towels on the mattress to soak up the rain and we try to go to sleep again. Morning seems to come too soon after all the night-time commotion. We now understand why there were so many vessels in the attic. They were not only stored there, they were providing an essential service. This roof leaks in a spectacular way.

Chapter 29

Unpacking History

We've now emptied all seven trunks in the attic so we can carry these big chests down and store them in the barn. Some of the chests are pieces of art. All are wooden, some with dome tops, brass handles and locks. Others are less decorated and flat on top, but they're all very desirable. In one we find some lovely coach lamps and bundles of official papers wrapped in parchment. We indulge briefly in deciphering some of the old documents, finding them to be over two hundred years old. It looks like some of the land was exchanged for another bit of land and both parties signed a contract. The signatures are scratchy as if the person can barely write their name. There must have been a scribe in the village who drew up the paperwork for locals. When I arrived in Spain in the 1970s, there was still a lot of illiteracy. Many of the older folk didn't know how to read or write.

Some documents have the word *hijuela* at the top. I don't know the word and when I look it up the dictionary says 'little daughter' as a translation. It looks like a dowry list, dated 1857, itemising what a woman called Isabela brings to the marriage with Santiago, including:

Three flannelette night dresses

Seven underpants

18 embroidered bedsheets

12 embroidered pillow slips

4 table cloths

One quilt

A dress for church

Who was the Isabela at the centre of this agreement? Feasibly it might have been Soledad's great-great-grandmother. Did she ever get new underpants during the marriage or was she made to make them last a lifetime? Some of the corsets and long johns we found in the attic were certainly made to last, some are more darn than the original material. These dowry papers were signed by both the husband-to-be and the father. Meanwhile, I suppose Isabela was busy embroidering the table cloths. How times have changed, but how few years have passed since this was the norm.

Several other handwritten documents are birth, death and marriage certificates dating back to the late 1700s. Others are records confirming the buying and selling of bits of land. In a notebook with dates from the early 1900s, someone has calculated each year how much grain he will grow and how much he can sell it for. We're racing to get the house ready for the big roof repair and can't indulge in reading these tantalising records in too much detail now. I wrap them carefully again and place them in the same trunk, which is now in the barn. I can't wait to have the time to get to these papers and see exactly what they are. It would be right to offer them to the vendors but not until after we've had a good look.

When we get home from a trip to the nearby museum, we have another visitor waiting. His name is Andres, he tells us, and he's the builder who put the roof on the barn twenty-two years ago. He did a good job; it still looks particularly solid. Unfortunately, he was never paid and would like us to make up for this as we are the ones benefitting from the new roof. He tells us a long story about Soledad's 'scoundrel' son, Leonardo, and how he was the one who arranged for the new roof and then did not pay. I explain that we have bought the house free of any debts and don't feel responsible for Leonardo not paying him twenty-two years ago. Would he like to see the contract that confirms that we bought the property debt-free?

'No, I will take your word for it,' he concedes with a sad little smile.

I give him Xavier's telephone number, as the contact for the vendors, and suggest he should talk to him. Andres is a nice old fellow, now retired, but he still does odd jobs, he says. We have heard his name around town as he's a well-respected builder. He shuffles off after a while, conceivably disappointed that these supposedly crazy foreigners did not feel the need to pay Leonardo's dues.

Xavier rings the next day to apologise for the visit from Andres. He wants to make sure we are not unduly alarmed by the claim for payment. He's spoken to Andres and explained it's all Leonardo's liability. Again, we hear about what a disappointment Leonardo has been to his family. Such a clever child with so much promise until he went off the rails. I now understand better why Xavier placed such importance on changing the locks on the house. In hindsight I think he might have been worried that Leonardo still has some keys to his old home and may come to rob us some time in the future.

~

Alex screws a new bulb into the light socket of the small room on the ground floor we think was the *trastero*, the junk room. After he's been clearing trash for a while he calls, 'Come and have a look at this!' When I come in, he shows me some pencil marks on the wall. We take photos to make the images bigger and decipher dates, the

259

names of Soledad and her sister, Catalina, and their heights. This was the room set up for the slaughter of pigs the locals have told us about. Perhaps they weighed the children here along with the pigs. We'll have to find out how to preserve these pencil marks on the whitewash, as they're part of the wonderful history of the house.

In the *trastero* ropes and wire are strung between the ceiling beams. Remnants of dried garlic, paprikas and herbs are suspended from these wires. Above each bunch there's a lid from a tin, rodent control the old way. Rats and mice would not be able to get around these.

~

Little by little we make ourselves more comfortable in the house. There are bits and pieces of furniture we use to make the house a little more homely. We get to know the neighbours and other locals a little better as time rolls on. Summer fades into autumn and then into early winter as we work in the garden and plan what needs to be done to the house to make it more liveable. It's still a bit like camping, which is fine while the summer lasts but as the season changes it gets tougher to have those cold showers.

The winters are very severe in this part of Castile. As it is now, the roof will further collapse with the weight of a good dumping of snow. We asked Paco a few weeks ago to give us a quote to repair the roof and put a wood heater in as we'll need it soon. We're totally dependent on Paco getting this done before the first snowfalls.

We're having lunch in one of the bars when Paco finds us to hand-deliver the quote for the roof repair. It's very reasonable and we accept it on the spot. He promises to repair the roof before the first winter snow, so that it does not collapse any further. We believe him. For some reason Paco inspires confidence. We offer to pay a deposit as we know he needs funds to buy the wooden beams and other materials.

' No need.' He laughs and waves his hand in a dismissive sort of a way. 'Don't worry about it. It will be done before winter.'

Out of the blue, just before the Spanish winter really sets in, Paco arrives with some large machinery, blocking the entire street of Calle del Huerto. In no time there are multiple men on the ridge loading a conveyer belt transporting the roof tiles down to the road. The old handmade tiles are carefully stored before they go back on the roof once the rotten beams have been replaced. Paco has started the repairs just before the first snow arrives, as promised. After a few very dusty days we have an insulated roof without a hole.

It's mid-winter, we have no hot shower and still only an illegal electrical connection that will not take a heater. We can't get the electricity upgraded until all plans for restoration are approved by the council. It's freezing and snowing but now Paco has put in the wood heater we can survive the sub-zero conditions. We've furnished the old kitchen with some of the furniture stored in the barn. A round table and a few chairs. A low wooden chair sits next to the hearth under a window that looks out over the river below. The poplar trees lining the river are bare, allowing us to look through the branches to see the snow-capped mountains in the distance.

On the first day after the heater goes in we crumple some newspaper, get a few dry sticks from the garden and some timber left over from the roof repairs to coax some modest flames in the wood heater. Paco phones to check if we're home.

'Go and stand in the street,' he demands. 'I'm driving by to give you two a gift.'

We stand rugged up in the street in the fading light of the last sunrays. Within minutes he comes around the corner with a big truck loaded with firewood.

'This is the good stuff, oak. It should keep you warm for longer.'

He offloads the timber by tilting the truck backwards. It's getting dark and now there's a load of lumber all over the road.

'Don't worry about that,' he says, waving his arms about. 'Nobody comes through this street in the evening.'

We stoke the new wood heater with Paco's gifted oak into an inferno to heat at least one room. The metre-thick walls will take time to warm up. A few days ago we raided the many wooden trunks to put old blankets on the bedroom floor to cover the gaps between the floorboards, where cold air comes up from below. At night we fill some hot-water bottles with boiling water from the little gas burner. This will do for now.

~

There's no summer crowd now, in the middle of winter. In the bar we're treated like locals. Alex gets slapped on the shoulder by every farmer, while I get kissed on both cheeks by stubbly blokes and all the women. We've slipped into the rhythm of the village, buying the daily bread from Cristina in the *panadería*, a coffee in one of the bars, a glass of wine and some tapas in the evening.

When we first arrived last year we were introduced to the only other foreigner in the village. Ricardo (I assume he once was Richard) is a Californian who arrived as a hippie in the 1960s and married a local girl from the next village along. Every morning he saunters over to the bar at mid-morning, sits on the terrace with a cigar and a glass of sherry and chats to the other regulars. He wears a fedora and a silk scarf in sharp contrast to the farmers in their muddy work clothes. Yet he's very much part of the fabric of this community. Richard is a real life example of how you can be a foreigner and belong at the same time. Living here, we will never *not* be foreigners, but we will perhaps be *their* foreigners.

We've been planning the restoration of the house for a few months and now that Paco has done the roof we ask him to do some more work for us. During the day we're racing about in the nearby capital of Soria, selecting tiles for the bathroom and the floor in the main farmhouse kitchen. Choosing a hot-water system, stove, fridge, washing machine and the like. Paco takes us to his *nave*, a humongous barn storing materials he's removed from old houses he's renovated over the years. He lets us select a bath, sinks, doors and all sorts of things to make sure the river cottage retains its old-world look.

In the evenings we come back to a freezing house until we get the fire going again. In the one warm room we heat up water for sponge baths next to the fire. Alex spends his evenings drawing designs to discuss with the architect, while I read a book or scribble in my notebook by the fire. Paco organises an architect, José Luis, from Madrid to come and draw up the plans we need for council approval. We want to knock out two internal walls to have an open-plan kitchen-diner-living room, some bigger windows to the garden to bring in more light and a new bathroom. We're careful to respect the old bones of the place and keep the authentic farmhouse style.

~

Another random act of kindness befalls us the next day. We get up to find there's no water coming from the taps. Bugger! I remember this from living in Holland. If it gets cold you must turn the water off at the meter or the pipes will freeze. We make do with the bottled water from the fountain until midday, when Alex, for some reason, has a look at the mains tap on the street. Someone has turned it off. Bless their cotton socks! Someone must have thought,

'It's going to be six below zero and those Australianos will have no idea. I'd better turn the water off for them.' Some lovely neighbour has saved our old water pipes.

Despite the cold, the winter season is exhilarating. We love to see the country around us with a good layer of snow. The new roof gets tested with a heavy fall and passes with a gold star. Snowflakes drift by the French doors in the bedroom as we look out to see the neighbours' roofs now covered in white.

Paco finally gives us an invoice for the roof and the wood heater so we can pay him. He continues to bring people to the house who are going to do the various trades to get the house more liveable. The carpenter, Felipe, is going to make the new window shutters to replace the ones eaten out by woodborers. The electrician, Emilio, who happens to be his nephew, will rewire the house for us and make the electricity connection all legal. The plumber, Fernando, comes to inspect. Various specialists in repointing the stone walls and rebuilding the collapsed wall of the ruined dairy are also consulted.

Alex's Spanish is improving dramatically. He's learning a lot of new building vocabulary at the moment: sewerage, roof, insulation and beams are all words rolling off his tongue in Spanish. He still uses the neighbourly advice, *poco a poco*, little by little, when locals in the bar ask after our progress. He has developed an appreciation of the local *gastronomía* and can order a plate of wild mushrooms with a glass of red wine, no trouble.

After all the specialists have been to quote on their expertise, Paco is able to give us his final estimate. It's very reasonable and we again accept on the spot. There's no contract, just a handshake with both of us. It feels wrong to ask for more.

Paco is available to do our job next before he starts another big project. We have no idea if the plans have been signed off by council, but Paco is not worried. After all, his wife is the mayor of this village and the surrounding ones. While Paco does the wall breaking, the house will not be liveable. We contemplate what to do and in the end decide it may be easier to go back to Sydney in the meantime and sort out Alex's visa status from there.

Julian, the neighbour who showed us his house next door, comes to our table in the bar because he's heard we're leaving tomorrow. He reminisces already about the good neighbours he has gained and wishes us safe travels home and a speedy return. One loose bottom tooth wiggles with every word he speaks. I think this is a recent change, as I've not noticed the tooth the last few times we chatted. I concentrate on his words, trying to look in his eyes instead of glancing down at the wriggling tooth. I get a hug before he saunters off home. As we are getting up to leave, the barman comes from behind the bar to shake Alex's hand and kiss me on the cheek.

Later, Mari-Carmen of the Chorizo drops by with three antique water jugs. They look like family heirlooms.

'I have several others just like these,' she says. 'Too many! They will look *fabuloso* on your mantelpiece.'

Mari-Carmen and I have enjoyed a bit of time together now. We've become friends. I promise we'll return soon and we give each other one last hug.

In the late evening, Rafael del Punto Limpio stops by to wish us *buen viaje*. His old four-wheel drive is parked on the road next to our house. The charismatic old bachelor has a car full of women. They're all former village residents returning for the long weekend. Some of these women may have been the inspiration for Rafael's sculptures titled, *Woman Waiting for Her Lover*. They are off to have a good time in the next town. After all, it's only eleven o'clock, the evening is just beginning.

~

We have gained so much more than a stone house by a river. We've made new friends, seen more castles than you can poke a stick at, learned about the Romans, the Visigoths and the wars with the Moors. We've taken appropriate advantage of the *gastronomía* of this region. Fantasies of sitting on cobblestoned terraces drinking fabulous wine and eating tapas were realised. We've eaten enough pork to last us the rest of the year. We've lived through the fiestas of several towns and villages, each honouring a different patron saint, all fully embraced by the locals.

History is everywhere in these parts – every castle, town, village or unimportant-looking hill is a place where a critical event took place. If nothing important happened, there will be at least a myth or a fiesta to commemorate a saint who may or may not have lived there. Myth, legend and history combine flawlessly to make each and every spot the setting of something significant.

It's our last night in Soledad's house for now. Our house. It's starting to feel like a home despite the primitive conditions. There has been some hard work, labouring with sore backs being ignored so we can be up and at it again the next day. Our lives have been full of renewed vigour, our appetite for this work is surprising. It's not the move to Spain we planned, lazing about, doing a bit of sightseeing and lots of eating and drinking. We have mixed feelings about leaving. We would like to be here longer and get more done. We've packed the house up as best we can to withstand Paco and his troop of builders, who will arrive soon. We've covered all the furniture in the house and the barn with large sheets of plastic.

If you live long enough, circles close. What began as a sentimental return to Spain, because I lived there as a young woman, ends with buying a ruin and living here again. Meeting Alex on the Iberian Peninsula and going on this journey together decades later just confirms everything I love about him. I sure picked a goody all those years ago. Those blue eyes, which mesmerised me when we met, still sparkle with a joy for life. Alex hasn't forgotten about his infatuation with Uncle Domingo's house, but he's fallen deeply for the river cottage and loves 'our village' too.

Early the following morning we turn off the electricity and the water at the mains. Driving away feels odd, leaving the river cottage and Soledad on their own to withstand the repairs. On the drive out of town, last night's snowfall dominates the ever-changing scenery along the road.

~

At the airport, Alex is nervous about leaving Spain as his visa has expired. Despite the Iron Lady's dire warnings, we have not received any correspondence about a decision to grant or not grant a visa extension. We have the piece of paper that states that an extension was requested. However, permission to remain in Spain hasn't been officially given. If the passport control officers are not pleased with his visa status, Alex could be refused entry into Spain for at least twelve months. Not a good prospect for someone who's just bought a house and is embarking on a renovation.

The walk-through passport control is uneventful but Alex looks so guilty I'm surprised they don't pull him out of the line to interrogate him. He would never have made a good smuggler or a spy. The officer doesn't even look for arrival dates as he slams down his exit stamp. Obviously, he doesn't care very much; if you're leaving the country, you can't be much of a problem. Alex finally exhales as he exits the passport lane. In hindsight, the Iron Lady has done well by us. She has worked the system to delay things long enough for us to do everything we wanted. I will have to start calling her by her proper name from now on.

We never heard again from any of the authorities we approached for information about Uncle Domingo's house, not about the sewerage or if the Diputación would allow the road to be dug up for sewerage, or if the electricity could be connected, or what it would cost to put the water on. Not a word. Zip. *Nada*!

~

At the airport we read some news for the first time in a few weeks. A virus, originating in China, has made its way to Italy. It sounds a little worrying. The gravity of these events is hard to grasp at first. Within weeks the whole world is locked down, a profound moment in the history of our planet.

Chapter 30

Postscript

It feels strange to be back in Sydney. We leave our backpacks leaning up against the bedroom wall, reluctant to unpack more than our toiletries. Unpacking feels like an ending we're not prepared for. We plan to go back to San Juan de Soria once Paco has finished the planned restoration.

The experience in Castile has emboldened us, knowing that, within reason, we can do whatever we want with our life. Within days we're talking about selling our house on the northern beaches. It will free up the funds we need to make the river cottage even more perfect, with a functional kitchen and a bathroom with hot water. Living in a small town is something we've always wanted to do but was impossible as our jobs were tied to the city. Spain taught us that we were craving community, living in a small town or village.

Within a few weeks of coming back to Sydney our house is listed for auction. We're on a rollercoaster and every now and then we look at each other in dismay; are we being brave or foolish? The house sells before auction and things get real. We're now the owners of a semi-ruin on the other side of the world, but otherwise homeless. We haven't heard from Paco since we left Spain.

Spain, including the province of Soria, went into severe lockdown soon after we left. Like the rest of Europe, they have suffered through one wave of surging infections after another, severely impacting all lives and causing many deaths. The lack of news from Soria is concerning. We have no idea if Paco is dead or alive.

We do hear from *notario* Alejandro. He has come up with the goods. The deeds to the property have been created and everything's legal. The river cottage is finally truly ours.

Our WhatsApp messages to Paco go unanswered for months. We're still hopeful he'll be true to his word but we're getting nervous. Meanwhile we devise Plan B. We can't leave Australia, Spain is in the grips of a deadly pandemic, we have sold our house in Sydney and need somewhere to live. Soon.

Again, we go traipsing about the countryside to look at houses. If we buy something modest in the country we'll have somewhere to move after the settlement of the house in Sydney and still have enough money left over to complete the rescue of the river cottage.

We're moving very fast on major life changes, friends and family are starting to look at us with concern. We find a handsome 1920s timber cottage in a lovely village on the north coast of New South Wales in Gumbaynggirr Country. Valleys and river flats of deep green, studded with black-and-white dairy cows. Just like the Dutch village I grew up in. Unlike that Dutch village, it's close to the beach as well as the mountains. Both houses settle on the same day. For people taking lots of risks, we seem to be quite lucky. We have somewhere to go and be safe during this strange time.

~

As this virus continues to cause havoc around the world, we are getting used to yet another life. Meanwhile, Alex has planted a garden bed with fragrant Mediterranean plants like lavender, thyme, basil, oregano, sage and rosemary to keep a bit of Castile wafting through our lives. We grow our veggies, go for walks, chat to neighbours over the fence and adapt to the new circumstances. It's not the river cottage but it will do for now as we continue to dream of Spain.

~

Eighteen months later, out of the blue, a WhatsApp message arrives from Paco. Due to the time difference between the two countries, it arrives during the night. Alex is the first to see it when he wakes up. His whooping for joy wakes me. There are no words in the message, just a few photos. One of a small excavator parked inside the river cottage in what is now an open-plan kitchen and living room. We're surprised to see an excavator, we had envisaged a couple of workers with hammers and chisels rather than modern machines. Another photo shows a picture window to the river, big enough for a wide window seat. I imagine I'll read many books in that very spot. Paco knows we're not able to come back for now. Therefore, he is not in a hurry to get the work completed but he's made great progress. Seeing photos of what we've imagined is thrilling. We look forward to going back, making more connections and having old friends and family visit us in the river cottage, sharing this remote part of Spain with them.

Thinking as positively as possible, given the circumstances, I'm hoping we can get back in the next European spring. There are many jobs waiting for us – cleaning the fire-blackened beams in the kitchen, white-washing the walls, restoring more of the antique furniture in the barn. We've had many chats about creating a perfect garden and I can't wait to get some Spanish soil under my fingernails as we plant our first grapes and lay out the garden.

In a world in flux, there's an ancient cottage perched above a little river with both feet firmly planted in times gone by. One age-old cottage rescued, a future for perhaps another century. We are looking forward to being welcomed back into the fold of our small village community. We'll go back as soon as it is safe to do so. We're lucky bastards.

We message to Paco to thank him for the update and ask him to send us an invoice for the work to date. He sends back a message saying: 'You can pay me when you come back.'

Acknowledgements

My previous books were all about animals and zoology, but for some reason this book about Spain pushed the animals aside for a while. It wanted to be written and I had to get it out. It all began in Spain, a long time ago ...

Thank you Joanne Riccioni, my writing coach, for helping me shape my thoughts about how to present this jumble of stories into something people may read!

I am grateful to Affirm Press for taking a gamble on someone who normally writes books about wild animals. Thank you Natasha Seymour, Martin Hughes and Kerry Davies for manuscript midwifery and your precious encouragement. Thank you kindly.

I am indebted to my sister, Elsa, who came and gave a hand to clean Soledad's house after we'd just bought it. She was also one of the first readers of an early draft and read the whole manuscript in English, not her first language. She corrected some details about Spain and told me she loved it, which gave me a little boost to continue. My Australian pseudo-sister Alison and our friend Dave came on a little Camino walk with us and did not think we were too crazy for buying a ruin. They are the friends you want! Alison also read through an early draft and raised some good points that needed to be clarified. She also encouraged me to be more generous when writing about the Iron Lady than I was prepared to do. She won.

Good people who don't really have the time read an entire manuscript did so because I asked; Liz Spielman, Renske de Jong, Bob van der Valk, I owe you a big favour, let me know how I can repay you!

Leonie Henschke provided a professional manuscript assessment, the first comments by someone who's not my friend or my family! She did not know me at all but did the review as a favour to another friend and fellow writer, Kim Hodges. Thanks to you Kim for asking for a favour on my behalf!

Thanks also to the Bellingen writers group, WoW, who provided critiques on a few excerpts. Thanks to all and Anny Ventura in particular, who reviewed a few chapters. There were some other chapters I was keen to get opinion on, and Madelon Willemsen obliged and said that Paul Andrew, her late husband and my good friend, would have said, 'You're going on a bit'. So I tried to be more to the point.

As always, thanks to Alex, who will come and have an adventure with me any time. I still love those blue eyes!